MY PEOPLE

The Portraits of Robert Henri

Sponsored in part by a grant from the
NATIONAL ENDOWMENT FOR THE ARTS

with additional support provided by the
GERALD PETERS GALLERY, NEW YORK

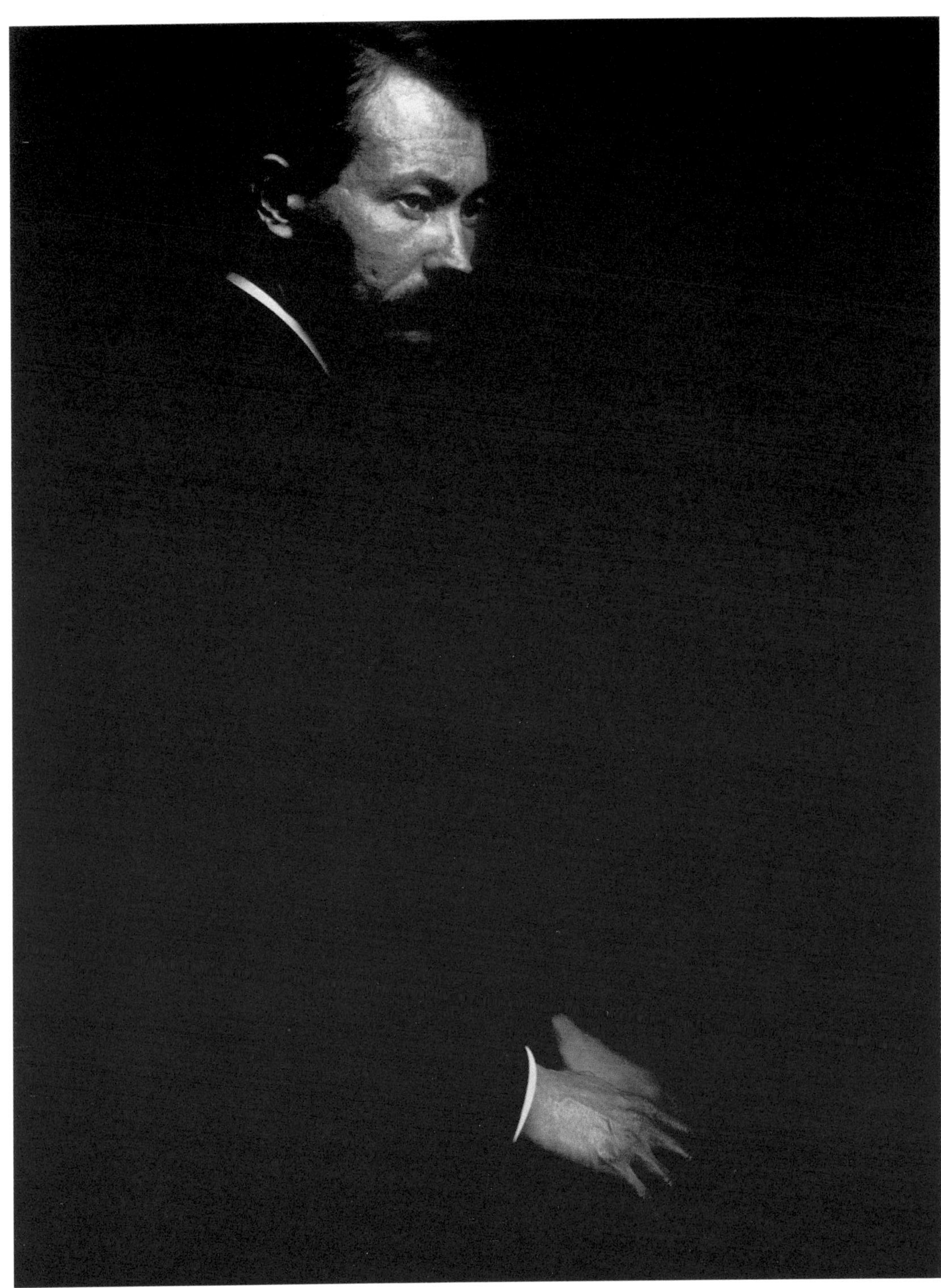

Gertrude Käsebier (1852–1934)
Robert Henri, c. 1907
Silverprint toned and coated to simulate gum print
Sheldon Memorial Art Gallery, University of Nebraska-Lincoln, F.M. Hall Collection

MY PEOPLE

The Portraits of Robert Henri

VALERIE ANN LEEDS

with contributions by
William Innes Homer
and
Michael Quick

ORLANDO MUSEUM OF ART
1994

Distributed by the University of Washington Press
Seattle and London

Published on the occasion of the exhibition

"MY PEOPLE": The Portraits of Robert Henri

Exhibition Itinerary:

ORLANDO MUSEUM OF ART, Florida
October 22, 1994–January 8, 1995

MUSEUM OF ART, Ft. Lauderdale, Florida
February 5–April 2, 1995

THE COLUMBUS MUSEUM, Georgia
April 30–June 25, 1995

Distributed by
UNIVERSITY OF WASHINGTON PRESS
P. O. Box 50096
Seattle, Washington 98145

Printed in the United States of America

Design: Robert Hellier
Editor: Sheila Schwartz
Printed by: Promocom Printing, St. Petersburg, Florida

Library of Congress Cataloging-in-Publication Data
Leeds, Valerie Ann, 1958–
My People: The portraits of Robert Henri / Valerie Ann Leeds; with contributions by William Innes Homer and Michael Quick.
p. cm.
Catalog of 1995 traveling exhibition: Orlando Museum of Art, Museum of Art of Fort Lauderdale, and Columbus Museum in Georgia.
Includes bibliographical references.
ISBN 1-880699-03-6
1. Henri, Robert, 1865-1929—Exhibitions. 2. Portrait painting—19th century—United States—Exhibitions. 3. Portrait painting—20th century—United States—Exhibitions. I. Henri, Robert, 1865-1929. II. Orlando Museum of Art. III. Fort Lauderdale
Museum of the Arts. IV. Columbus Museum of Art. V. Title.
ND237.H5A4 1994
759.13—dc20 94-27381
CIP

COVER: *La Madrileñita,* 1910
Oil on canvas, 24 x 20 in.
Private collection

PHOTOGRAPH CREDITS

The photographs in this publication have been supplied by the owners as cited in the captions. The following applies to photographs for which additional acknowledgment is due.

James Madden, Chattanooga, Tennessee
(cats. 4, 10, 59)
Ali Elai, Camerarts, New York
(cats. 11, 13, 25, 35, 40, 41, 52)
Thomas Gessler, St. Petersburg, Florida
(cat. 39)
Theodore Flagg, Orlando, Florida
(cat. 9)
Eli Albalancy, Wynnewood, Pennsylvania
(cat. 37)
Lee Stalsworth, Washington, D.C.
(cats. 20, 55)
Tom Duvrock, Houston, Texas
(cat. 58)
Williams and Williams
(cat. 15)

Contents

Lenders to the Exhibition

ALBRIGHT-KNOX ART GALLERY, BUFFALO, NEW YORK
THE ART INSTITUTE OF CHICAGO, ILLINOIS
MRS. MARTIN ANDERSEN
MR. AND MRS. W.J. BOWEN
THE BROOKLYN MUSEUM, NEW YORK
CANAJOHARIE LIBRARY AND ART GALLERY, NEW YORK
COLBY COLLEGE MUSEUM OF ART, WATERVILLE, MAINE
THE COLUMBUS MUSEUM, GEORGIA
THE CORCORAN GALLERY OF ART, WASHINGTON, D.C.
CUMMER GALLERY OF ART, JACKSONVILLE, FLORIDA
GIBBES MUSEUM OF ART, CHARLESTON, SOUTH CAROLINA
MR. AND MRS. CYRUS W. GRANDY, V
BETTY CAVANNA HARRISON
HIRSHHORN MUSEUM AND SCULPTURE GARDEN, WASHINGTON, D.C.
HUNTER MUSEUM OF ART, CHATTANOOGA, TENNESSEE
JANET LE CLAIR, ESTATE OF ROBERT HENRI
LOS ANGELES COUNTY MUSEUM OF ART, CALIFORNIA
LOWE ART MUSEUM, UNIVERSITY OF MIAMI, CORAL GABLES, FLORIDA
MEMORIAL ART GALLERY OF THE UNIVERSITY OF ROCHESTER, NEW YORK
THE METROPOLITAN MUSEUM OF ART, NEW YORK
MILWAUKEE ART MUSEUM, WISCONSIN
MINNESOTA MUSEUM OF ART, ST. PAUL
MISSISSIPPI MUSEUM OF ART, JACKSON
MONTGOMERY MUSEUM OF FINE ARTS, ALABAMA
MUSEUM OF FINE ARTS, MUSEUM OF NEW MEXICO, SANTA FE
MUSEUM OF FINE ARTS, ST. PETERSBURG, FLORIDA
NATIONAL ACADEMY OF DESIGN, NEW YORK
NEW ORLEANS MUSEUM OF ART, LOUISIANA
THE PARRISH ART MUSEUM, SOUTHAMPTON, NEW YORK
PENNSYLVANIA ACADEMY OF THE FINE ARTS, PHILADELPHIA
THE JOHN AND MABLE RINGLING MUSEUM OF ART, SARASOTA, FLORIDA
SAN ANTONIO MUSEUM OF ART, TEXAS
SAN DIEGO MUSEUM OF ART, CALIFORNIA
SCRIPPS COLLEGE, CLAREMONT, CALIFORNIA
SHELDON MEMORIAL ART GALLERY, UNIVERSITY OF NEBRASKA-LINCOLN
MR. AND MRS. TERRY STENT
EDWIN A. ULRICH MUSEUM OF ART, WICHITA STATE UNIVERSITY, KANSAS
VIRGINIA MUSEUM OF FINE ARTS, RICHMOND
THE WARNER COLLECTION OF GULF STATES PAPER CORPORATION, TUSCALOOSA, ALABAMA
WESTMORELAND MUSEUM OF ART, GREENSBURG, PENNSYLVANIA
WHITNEY MUSEUM OF AMERICAN ART, NEW YORK
WICHITA ART MUSEUM, KANSAS
PRIVATE COLLECTIONS

The exhibition

"MY PEOPLE":

THE PORTRAITS OF ROBERT HENRI

and the related programs were made possible

with the generous support of:

OFFICIAL SPONSOR

The National Endowment for the Arts

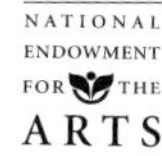

CONTRIBUTORS

Gerald Peters Gallery, New York

Spanierman Gallery, New York

Allison Gallery, New York

SPONSORSHIP SOCIETY

BENEFACTOR

Institute of Museum Services

SPONSORS

Council of 101

The Pino Family Foundation

PARTNERS

David and Judy Albertson

The Raymond E. and Ellen F. Crane Foundation

Goldman, Sachs & Company

Helmuth, Obata and Kassabaum, Inc.

The George W. Jenkins Foundation

South Trust Bank of Orlando

Spanierman Gallery, New York

Richard W. Zipperly

PARTICIPATING FELLOWS

Pam and Dale Lindon

Jacqueline Everhart McMullen

Francine and Neil Newberg

Sonny's Real Pit Bar-B-Q

Hans W. Tews

The Orlando Museum of Art is member supported
and sponsored in part by
United Arts of Central Florida, Inc.,
the National Endowment for the Arts
and
the State of Florida, Department of State,
Division of Cultural Affairs and the
Florida Arts Council.

Foreword

In keeping with the Orlando Museum of Art's mission to originate and tour major exhibitions complementing its own permanent collection of nineteenth- and twentieth-century American art, the Museum is pleased to present "'My People': The Portraits of Robert Henri." Curated by the Museum's Curator of 19th- and Early 20th-Century American Art, Valerie Leeds, this exhibition includes exemplary portraits by one of America's premier artists (1865–1929). While Robert Henri's life work was dominated by portraits, no museum exhibition has been devoted solely to surveying these works. After a great deal of research and contact with some of the nation's most important museums and private collectors, Valerie Leeds carefully selected approximately sixty paintings for this first major retrospective of Henri's portraits.

This exhibition traces Henri's development as a portraitist over a period of three decades, and includes a broad range of subjects, from formal portraits of art and literary figures, friends, and family to informal portraits of people of diverse races and cultures whom Henri saw in his extensive travels. His late portraits are almost exclusively devoted to the subject of children.

This catalogue is enhanced by the insights on Henri offered in essays by two leading art historians: noted Henri scholar Dr. William Innes Homer, University of Delaware, and Michael Quick, former Curator of American Art at the Los Angeles County Museum of Art. In addition, Michael Quick will be giving a lecture on the exhibition at the Orlando Museum of Art.

Following its debut in Orlando, this exhibition will travel to the Museum of Art, Fort Lauderdale, and The Columbus Museum, Columbus, Georgia. More than 20,000 people of all ages will enjoy Henri's portraits and a variety of educational programs related to the exhibition in Orlando. An additional 40,000 visitors are expected to view the exhibition on tour.

An exhibition of this stature, and its related programs, would not have been possible without the generous support of a substantial number of organizations and individuals. Their support has been critical to helping the Museum fulfill its commitment to showcase exhibitions of important nineteenth- and twentieth-century American art and share them with other institutions.

We are pleased that the exhibition earned support on the national level through a grant from the National Endowment for the Arts. Our sincere gratitude also goes to the exhibition contributors: Gerald Peters Gallery, New York, Allison Gallery, and Spanierman Gallery. In addition, this exhibition—and all the Museum's programs—could not go forward without the ongoing funding of the Sponsorship Society, the Institute for Museum Services, the State of Florida, Department of State, Division of Cultural Affairs and Florida Arts Council, and United Arts of Central Florida, Inc.

We are indeed fortunate to have obtained loans for this exhibition from more than forty prestigious public and private collections, including The Art Institute of Chicago; Hirshhorn Museum and Sculpture Garden, Smithsonian Institution, Washington, D.C.; Los Angeles County Museum of Art; The Metropolitan Museum of Art, New York; and the Whitney Museum of American Art, New York, among others. We are also deeply grateful to all the private collectors who are generously sharing their treasures with the public. Finally, I would like to thank the Museum's Board of Trustees and staff for their support of this exhibition and the related programs.

Marena Grant Morrisey
Executive Director

Preface

As the fourth generation to have been entrusted with the care of the estate of Robert Henri, I should like to congratulate the Orlando Museum of Art for organizing this exhibition.

Throughout his career, Henri described his "people" in text and on canvas. They have lived on for all the world to see and to know as he saw and loved them. They have traveled and been in the hands of hundreds of museums, galleries, and collectors. There is no doubt that this assemblage of his most cherished subjects shall be remembered for years to come . . . and Henri will live as long as they.

Janet Le Clair

Acknowledgments

An exhibition of this scope could not have been assembled without the assistance and support of numerous individuals and institutions. First, and foremost, deepest gratitude must be expressed to all the lenders for sharing their works of art and allowing them to be a part of this exhibition. George Neubert, Sheldon Memorial Art Gallery, University of Nebraska-Lincoln, Janet Le Clair, Mr. and Mrs. Terry Stent, Judith O'Toole, Westmoreland Museum of Art, Greensburg, Pennsylvania, James Demetrion, Hirshhorn Museum and Sculpture Garden, Linda Bantel, Pennsylvania Academy of the Fine Arts, and Ilene Fort, Los Angeles County Museum of Art, deserve added thanks for agreeing to multiple loans from their collections that proved crucial to the show.

Janet Le Clair is owed special acknowledgment for her unfailing generosity and encouragement in numerous ways from the project's inception. Throughout the process of organizing the show and preparing the catalogue, she freely and graciously shared her invaluable knowledge, provided information and documentation, and patiently answered numerous queries. Particular gratitude is due Reagan Upshaw and Gerald Peters, Gerald Peters Gallery, New York, for their interest and generous support of the catalogue. Also Gavin and Ira Spanierman, Spanierman Gallery, New York, and Glenn Peck, Allison Gallery, New York deserve special recognition. Marena Grant Morrisey, Executive Director, and The Board of Trustees of the Orlando Museum of Art provided the vital support necessary to see the project through to completion. We are fortunate to have had the cooperation of other museums who are participating in the tour. In particular, we are grateful to our colleagues Thomas Butler and Karol Lawson, The Columbus Museum, Georgia, and Kenworth Moffett of the Museum of Art, Ft. Lauderdale.

Many individuals assisted in locating and facilitating the loan of key Henri paintings: Glenn Peck, Allison Gallery; Robert Workman, American Federation of Arts; Betty Campanile, Campanile Galleries, Chicago; Pat Bridwell, Center for the Arts, Vero Beach, Florida; Hugh J. Gourley, III and Lynn Marsden-Atlass, Colby College Museum of Art, Waterville, Maine; Stuart Evans, Cummer Gallery of Art, Jacksonville, Florida; Alexander Nyerges, Dayton Art Institute, Ohio; Reagan Upshaw, and Gerald Peters, Gerald Peters Gallery, New York; Michael Owen, Michael Owen Gallery, New York; Michael Milkovich, Museum of Fine Arts, St. Petersburg, Florida; Linda Bantel, Pennsylvania Academy of the Fine Arts; Douglas Hyland, San Antonio Museum of Art; John H. Surovek, John H. Surovek Gallery, Palm Beach; Paul Chew, and Judith O'Toole, Westmoreland Museum, Greensburg, Pennsylvania.

Many people were exceedingly helpful in supplying information and documentation relating to Henri's portraits: Feay Shellman Coleman; Katherine Lawrence, Dixon Gallery and Gardens, Memphis, Tennessee; Jacquelyn Casey, Hunter Museum of Art, Chattanooga, Tennessee; Thomas McNamara, Achill Island, Ireland; Beatrice Epstein, The Metropolitan Museum of Art; Suzanne Decker, Museum of Fine Arts, Houston; Ron McCarty, The John and Mable Ringling Museum of Art, Sarasota, Florida; Karen Merritt and Karen Williams, Sheldon Memorial Art Gallery, University of Nebraska-Lincoln; Helen Farr Sloan; Pamela King, Telfair Academy, Savannah, Georgia; and Charles Hilburn, The Warner Collection, Gulf States Paper Corporation, Tuscaloosa, Alabama. Special acknowledgment is also due to the following: Lee Ann Dean, and Harriet Memeger, Helen Farr Sloan Library, Delaware Art Museum, Wilmington; Rafaela Ellis; Helen Sanger and Lydia Dufour, Frick Art

Reference Library; Debra Force, Hirschl & Adler Galleries, New York; David Smith, Research Division, New York Public Library; and Helen Farr Sloan.

The staff of the Orlando Museum of Art showed outstanding dedication to this project. In particular, the exceptional efforts provided by Betsy Gwinn, Exhibitions Assistant, who was involved in every phase of the exhibition, were essential to the realization of the project. Grateful appreciation also goes to Andrea Farnick and Hansen Mulford for their additional assistance with many aspects of the exhibition and catalogue.

I am indebted to both William Inness Homer and Michael Quick for their contributions to the catalogue, and their belief in the project. Both scholars bring a specialized knowledge to the subject, and I am grateful for their thoughtful insights. They generously shared ideas and information, and their advice and involvement are greatly valued. Additional contributions to the catalogue were made by Bob Hellier, who provided the elegant catalogue design, and Sheila Schwartz, whose editorial skills were indispensable.

V.A.L.

Robert Henri as a Portrait Painter: An Introduction

WILLIAM INNES HOMER

When people think of Robert Henri as a painter, they usually envision him as the leader of the Ashcan School (a misnomer for a group more appropriately called the New York Realists, also members of The Eight), a vital force for reform in the early twentieth-century art world. In this connection, unidealized scenes of everyday life—views of New York City working people and slums—immediately come to mind. Henri is often associated with images of this kind that were made by the painters he influenced, other New York Realists such as John Sloan, William Glackens, George Luks, and Everett Shinn, though in fact Henri himself painted relatively few scenes that chronicled the city and its inhabitants. Indeed, when Henri's life work is reviewed, it will be found that there are far more portraits than any other kind of subject matter. Yet, oddly enough, no major survey has been undertaken that is devoted solely to Henri's portraits, an essential portion of his creative output.

Henri did not start out with a dominant interest in portrait painting. His first decade of independent production, the 1890s, was filled with a variety of other subjects—beach scenes, interiors with figures, cityscapes (primarily of Paris), often filled with people. Toward the end of this decade, however, he began to turn to portraits, though he did not make any large number at that time.

In the opening years of the twentieth century, Henri came into his own as a portrait painter. He gave his attention both to full-length subjects, handled rather formally, as well as to more intimate portraits of his friends and family, including himself. In the former category we find works intended to impress the juries of the National Academy of Design and similar exhibitions, as well to please an occasional client who would order a commissioned portrait. In the latter category there are images of people Henri asked to pose just because he found them interesting; in these we discover a looser and more spontaneous mode of expression—the vigorous brushwork and rapid paint handling for which he is best known.

In his earliest portraits, Henri utilized a dark palette, reminiscent of Velázquez, Rembrandt, Hals, and Manet, masters who served as models for his manner of painting at the time. He learned to work not only with dark, contrasting tonalities, but also with aggressive, animated brushwork, which is particularly reminiscent of Hals. While there may be some superficial similarities between Henri's work and that of John Singer Sargent, with its bravura paint handling, the former was far less polished in technique. For Henri, vigorous execution symbolized freshness and uninhibited spontaneity. This kind of spontaneity, however, was counterbalanced by Henri's disciplined knowledge of construction and anatomy, which he had obtained during his studies in Philadelphia and Paris. He would tell his students in words that recall the advice of Thomas Anshutz, one of his teachers, "Think of solidity as you work" or "Study muscles so that you know the nature of what you use. Where each comes from and goes to, and its part of the action in hand." It is rare to find a Henri portrait, particularly among the earlier works, that is not constructed as a solid mass in space, with a convincing sense of anatomical structure underlying the subject's flesh.

Robert Henri defined the portrait in a broad and universal way. At home in New York City and especially on his various travels in the United States and trips to Europe, he would seek out "types," individuals previously unknown to him whom he would ask to pose for a portrait. These were non- commercial efforts executed simply because the character of the subject attracted him. He began to call these "My People," sitters who represented a cross-section of races and cultures. Whether in Spain, Holland, or later Ireland, he would select individuals whose appearance and costume would reveal some telling truth. As he said, he liked to paint "My People," "whoever they may be, wherever they may exist, the people through whom dignity of life is manifest, that is, who are in some way expressing themselves naturally along the lines Nature intended for them." His subjects came not only from foreign countries but also from the United States, where he sought out blacks and Chinese Americans, along with Mexicans, Native Americans, and gypsies. His outlook was clearly international, as witnessed by the diverse backgrounds of his sitters. His constant attention to these types speaks of his reaction to the evils of nationalism and "patriotism" that impelled Europeans, with help from the United States later on, through four years of war between 1914 and 1918

Henri refused, as was his habit, to fight for a cause through any organized institution. As he said: "No blind, intense devotion for an institution that has stiffened in chains of its own making. My love of mankind is individual, not national, and I always find the race expressed in the individual." Although Henri's interest in the working classes has been interpreted (though less often, recently) as evidence of his alleged socialism, he was not connected to that movement, but was, rather, a philosophical anarchist. His fear of institutions and his belief in the individual and his or her capabilities speak of his anarchist leanings, and in the end his portraits are a celebration of the power and potential of the individual, as opposed to any form of collective ideals.

Not every one of Henri's portraits is successful. There are some that are not fully realized. These aberrations are to be expected, given Henri's method of painting. In a sense, he was existential in his relation to his subject and in his execution. He believed the artist should work as quickly as possible, using spontaneous brushstrokes that would express his personal feeling about the sitter. He wrote that the goal of painting is "not to make a picture—however unreasonable this may sound. The picture, if a picture results, is a byproduct and may be useful, valuable, interesting as a sign of what has passed. The object, which is back of every true work of art, is the attainment of a state of being, a state of high functioning, a more-than- ordinary moment of existence." Henri's statement applies particularly well to his portraits, works in which the artist aspires to a state of lively psychological tension when confronting another human being. If his sympathy with that individual was successfully translated into pigment on canvas, then the portrait worked. But if he did not attain that "state of high functioning," the outcome would not be everything the artist or his audience might have wished it could be.

As Henri entered the second and third decades of this century, he gained more and more control of the issues of color. Thanks to his knowledge of the theories of Hardesty Maratta, beginning around 1909, his palette opened up into a far wider range of hues than before, and from that point until his death in 1929, he established his color compositions in advance, arranging colored tones throughout the canvas so that a pre-planned harmony would prevail. This system gave an added dimension to Henri's portraits—a vivid and often brilliant impact that, combined with his increasingly vigorous brushstroke, helped generate works of unusual vitality and presence.

In the late portraits, particularly those Henri executed in Ireland, his execution became increasingly spirited, sometimes to the point of superficiality. However, when he was successful in bringing off the existential psychological encounter between himself and the subject, his portraits demonstrate a vigor and presence unmatched by any other painter of his time.

The Portraits of Robert Henri

VALERIE ANN LEEDS

The myth of Robert Henri, a complex man of great influence and personal magnetism, often overshadowed his art. His lifelong campaign to provide emerging artists with an alternative forum for exhibiting their work and his role as the driving force behind The Eight, the insurgency movement against the policies of the National Academy of Design, have earned him renown as the mastermind of this artistic rebellion. Moreover, Henri was one of the most influential teachers in America. Along with Thomas Eakins and William Merritt Chase, he shaped a generation of painters while teaching art privately and at a number of schools and organizations, including the School of Design for Women, Philadelphia, the New York School of Art, and the Art Students League. His charismatic personality and inspiring approach encouraged students to express their own artistic individuality, free from stylistic doctrine.

Henri's legendary reputation as a teacher and his leadership of the anti-academic New York realist painters continue to eclipse Robert Henri, the painter. Yet the body of work he produced during a career of more than thirty years represents a turning point in American portraiture. Unlike the more established fashionable portraitists, William Merritt Chase and John Singer Sargent, Henri promoted the painting of life. His refusal to flatter or focus on superficially pretty subjects earned him the epithet "Manet of Manhattan." Although strong parallels do exist between the early work of Henri and Manet, such as their shared approach to realism in portraiture, fascination with the culture and aesthetic of Spain, and strong Old Master influences, it could be said that Thomas Eakins provided an even more powerful model and was Henri's artistic mentor. Of Eakins, Henri wrote in 1917:

> *Eakins was a deep student of life and with a great love he studied humanity frankly . . . . In the matter of ways and means of expression—the science of technique—he studied most profoundly . . . . His vision was not touched by fashion. He cared nothing for prettiness or cleverness in the life or in art. His quality was honesty . . . . Personally, I consider him the greatest portrait painter America has produced.*[1]

It was in this tradition of American realism that Henri fashioned his own course, away from the world of commissioned portraits and commercial success. Guy Pène du Bois, a student of Henri and an advocate of his brand of realism, characterized his position:

> *Robert Henri seeks to express himself . . . . Henri, the portrait painter, in American art is almost a solitary figure. That is why he is called a modern . . . . He paints his own idea of the sitter—That is a method which since the eighteenth century, has gone out of fashion . . . America is shocked by Henri as Paris was shocked by Manet. He dares to express his opinion, and that is an error from the popular point of view. The populace demands pretty portraits.*[2]

The particular triumph of Robert Henri as a portrait painter rests with his ability to extract the spiritual essence and personality of a subject, without flattery, and translate it into paint. "Historically, portrait painters have often sought to discover some central core of personhood as the proper object of their representation . . . . That invisible core of self was always hard to grasp and even harder to portray."[3] Henri's rendering of a likeness through gesture and expression are central to his accomplishments in portraiture. As he painted, so he instructed his students:

> *The making of a good portrait is the use of intelligence of what is essentially the features of that person, the gesture to be painted. By that I mean the something that enables you to recognize your friends a block or two away.*[4]

Henri found this "something" by forming a relationship with the individual he was painting. He attempted to establish an emotional empathy with each sitter, and was drawn to subjects that evoked a personal response in him:

> *The people I like to paint are "my people," whoever they may be, wherever they may exist, the people through whom dignity of life is manifest, that is, who are in some way expressing themselves naturally along the lines nature intended for them. My people may be old or young, rich or poor . . . . But wherever I find them, the Indian at work in the white man's way, the Spanish gypsy moving back to the freedom of the hills, the little boy, quiet and reticent before the stranger, my interest is awakened and my impulse immediately is to tell about them through my own language—drawing and painting in color.*[5]

Between 1892 and 1894, before Henri's signature style emerged, he had worked in an Impressionist mode, painting bright landscapes, using a light palette and abbreviated brushstrokes. However, by the end of the decade, few works by Henri exhibited even remnants of the Impressionist style, though confusion about whether he should be categorized as an Impressionist or a Realist continued for some time. As late as 1904, he was still being called an Impressionist, though he had long abandoned the style in favor of dark, monochromatic single figure portraits.[6] The most pronounced influence on Henri's portraits was exerted by the Old Masters—Diego Velázquez, Rembrandt van Rijn, Frans Hals, and Francisco Goya, whose paintings he had seen at the Louvre, the Prado, and museums in Holland and Belgium. Henri commented: "Here [Paris] I have done five times more work already than I did all last winter. The influences are the best—I go a good deal to the Louvre."[7] References to Velázquez, Goya, and Hals appear in other letters sent from Europe.[8] Two works from 1898, *The Man Who Posed as Richelieu* (cat. 1) and *The Woman in a Manteau* (The Brooklyn Museum, New York), represent the genesis of Henri's signature style. Though they recall portraits by Velázquez and Manet, Henri has here begun to define an individualized approach, abandoning broken Impressionist brushstrokes in favor of loose painterly brushwork, and returning to the dark palette of Dutch seventeenth-century portraiture.

Painted while in Paris, *The Man Who Posed as Richelieu* follows the three-quarter length portrait frequently seen in Spanish portraiture, and has a certain stylistic temperament that suggests Old Master portraits. The portrait was painted from a model who had objected to being depicted in his street clothes, so Henri instead painted him as Cardinal Richelieu.[9] Armand de Richelieu was a powerful French cardinal and chief minister of King Louis XIII. Philippe de Champaigne's imposing full-length portrait of Richelieu (c. 1635) hung in the Louvre, and Henri most certainly knew it from numerous visits there. Henri's notes reveal his intention in the painting: "a veritable rascal in a blouse, mustache and imperial . . . . Eyes piercing but of uncertain regard. Very hardy painting."[10] The portrait was shown in Henri's second one-man exhibition, held in 1902, at the Pennsylvania Academy of the Fine Arts, which included over forty of his paintings. One Philadelphia critic felt that Henri's portrait was unsuccessful:

> *If I were Mr. Robert Henri, I would give up painting portraits and become a landscapist, for such a head as* The Man Who Posed as Richelieu *is satanic in its expression. There is a rumor that this is a portrait of Whistler . . . . Certainly it resembles him. It has a demonic look.*[11]

Although Henri had begun to receive some complimentary reviews, the taste for Impressionist portraits of comely subjects still generally prevailed.

By 1902, the year Henri painted *Portrait of Miss Leora M. Dryer in Riding Costume* (cat. 2), and *Young Woman in Black* (cat. 3), he had shed a degree of the technical awkwardness evident in his earlier portraits. These two paintings reveal a confidence in approach that affirms his place among the foremost American painters. The critical and popular response that these works received when exhibited testify that Henri had by this time attained a certain status as an artist. Painted after he returned from Europe to live in New York, the *Portrait of Miss Leora M. Dryer* was executed over a three-day period in May. When shown at Henri's Pennsylvania Academy of the Fine Arts exhibition in November, it was singled out as a "fresh portrait of youth" by one critic, while another proclaimed that "of the portraits, probably the most distinguished is that of Miss Leora M. Dryer, a young lady in a black riding suit."[12] Dark in overall tonality, this formal full-length portrait is one of Henri's most successful early efforts. The largely monochromatic scheme is relieved only by brief flashes of color. The painting shows a transition away from the more direct influence of Velázquez and Manet in its softer blending and less somber disposition.

In November 1902, Henri began a large full-length painting of professional model Jesseca Penn, *Young Woman in Black*. This portrait ultimately became one of his most widely praised, and it effectively launched his career. Shown at the Pennsylvania Academy of the Fine Arts 1903 exhibition, it was compared to the refined society portraits of Sargent:

> *Of all, not even excepting the Sargents, there is nothing better than Robert Henri's portrait of a girl in black velvet jacket, black skirt and hat, relieved by a glimpse of the white waist beneath her coat. Painted in the low key Mr. Henri delights in, the figure rounds out from the canvas in a masterly way and the delicate beauty of the face makes a vivid appeal to the spectator.*[13]

Other critics concurred, pronouncing it one of the great portraits. When the painting was again presented in a group show at the National Arts Club in 1904, which included works by Glackens, Luks, Sloan, Prendergast, and Davies, it was again lauded. Charles De Kay declared Henri a rival of Whistler:

> *Mr. Robert Henri may be said to lead this procession . . . so distinguished are the figures he offers. The "Young Woman in Black" has been seen at earlier exhibitions, but it is always a pleasure to look on it again. The sweet pensive face without a touch of commonplace . . . show[s] that there are others beside Lavery of the Glasgow artists who can run Whistler hard for honors.* [14]

Young Woman in Black, showing the artist's confident mastery and skill, was Henri's first major, fully realized portrait, and the definitive work of his early style. The enthusiastic reviews that accompanied its frequent showings created a wave of publicity that helped to establish his reputation.

By 1903, Henri's steady output consisted principally of portraits. Drawing on the example of Whistler, Manet, and Velázquez, Henri continued to paint sober full-length, life-size portraits in a grand manner intended to impress exhibition juries. Dramatically dark figures and backgrounds with intensely lit features mark these early efforts. The strength of these portraits derives from the minimal approach Henri used: plain, shadowy backdrops from which the figure emerges, with attention focused on the face. Henri believed that the figure should dominate but function within the background. The background, he felt is

> *more air than it is anything else. It is the place in which the model moves . . . . The spaces on either side of the head and above the head can do so many things good and bad to the head and the figure . . . that it is remarkable how little attention is paid to them . . . .*
> *From my point of view the simpler a background is the better the figure in front of it will be, and . . . the better the figure is the less the observer will need entertainment in the background.*[15]

Henri's *Self-Portrait* (cat. 4), painted in 1903, followed these concepts, as did a series of portraits he painted in 1904 that includes his brother, John Sloan, Eugenie Stein, and James Preston (cats. 5, 6, 8, 9). Henri noted that he started and completed his self-portrait on June 8.[16] He was by now able to produce finished works quite rapidly, sometimes in one sitting, though generally they were executed over the course of two or three days, like the portrait of his brother, Frank L. Southrn (cat. 5). It was begun on January 10, 1904; Henri worked on it for one hour the following day, and completed it on January 12.[17] Like his self-portrait, the work shows a strong highlight on the right side of the face and collar while the rest of the figure recedes into the darkness. Both portraits convey a sense of the subject's physical presence by the indirect gaze, and are painted from similar angles though with reverse sides of his face in shadow.

Portrait of Frank L. Southrn, M.D. was shown in the 1904 National Arts Club exhibition shortly after it was completed and received this critical assessment: "vigorous brushwork is seen in *Portrait of Frank L. Southrn,* where the high light on the nose gives one the idea that the organ has received a blow that indents the face."[18] Another critic, however, was more positive. He remarked that the portrait appeared "so true to life . . . and so well has the character been written in on the canvas. The brow is strongly painted and the eyes, nose and mouth speak for themselves."[19] Though the portrait was critically well-received, Henri must have harbored some reservations about the painting, for he later noted that he had "painted on portrait of Frank done about a year ago. Gave it up finally and rubbed all the new work off leaving it as it finally was."[20]

Shortly after painting the portrait of his brother, he completed the full-length *Portrait of George Luks* (fig. 1), followed by the portrait of his friend and fellow artist, John Sloan (cat. 6), painted on January 30 and 31, 1904.[21] In this formal portrait, Sloan is shown fashionably turned out, with his left hand in his pocket and a hat in his right. The portrait is in the three-quarter length format with which Henri periodically experimented. As in his self-portrait, Henri employs a smoky monochromatic background, similar in tone to that of Sloan's attire, which makes the figure appear to emerge mysteriously from the shadows.

Though at times Henri hired professional models, during this period he executed a series of portraits of friends, family, and acquaintances. His first wife, Linda, was a frequent model; in addition to Sloan and Luks, others from his social sphere who sat for portraits include Edith and William Glackens, Charles Grafly, James Preston, Thomas Anshutz, and Elmer Schofield. Members of his family and close friends served as models from time to time throughout his career, yet between 1904 and 1906, Henri used such sitters predominantly.

Another painting which proved to be critical to Henri's growing reputation was *Lady in Black (Mrs. Robert Henri)* (cat. 7). The work was shown at the 1904 Society of American Artists exhibition, the 1904 Universal Exposition in St. Louis (where it won the Silver Medal with *Young Woman in Black*), and at The Art Institute of Chicago in 1905, where it won the Harris Prize. It was also shown in 1906 at the Pennsylvania Academy of the Fine Arts show; there it was one vote short of receiving the Temple Prize.[22] The work generated positive reviews and recognition for Henri as one of the preeminent portrait painters in America. A notice from The Art Institute of Chicago's exhibition stated:

> *The natural first mention, and unquestionably the finest single canvas in the show, is the "Portrait of Lady in Black" by Robert Henri . . . . Dignified and strong, executed with a masterly power over technical difficulties, and a searching insight for character, this work is nearly, if not quite, the last word yet said in American portraiture.*[23]

A review of the 1904 Society of American Artists show also proved flattering, favorably comparing Henri's *Lady in Black* to Sargent's *Portrait of the Misses Hunter*—the attractive and elegant type of society portraiture from which Henri became more and more removed:

> *the Sargent "Portrait of the Misses Hunter" attracts general attention . . . . Everything about the canvas, its position, brilliancy of color and soft draperies around the frame tends to make it the dominant picture in the room. It is surpassed however, in real worth by another portrait that hangs near by. Robert Henri's full-length figure of a young woman. Painted in the familiar manner, the figure emerging from a dusky background, it is vibrant with life and dignity. It is the finest thing in the room . . . .*[24]

Henri's portrait of his wife presents her in black silk, leaning on a brown high-backed sofa against an even darker ground, highlighting only her face and a border of white lace. Henri became associated with painting portraits of woman in monochromatic schemes of black or white through a number of works he painted between 1902 and 1904. These single-figure, large-scale portraits often generated pointed comparisons between his work and Whistler's, and sometimes that of Chase as well. As Samuel Isham commented about Henri's works:

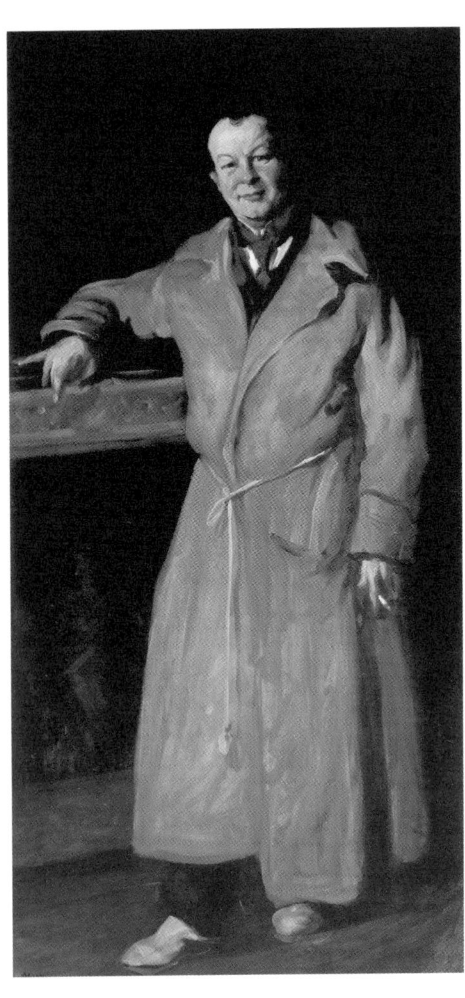

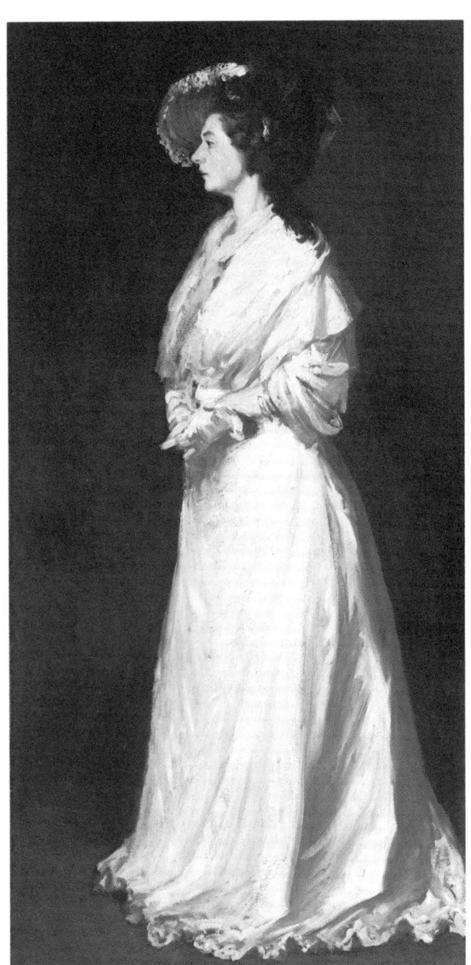

> *Their interest lies in their application, which in the present case has something of the tradition of Manet and something of the sentiment of Whistler, both tempered by individual originality . . . .*
>
> *Robert Henri is perhaps the most characteristic of this younger group, for although he is, strictly speaking, a portrait painter, his best works are not from the casual sitter . . . , but from carefully chosen models . . . . The girls in "white" or "black" of Henri are modern, complex, and rather mysterious, as they stand slender and graceful with their faces showing bright against the dark background. The workmanship . . . is broad and sure, insistently masterly, with great richness of surface and harmony of tone in the simple schemes of black and white and flesh color.* [25]

Precedent for this type of female portrait can be found in a series Chase painted in the 1880s and 1890s. Among these are *Portrait of a Lady in Black,* 1888 (The Metropolitan Museum of Art, New York); *Memories (Woman in White),* c. 1888 (Munson-Williams-Proctor Museum of Art, Utica, New York); *Woman in Black,* c. 1890 (Smith College Museum of Art, Northampton, Massachusetts); and *Young Girl in Black,* c. 1899 (Hirshhorn Museum and Sculpture Garden, Washington, D.C.). Although Chase and Henri became adversaries, with Chase representing the academic establishment and Henri the radicals, both artists had sometimes used similar idioms, particularly in their earlier work. Their formative influences in portraiture were inspired by their regard for the Old Masters, and later they also paid homage to Whistler's tonal abstractions, such as the noted *Symphony in White, No. 1: The White Girl,* 1862 (National Gallery of Art, Washington, D.C.).

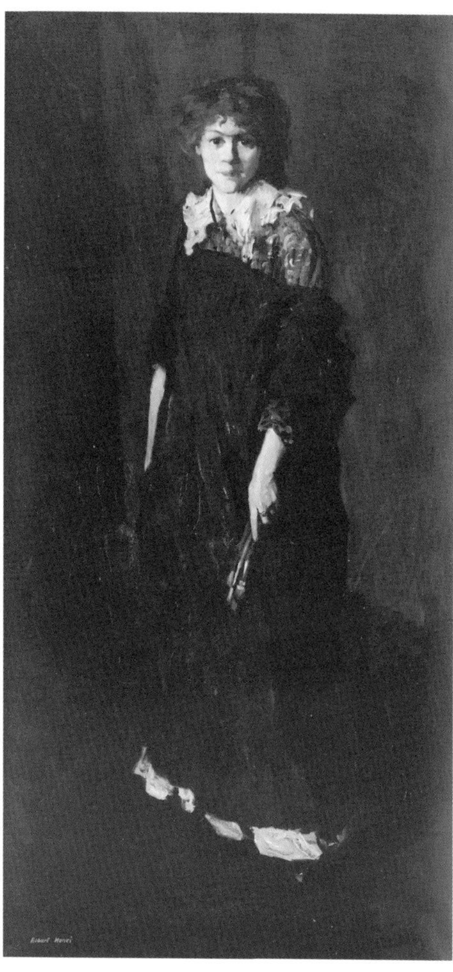

Fig. 1 (Opposite, left)
Portrait of George Luks, 1904
Oil on canvas, 76 1/2 x 38 1/4 in.
National Gallery of Canada, Ottawa

Fig. 2 (Opposite, right)
Young Woman in White, 1904
Oil on canvas, 78 1/4 x 38 1/8 in.
National Gallery of Art, Washington, D.C.,
Gift of Violet Organ

Fig. 3 (Left)
The Art Student (Miss Josephine Nivison), 1906
Oil on canvas, 77 1/4 x 38 1/2 in.
Milwaukee Art Museum, Purchase, Acquisition Fund

Another Henri portrait that evokes Whistler's female portraits is *Young Woman in White,* 1904 (fig. 2). This painting depicts Eugenie Stein, a professional model, known as "Zenka of Bohemia," who became part of Henri's extended circle. She posed for both Sloan and Henri, and was among Henri's favorite models. Sloan once noted that "Stein (Zenka) called and we enjoyed her visit as usual. She's a great girl, so ingenuous, so paintable, the best professional model in New York probably . . . ."[26] *Zenka (Portrait of Eugenie Stein)* (cat. 8) pictures her in a less romanticized manner than *Young Woman in White.* Here Henri returns to a somber palette of gray-green against a dark background. Effects of chiaroscuro, conveyed by the brush, delineate the features and planes of the face in sharply contrasting light and shadow. The elaborately tall hat angled on her head theatrically casts the upper part of her face into shadow.

Another member of Henri's circle was the artist James Preston, who appears in *Portrait of James Preston* (cat. 9). Preston was a friend of Henri's from Philadelphia, before they both eventually moved to New York. Henri's portrait, painted over three days in April and May 1904, again uses murky tonalities of gray-green against a darkened brown ground together with light highlights to accentuate his chiseled features. Typical of Henri's 1904-06 portraits, the depiction is forceful and dramatic, in part due to the straight-on gaze of the subject and the direct light source that casts half the face in shadow. Ira Glackens related that Preston "was famous for being dapper. He had . . . the bright and quizzical look of a bird, and he has always been a favorite on sight of everyone from infants to octogenarians."[27] Henri's portrait communicates Preston's characteristic sense of style and charm. Tall and thin, Preston's elegant figure lends itself to the elongated full-length format. The sitter's pose, with one hand in his pocket, the other holding his pipe, creates an air of casual realism.

Other important portraits of the period that depict Henri's friends and acquaintances include full-length paintings of George Luks, Josephine Nivison, Edith Dimock, and William Glackens. *The Art Student* (fig. 3), a portrait of Josephine Nivison (who later became Edward Hopper's wife), and the *Portrait of George Luks* (fig. 1) are seemingly naturalistic and informal. Nivison is depicted in a painting smock holding her brushes, and Luks is shown casually leaning against an empty frame while smoking a cigarette. Henri's portrait of William Glackens (cat. 10) differs from these two examples in its established formality. Glackens recalled posing for Henri:

> *He started me off this afternoon and it promises to be a pretty good picture. He had a curious habit recently of painting one side in a brilliant light and the other in a deep shadow. I don't think all heads are applicable to that effect, especially for portraits. I have on a gorgeous white vest that I purchased for $1.50 on the way up there.*[28]

Glackens is shown slightly turned away, holding an elegant horn-handled cane in his hand. The restrained appearance and formal dress of the portrait evoke traditional Grand Manner portraits more than do Henri's representations of George Luks or Josephine Nivison. Marked parallels can be seen in Henri's style and interpretation to Velázquez's portrait of King Philip IV of Spain (c. 1623-27; Museo del Prado, Madrid), which Henri must have seen on his trip to Madrid in 1900.[29]

Late in 1904, Henri painted three full-length portraits of a model, Anna Maria Bustamente, dressed as a Spanish dancer, which were probably influenced by his earlier trip to Madrid. *Spanish*

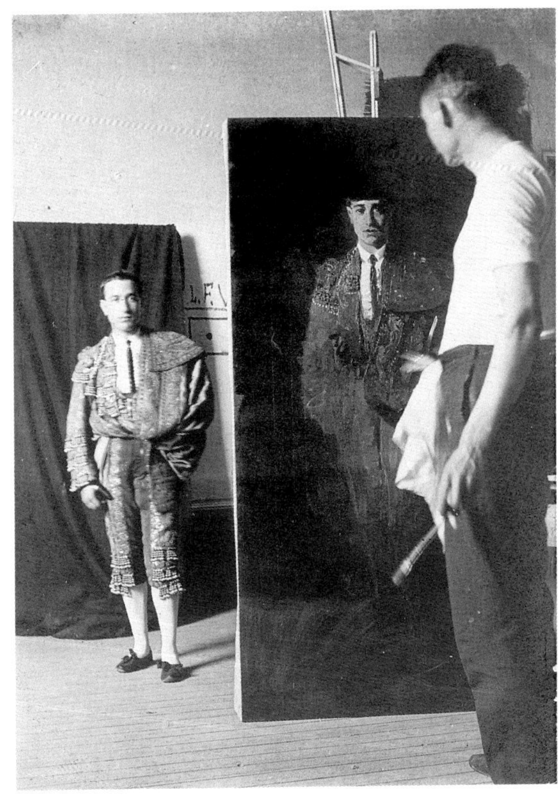

Photograph of Henri painting Asiego, Madrid, 1906. Collection of Janet Le Clair

Dancing Girl (cat. 11), the first of the series, was painted in his New York studio, four years after his first visit to Spain. The country had made an indelible impression on him, both artistically, through the work of Velázquez and Goya, and spiritually. Spain continually offered artistic inspiration to Henri as seen in his repeated use of Spanish subjects throughout his career.

In the summer of 1906, Henri returned to Spain with a New York School of Art class, and stayed on to paint in Madrid after the class ended. His imagination was stimulated by the Spanish aesthetic and culture resulting in a prolific period of work. During the remainder of the summer, he completed a number of important canvases, including two versions of *Modiste of Madrid, Portrait of El Matador Felix Asiego, La Reina Mora* (cats. 12-14), and *Gypsy with Guitar* (fig. 4), among others.

Modiste of Madrid (cat. 12), painted in July 1906, is the first of two variations. The portrait exhibits a loose and painterly style with visible brushstrokes. Henri described the subject as having "black hair, large eyes with strong lashes, full face. Black shawl with fringe. White waist full bust. Black fan in right hand."[30] He went on to paint another similarly posed version, which he noted in his diary on August 10: "completed without model second full length of 'the modiste' . . . . think it an excellent likeness of the girl."[31]

Later that summer, Henri befriended a bullfighter in Madrid, Felix Asiego. He wrote extensively of Asiego:

> *We have made the acquaintance of a Matador "Felix Asiego." We saw him at the Madrid Plaza des Toros in a fight about three Sundays ago—a handsome and graceful man—he is not more than twenty-two . . . and has studied law but did not want to give up his idea of glory in the bull ring . . . . he is indeed very popular and attracts attention all over Madrid.*[32]

Captivated by the heroic romanticism of bullfighting, Henri's letters from the summer are filled with references to the major pastime of Spain and to Asiego. He later described the portrait he painted of the young matador (cat. 13):

> *My portrait of Asiego is done—full length. It is much thought of . . . . He is in full costume as he appears just before the grand entry into the ring . . . . He . . . appears before a dark background—full face his right hand hanging as his side—I had much trouble with the hand on account of his hand being bandaged up—he was wounded by the bull three Sundays ago and the injury to his hand was considerable.*[33]

Henri's detailed account of the portrait includes a description of Asiego's sumptuous costume of green and gold, with a purple and gold cape. He also noted that he believed he had captured the typically serious expression and sense of apprehension in the bullfighter's face just before he enters the ring.[34] *Portrait of El Matador Felix Asiego* was one of three works Henri submitted to the 1907 National Academy of Design Annual. It was dropped a grade by the Academy rating system, and he ultimately withdrew the painting, along with another work. In addition, he felt that the works of his associates had been unjustly rejected for exhibition—these events collectively became the catalyst for his revolt against the Academy, and resulted in the formation of the alternative exhibition of The Eight at the Macbeth Galleries.[35]

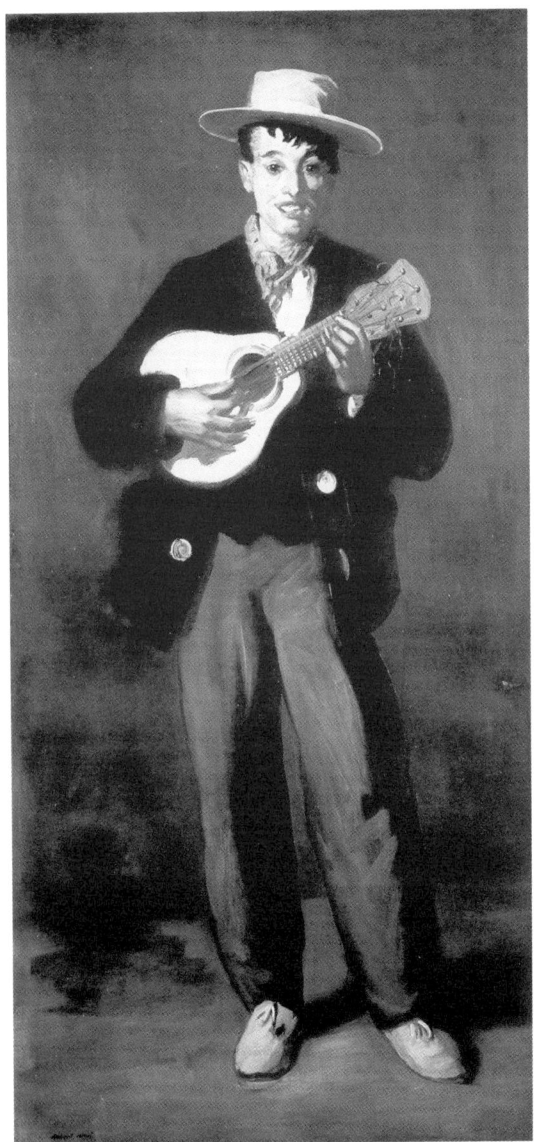

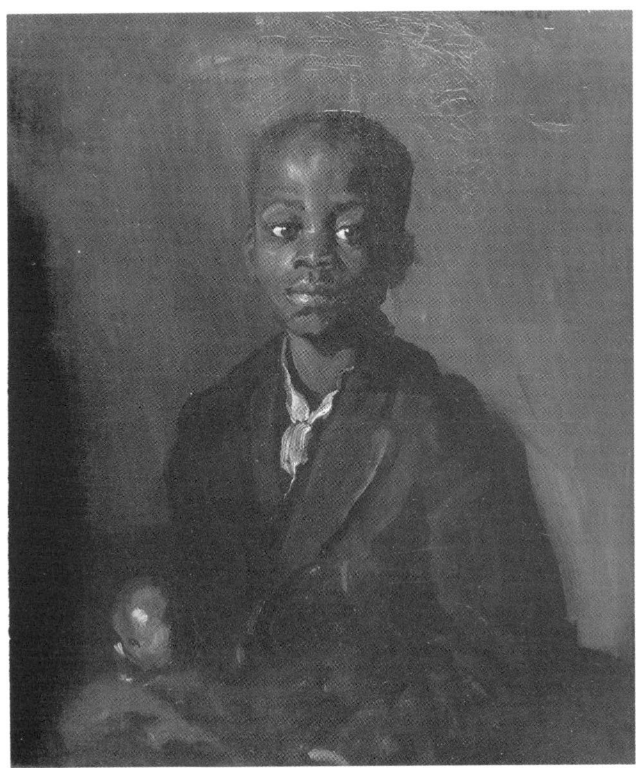

Fig. 4
Gypsy with Guitar (Gitano), 1906
Oil on canvas, 78 x 37¾ in.
The Chrysler Museum, Norfolk, Virginia
Gift of Walter P. Chrysler, Jr.

Fig. 5
Portrait of Willie Gee, 1904
Oil on canvas, 32¼ x 26¼ in.
The Newark Museum, New Jersey, Anonymous Gift, 1925

All the works painted during Henri's stay in Spain have an aesthetic connection to the work of Velázquez, Goya, and Manet, though the effect is most pronounced in *La Reina Mora (The Moorish Queen)* (cat. 14). *La Reina Mora* is a portrait of Milagros Moreno, a well-known Andalusian dancer. After seeing her dance at the "Actualidades," a center for Spanish dancing, Henri said of her performance, "on the stage she is almost savage in her dance—a fierceness that is terrible. I saw her earlier in the season."[36] This is one of his most memorable portraits, capturing with assurance, Moreno's vivid and decorated costume and smoldering sensuality. He had gone to the dancer's house, and selected her outfit from a multitude of elaborate and expensive costumes.[37] As he reported in a letter that September, he was satisfied with the portrait: "I did a large full length portrait of . . . a brilliant dancer in a white shawl with embroidery in brilliant red and colors. White skirt, stockings and shoes all white a blue ribbon over one shoulder . . . flowers in her jet black hair, pearl necklace with diamond cluster and pendant pearls, rings—a very brilliant piece of color."[38] By this time, Henri's technique allowed him to complete a large scale portrait in an even more accelerated fashion. He mentions that "this big portrait was rather a rapid piece of work—three sittings of two hours each—I had to work fast to be sure to get her before she got tired."[39] The portrait is executed in a more assured and mature style than anything he had previously attempted and captures the charismatic aura of this confident performer. Despite the specificity and realism, Henri's *La Reina Mora* also recalls a portrait type of Spanish dancer found in Goya's *The Duchess of Alba,* 1799 (The Hispanic Society of America, New York) and Manet's *Lola de Valence,* 1862 (Musée d'Orsay, Paris), which likely served as models, if only in concept. The most prominent American precursors to Henri include Chase's *Carmencita,* 1890 (The Metropolitan Museum of Art, New York) and Sargent's, *El Jaleo,* 1882 (Isabella Stewart Gardner Museum, Boston) .

During mid-September, while modeling for *La Reina Mora,* Milagros Moreno broke a number of appointments with Henri. To fill the time, he located a gypsy family who posed for him. He first depicted the young mother and her child, and then he painted the husband in a full-length portrait, *Gypsy with Guitar,* 1906 (fig. 4). Henri described him as

> *a dandy . . . , on his head a sombrero like the bullfighters wear with flat brim over jet black loose hair . . . jet like eyes—these people show the light of life in their eyes . . . —a rich red roll of handkerchief about the neck—velvet—or heavy plush coat with enormous mother of pearl buttons. Cut short—"chulo" style—a style peculiar to Spain . . . . I painted him in his loose swing, a Spanish guitar in his hands playing and his face in a reckless devil may care song.*[40]

Following the full-length portrait, Henri also undertook a three-quarter length portrait of the same subject, *Gypsy with Cigarette* (IBM Collection, Armonk, New York). These Spanish gypsy subjects are presented with great nobility, and show strong contrasts with a rich palette, a robust painting style, and broad flat areas of color that stylistically recall portraits by Manet.

During the first half of 1907, preoccupied with planning The Eight exhibition in addition to his regular activities, Henri produced few works. Among them were a group of portraits of the model Jesseca Penn. The first of the series, *Young Woman in Yellow Satin* (cat. 15), is a traditional formal portrait, painted in a restrained manner. The lightness of the overall palette represents a departure from the predominantly somber tonal scheme of many of Henri's early portraits. The work is a study in textural contrasts that highlight the model's hair, complexion, and the satin fabric of the dress. Henri entered the painting in the Winter exhibition of the National Academy of Design, and subsequently toured it to a number of institutions over the next couple of years.

In the summer of 1907, Henri went to Holland to teach a New York School of Art class. After visiting Haarlem, Volendam, and Amsterdam, a new influence became evident in his work. The paintings he produced in Holland that summer reflect the direct influence of Dutch seventeenth-century masters, as in *Laughing Child, Martche with Hat,* and *Dutch Fisherman,* (cats. 16–18). The broad brushwork, a liberated and abundant application of paint, earth tones, and the dark backgrounds that Henri used during this period mirror the stylistic traits he saw in the portraits of Frans Hals and Rembrandt. Henri wrote from Holland that "the people here are certainly mighty interesting looking . . . . Frans Hals painted them—men and women—wonderfully and the pictures by Hals, Rembrandt, and many others . . . are a great treat to see."[41] Initially, Henri was not impressed with Holland, perhaps because the memory of Spain was still so vivid, but he soon developed a warm appreciation for the country and its people.

I have been very busy—have found much to do. Last week I painted a head of a child every day. These little Dutch children are wonderful to paint.—No wonder Frans Hals painted such smiling people—all Holland has red apple cheeks, white heads, smiles—they are very kind—happy people—my old view of them is all changed. [42]

His stay in Holland proved to be an important and productive time for Henri. He painted numerous small-scale portraits, many of children. *Dutch Fisherman* and *Laughing Child,* both executed in Haarlem, were later shown in The Eight exhibition, and *Laughing Child* was purchased directly from the exhibition by the art patron Gertrude Vanderbilt Whitney for her collection. And, *Martche with Hat,* also painted in Haarlem, was shown at the National Academy of Design 1908 exhibition.

While in Haarlem, Henri's attention focused on two Dutch girls, Cori Peterson and Martche, who were a marked study in contrasts. Henri commented on Cori: "all the time I have been here I have painted over and over again a little roistering white headed red cheeked broad faced girl—I have done many heads of her, most of them laughing."[43] The Whitney painting is the first of a consecutive series of more than fifteen portraits Henri painted of Cori. Comparing the other model, Martche, to Cori, he said: "I have another little model—just the opposite type in character—thin, pathetic—pale—very interesting and just as Dutch as the other rollicking one."[44] Henri's different response to the two subjects is reflected in the contrasting manner of the execution of their portraits. *Laughing Child* is "very roughly painted thick paint with much rather pure red and blue in it,"[45] while *Martche with Hat* is more delicate in appearance with paler, blended tonalities.

Though rendered in a broad style reminiscent of Hals, the portrait of Martche is subdued in temperament, reflecting her fragility. She appears poised, with a thoughtful and mysterious gaze. It is more finely painted than the Cori portrait, with its bold, unpolished quality of brushwork. Henri painted approximately ten portraits of Martche, in which he experimented with various poses and different clothes. Several of the portraits also include hats, such as *Dutch Girl in White,* 1907 (The Metropolitan Museum of Art, New York).

Henri returned to New York in the fall and began teaching art classes at the New York School of Art. After a surge of creative energy during the summer, he produced few portraits during the remainder of 1907. One of his finest efforts was *Eva Green,* painted on Christmas Day (cat. 19). Henri's notes record a "tamoshanter hat . . . . Blue coat, blue ribbon showing and reddish ribbon sticking out from back of hair."[46] His portraits at this time, as seen in *Eva Green,* begin to display more emotional depth and a growing ability to achieve deeper characterizations through details of gesture, and expression than the works of several years earlier. Henri had previously depicted an African-American in the well-known *Portrait of Willie Gee,* 1904 (fig. 5). His interest in representing different types of people in his portraits can be traced to his deeply felt democratic views of humanity, and precedents can be found in the work of other artists he knew and admired, including his teachers, Thomas Hovenden and Thomas Anshutz, as well as Thomas Eakins and Winslow Homer.

Henri's emotional connection to Spain surfaces again in a series of portraits completed in the late summer and early fall of 1908. While visiting Spain in the summer of that year, where he taught a class, Henri returned to the subjects he had painted on his previous visit, particularly native gypsies, dancers, and matadors. In September, he wrote to John Sloan about what he had accomplished—"so far of importance, full length of a picadore, 3 full length dancers . . . —had a cold for a while, and did little then, and the material was hard to get to start with . . . ."[47]

This second group of Spanish portraits is broader in interpretation, exhibiting a looser style than those painted during his 1906 visit. Among the paintings he produced on this trip to Madrid was *Celestina* (cat. 20), a portrait of an old woman smiling.[48] In this unromanticized portrayal of a hag with a toothless grin, Henri presents her with great humanity and dignity. By finding character and nobility in an unprepossessing sitter, Henri reveals his bond to Frans Hals, seventeenth-century Spanish artists, and Goya, who frequently depicted the downtrodden. Recalling similar subjects painted by Hals, Henri noted:

> *Frans Hals liked them all for what they were and he gave his best to each one. Every bit of Frans Hals' painting is sheer invention. Examine the structure in the strokes which make the heads . . . . He saw life and people in his own peculiar way and he was a supreme master of the tools in his hand.*[49]

Many of Henri's lectures and writings refer to Hals, celebrating his technique and style. In Henri's own philosophy of art and subjective beauty, "the subject can be as it may, beautiful or ugly. The beauty of a work of art is in the work itself."[50] This exclusively formal emphasis, however, is not reflected in Henri's portraits, which frequently carry a strong affective message, moreover, the lowliest subjects he depicted were often his most emotionally stirring portraits.

One of the major canvases Henri painted while in Spain was of the dancer Manoleta Marequis, entitled *El Tango* (cat. 21).[51] About this portrait, one critic wrote, "we reach the note of greatest brilliance in these [Spanish] subjects . . . with *El Tango,* magnificent in arrogance of pose, in vitality of expression, and in the color and line of the flowered white shawl that forms the larger part of the costume."[52] The subject is boldly confident, with an earthy sexuality, and the penetrating characterization and realism in the portrait is communicated through facial expression, stance, gesture, and detail of costume.

In May 1909, Henri executed two full-length portraits of an opera singer, Mademoiselle Voclezca, in costume as Salome from the Richard Strauss opera. The first version (Mead Art Museum, Amherst College) shows the performer confronting the viewer with self-possessed confidence and an enticing look.[53] She holds a white shawl as a prop, which was eliminated in the later variant. In *Salome (No. 2)* (cat. 22), the model is shown dancing in a more animated pose. The costume, with a chiffon skirt, is decorated with embroidery, sequins, beads, and is a study of texture and movement. Like Sargent and Chase, Henri was fascinated with the charismatic dynamism of dramatic personalities and depicted dancers and other performers in a number of works, including *Spanish Dancing Girl, La Reina Mora, El Tango,* and *La Madrileñita* (cats. 11, 14, 21, 28).

In May 1908 Henri had secretly married Marjorie Organ, an illustrator, before he went abroad (his first wife had died in 1905). Following his return to New York in the fall, he became involved with various exhibition activities and teaching opportunities that distracted him from painting. Marjorie, along with other women, served as model for a number of the full-length portraits he painted during 1909, 1910, and 1911. This cycle of portraits shows female figures elegantly garbed in shawls, kimonos, or long dresses that produce an attenuated effect. On May 10, 1909, Henri began a life-size painting of Marjorie wrapped in a yellow shawl (cat. 23). John Sloan went to visit him on May 13, and saw "a new full-length of 'Marjorie.' It is a very good thing, the best thing he has painted of her in my opinion. A shawl wrapped around her, a perfect portrait and a work of creative imagination."[54] Sloan again mentioned the painting in comparison to another portrait Henri did of Marjorie about nine months later, saying, "I liked it as a work though in character it is not as true to her as the one in the yellow and purple shawl."[55]

Henri's diary notes reveal that Hardesty Maratta called on him on June 7, 1909, with a set of paints for him to try.[56] Maratta, an artist and theoretician, promoted his paints in association with a theory of color usage, based on a scale of tonal gradations that would uniformly systematize the palette. Color theory became of immense interest to Henri, who was fascinated throughout the remainder of his life by visual effects produced from regulated color harmonies. The *Blue Kimona* (cat. 24), executed on August 21, is Henri's first major effort after adopting the new method.[57] The overall brighter tonalities and unusual juxtaposition of colors represent Henri's tentative approach to the new paint system.

The model for the painting, Miss Waki Kaji, a Japanese-American, also posed for other Henri portraits, including *The Equestrian,* 1909 (The Carnegie Museum of Art, Pittsburgh), and modeled for Glackens and possibly Sloan.[58] *The Blue Kimona* was entered in the Philadelphia Art Club's 1909 annual exhibition shortly after being completed and won the Gold Medal. The portrait was favored by Henri, and he exhibited it extensively throughout his life.[59] In subject, it relates to the Orientalist themes that many American artists, following the French lead, began to take up in the mid-1880s.[60]

Betalo Rubino, a dancer noted for her striking features and unusual dramatic costumes, became another important model for Henri. During 1909 and 1910, he painted a series of portraits of her that include the three-quarter length, *Dancer in a Yellow Shawl,* 1910 (Columbus Museum of Art, Ohio) and a smaller, related work, *The Red Flower (Betalo in Spanish Chair)* (cat. 25). The latter was conceived as a full-length seated portrait, but Henri later cut it down to its current size in December 1910.[61] Betalo Rubino wears the same costume and gold bracelet as in the Columbus version, though her yellow and violet shawl has been shifted from the right arm to the left, and the added red flower serves as the focal point of the composition. *Girl with Fan* (cat. 26), a later reprise of the same theme, is a study of yellow tones, featuring Betalo's costume, a full-skirted yellow satin dress, for which Henri again employs purple accents. He sent the painting to the 1912 Pennsylvania Academy of the Fine Arts Annual Exhibition, where it was purchased for the Permanent Collection,[62] adding to an already growing list of institutions which had purchased Henri portraits.

Henri again traveled abroad in the summer of 1910, this time without the responsibility of teaching. June and July were spent in Haarlem, where he painted numerous portraits, including one particular model he used repeatedly, Jopie van Slouten, seen in *Dutch Joe (Jopie van Slouten)* (cat. 29). Earlier treatments of the same figure include *Jopie Laughing Boy* (Birmingham Museum of Art), and *Jopie Giggling Boy* (private collection). *Dutch Joe* shows Henri's ability to capture the effervescent personality of this subject. Critic John Cournos commented:

> *Henri has put on canvas quite a number of laughing boys, . . . but the most remarkable youngster of the kind he has just brought over with him from Holland. Surely in this case the artist blew breath into paint, and the result is a live, laughing boy . . . . This picture might be called a snapshot in paint, for it is amazing that an artist painting with a brush should have so successfully caught a child's momentary mood. Yet, despite its dash and brilliancy, there is more than mere virtuosity in this canvas.*[63]

The young Dutch boy became one of Henri's most characteristic portraits.

After spending time in Haarlem, Henri moved on to Volendam for July and August, and then to Madrid for the remainder of August and September. On September 15, he began a series of portraits of a young dancer of about fifteen, Josefa Cruz, the subject of *La Madrileñita.* The first "little girl of Madrid" was conceived as a full-length seated portrait in a scarlet dress, which the artist cut down to three-quarter size.[64] This painting was sold by Henri to the Telfair Academy of Art and Sciences in Savannah, Georgia; he wrote to Col. A.R. Lawton about the painting at the time of the sale:

> *I feel you will have in the picture "Madrileñita" one of the very best things I have painted. Perhaps you would be interested in the following data in reference to the picture. It was painted in Madrid. She is a very young girl, born and raised a dancer (that is, she is the niece of the celebrated teacher of dancing, Cansino of Madrid). Cansino trained her in the old dances of Spain. Although very young, she was already a very remarkable dancer at the time the painting was done, and it seemed to me she had in her carriage at all time much of the spirit and dignity of old Spain.*[65]

Another exploration of the "Madrileñita" theme is a bust portrait of the young girl in delicate tonalities of salmon-colored pinks, offset by muted green accents, painted on September 20 and 22 (cat. 27). Seen in side view, the young dancer appears pensive and slightly mysterious, and a sense of intimacy is apparent that is absent from the larger portraits.

Another version of *La Madrileñita* (cat. 28) was begun before the bust portrait, on September 19, and it is the only full-length, standing portrait of the model Henri painted. He started off using the red dress, but repainted the canvas several days later in the elaborate Spanish dancer's green and rose costume in which she appears in the smaller portrait.[66] In the full-size painting, Josefa Cruz is shown in bright green and pink, facing away in a dancer's stance with a hand on her hip. The intense shiny green fabric with pink ruffles decorating the dress forms a brilliantly colored visual arrangement. Henri's diary entries for the third week of September note that he went back and forth between the several different versions of *La Madrileñita,* reworking them and playing one against the other.[67]

1911 was a transitional year in Henri's stylistic development. Maratta was a continual visitor during this period, and color studies using the Maratta palette took up an increasing amount of Henri's time. Although he painted a number of portraits, he produced few forceful images. Portraits of fellow artists, literary figures, and family had been a constant endeavor in earlier years,

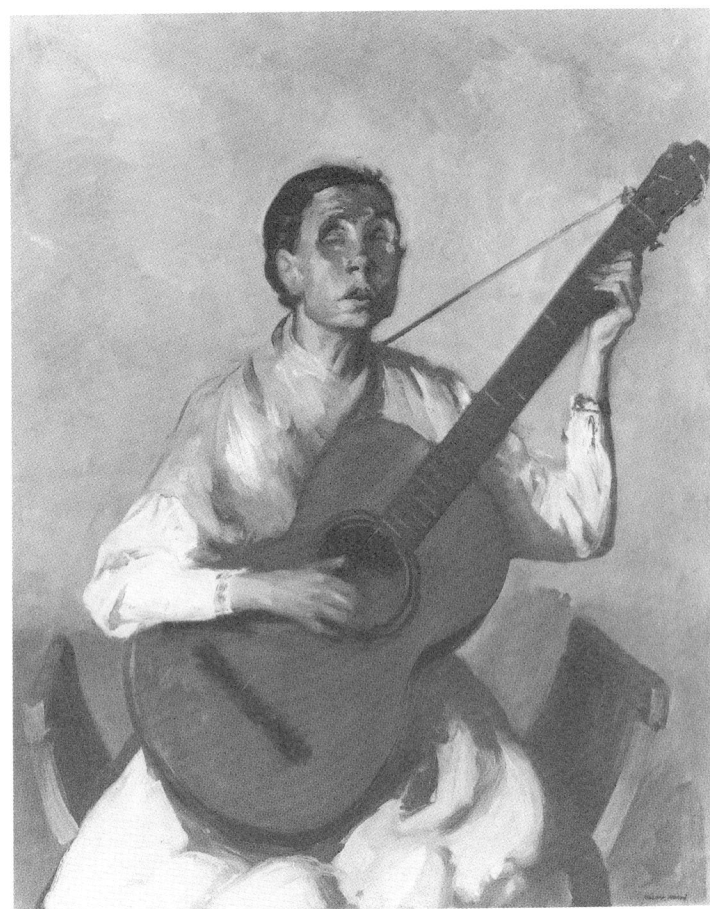

Fig. 6
Blind Spanish Singer, 1912
Oil on canvas, 41 x 33 1/8 in.
National Museum of American Art,
Smithsonian Institution,
Gift of Mr. J.H. Smith.

and Henri again looked toward his immediate circle for models. Among the notable subjects he painted during 1911 were Marjorie, portrayed in *The Brown Wrap* (Lauren Rogers Museum of Art, Laurel, Mississippi) and *The Masquerade Dress* (The Metropolitan Museum of Art, New York); and Mrs. Eulabee Dix Becker as *Lady in Black Velvet* (The High Museum of Art, Atlanta). In addition to painting his close friend George Bellows, Henri also produced portraits of fellow artists Carl Sprinchorn (Herbert F. Johnson Museum, Cornell University, Ithaca) and Randall Davey. He did not travel to Europe that summer, but instead visited Monhegan Island, Maine, in August with Marjorie, Davey, and Bellows. During that summer, Henri and Bellows both concentrated on painting varied views of the stark Maine coastline in numerous small panel paintings.

After Henri's return to New York, he executed a portrait of George Bellows (cat. 30). The picture, intended for the National Academy of Design, was to satisfy the requirements for Bellows' Associate Membership.[68] Though conceived as a formal portrait for the Academy, it is a personal and restrained rendition of Bellows that stylistically recalls Henri's earlier efforts of 1904. The generally dark tonality of the composition, with dramatic light modeling Bellows' face, looks to the Old Master sources Henri had relied on earlier in his development. Bellows saw Henri as a mentor and friend, crediting the older artist with guiding his formative artistic life.[69] Henri's portrait of his former student, whose rapid success rivaled, and even surpassed, his own, reflects the emotional warmth that existed between the two artists, as well as a sense of pride in Bellows' accomplishments.

Further rejecting notions of traditional society portraiture, Henri painted a group of portraits while in Spain during the summer of 1912 that were strong and compelling. This series includes

The Old Model (Archer M. Huntington Art Gallery, University of Texas at Austin), *Spanish Shepherd* (Akron Art Museum), *Blind Singers* (Hirshhorn Museum and Sculpture Garden, Washington, D.C.), and *Blind Spanish Singer* (fig. 6). Henri may have been responding in these works to the melancholy he perceived in the Spanish temperament. He wrote from Spain:

> *There are some wild looking gypsies and some children—there are no laughing Dutch children to do here—there is a more dramatic strain in these people. I have done one picture which I think is a very strong painting of a blind woman playing a guitar and singing—but it will not be a popular picture because it is of a terrible human tragedy and not a sentimental tragedy.* [70]

During this visit to Spain, Henri painted numerous canvases of the less fortunate, including peasants, gypsies and beggars. He may have found a precedent in images of the mendicant, especially those with physical deformities, in the work of Spanish artists, particularly Jusepe de Ribera and Goya, whose penchant for brutal realism and pathos in their work was well known. Although Henri repeatedly painted such comely subjects as the *The Green Fan (Girl of Toledo, Spain)* (cat. 31), and a series of a young Segovian girl, he was more often drawn to emotionally powerful, non-traditional subjects, even though they were considered unseemly by the academic establishment. One example is *Madre Gitana* (cat. 32) which conservative critic Royal Cortissoz singled out, while commending Henri's rejection of superficial subjects:

> *Though there is no imagination in Henri's paintings . . . there is a good deal of interesting characterization. He has painted Spanish and other exotic types, and they make a welcome contrast to the dull trou-frou of which we see so much . . . . He makes a positive personage out of the . . . matron of his "Madre Gitana." There are personalities mirrored in his canvases.* [71]

Cortissoz's criticism of the lack of imagination in the portraits refers to Henri's penchant for rendering truth in paint. Responding to the subdued temperament and winsome prettiness of the sitter in *The Green Fan (Girl of Toledo, Spain),* Henri painted the subject in warm and varied colors, but with subtle blending and shading. Though both works display a rich medley of color, in *Madre Gitana* he employed a hotter, more high-keyed palette, with rugged brushwork and raw pigment directly applied, producing a harsher appearance.

By 1913, although Henri was yet to produce much of his most original work, he found his influence and status waning within the art world. His marginalized role in the planning and presentation of the Armory Show and the overwhelming response generated by the innovations of the European artists' work shown there signified that Henri was no longer at the forefront of the progressive movement, nor a leading figure in the American art scene. The impact of the Armory Show had many ramifications for him, primarily the realization that American art was lagging far behind the European avant-garde, and that the style of realism which he practiced had become outmoded by the more modern styles of expressionism and abstraction.

Amidst the continuing reverberations of the Armory Show, Henri sailed for Ireland in June 1913 with Marjorie. They stayed until the end of September on the island of Achill, settling near the village of Dooagh. After first producing sketches and some paintings of the landscape, Henri returned to portraiture. Among other engaging subjects he depicted, including Johnnie Cummings and his wife in *Himself* and *Herself* (The Art Institute of Chicago), *Old Johnnie's Wife* (Indianapolis Museum of Art), and *Old Johnnie* (The Baltimore Museum of Art), and numerous Irish children, Henri found Brien O'Malley, a Gaelic storyteller, tourist guide, and one of the native eccentrics exceptionally interesting:

> *I painted today one of the great characters of the Island—he is "Brien," a guide to tourists up the Croaghan mountain—the one that slides off for 2,000 feet to the sea. He is 76, is quite certain that the earth stands still and does not revolve, and can take his tourists extra luggage on his back and climb up like a goat leaving his young followers to puff and heart fail* [sic]. *He has seen ghosts, fairies and gnomes . . . and claims descent from the celebrated lady who once ruled over this part of Ireland.*[72]

One portrait of O'Malley shows him in an overcoat with his walking stick, posed *en plein air,* a rarity in Henri's portrait compositions. A second seated portrait of him, *The Guide to Croaghan* (cat. 33), portrays the Irishman in dark formal attire, with a whimsical expression. A later composition, *My Friend Brien O'Malley* (Mint Museum of Art, Charlotte) presents the guide with his hat and pipe in a more informal portrait that introduces lighter tones of red, blue, and brown. O'Malley was reportedly pleased with the portraits, and was impressed with Henri's diligence and dedication to his work.[73]

Henri, constantly exploring new ideas and then reexamining methods and techniques he had previously employed, painted his mother in 1914 in a more traditional mode. *Portrait of Mrs. Richard H. Lee* (cat. 34) differs from much of the work he was producing at this time, the composition being staid and somewhat severe, with dark tonalities and restrained brushwork that recalls portraits he had painted more than a decade earlier.

However, a trip to southern California in the summer of 1914 led Henri to a period of experimentation in his portraiture. He drove to California with Marjorie and her sister, Violet Organ, known as Viv. The two women posed for portraits, alternating with Asian-Americans, Native Americans, and other models Henri located. The distinctiveness of the people and the ambiance had a pronounced effect on Henri's portrait style. The bright hues, variegated backgrounds, and a new sense of spatial openness infuse a look of modernity and freshness into these California portraits.

Viv in Blue Stripe (cat. 35) is one of a group of portraits Henri painted of Viv and Marjorie in hats, a group that also includes *The Beach Hat,* 1914 (The Detroit Institute of Arts) and *Portrait of Mrs. Robert Henri,* 1914 (San Diego Museum of Art). *Viv in Blue Stripe* represents a departure from Henri's previous work in the unprecedented impression of light and airiness created by the bright clothing and pale yellow and blue, undulating background. The black and blue striped bow provides a counterpoint to the vivid blue and white striped jacket and white hat. The stripes add an element of visual complexity atypical in Henri's portraits because of the tension created, which competes with the visage of the sitter. The portrait nevertheless achieves an overall sense of harmony through balance of color and composition.

Henri had been drawn to ethnic and cultural differences since his early trips abroad. Of his portraits of the diverse Southern Californians he encountered, he later remarked:

> *Since my return from the Southwest, where I saw many great things in a variety of human forms—the little Chinese-American girl, . . . and the Indian . . . —I have been reproached with not adding to my study of these people the background of their lives. This has astonished me because all their lives are in their expressions, in their eyes, their movements, or they are not worth translating into art. I was not interested in these people to sentimentalize over them . . . . I am looking at each individual with the eager hope of finding there something of the dignity of life . . . . I do not wish to explain these people, I do not wish to preach through them, I only want to find whatever of the* great spirit *there is in the Southwest. If I can hold it on my canvas I am satisfied . . . .*[74]

Viv in Blue Stripe and *Tam Gan* (cat. 36) were painted in La Jolla, California, where Henri was staying; other notable paintings he did there include three versions of a black newspaper boy, Sylvester.[75] He also ventured to San Diego in search of models, painting three portraits of Jim Lee, "the vegetable man." This portrait (cat. 37) was Henri's second attempt of the same subject. It is modified only in the facial expression, which Henri noted as "more awake with expression of quizzical humor."[76] Henri's egalitarian and populist beliefs are borne out in his portraiture by the noble bearing and dignity of presentation even in ordinarily unremarkable subjects.

The perceptive characterizations of *Tam Gan* and *Jim Lee* are created by a simplicity of structure that subordinates the design element of the composition. The bright and unexpected tonalities of the backgrounds set off the figures either through startling contrasts or monochromatic shadings. One critic said of the work Henri produced in California:

> *His schemes of color are brilliant, daring, unexpected, even startling. Yet somehow they are almost always right. His broad spaces of green and blue and red . . . never clash, though they often become deadly enemies under a feebler hand.*
>
> *But the facile rendering of the outward is with Henri only the attractive means by which he seeks—and finds—the really important ends. I am speaking now of his portraits . . . .*[77]

Critically, the portraits Henri produced during the La Jolla stay elicited strong, positive comments and were recognized as some of the most creative and artistically distinctive work he had produced. When an exhibition of the La Jolla portraits was held at the Macbeth Galleries in the fall of 1914, one reviewer observed:

> *Robert Henri has come back from the Far West with thirteen canvases . . . . They represent the extraordinary mixture of races that dwell along "the Coast" . . . and which, curiously enough, none of our painters . . . have thought to picture . . . . The bravura that was Velázquez and the humor that was Hals have passed from Mr. Henri's work within the past year and his art has assumed a phase more solidly brilliant than anything that has gone before. What is left is something infinitely finer, graver, more wonderful in color and in technique.*[78]

With the portraits Henri produced in California, the last conscious vestiges of Manet, Hals, and Velázquez disappeared from his work, and this period marks the advent of more original portraits, free of historical persuasion. These years represent a second zenith in Henri's career. Though no longer in the forefront of new developments in contemporary art, he continued to explore and reevaluate the direction he pursued in his own work.

Henri had been working with the Maratta color system for a number years, but more pronounced visual effects become apparent in the portraits of 1915, reflecting his increasing involvement with the theoretical aspects of painting. Among the recurring subjects he painted, which include a number of nudes, were portraits of a red-haired model, Edna Smith (cat. 38). This series of figure studies are less portraits focused on the individuality of the subject than explorations of the figure in an abstract and formalistic sense. The complexity of the palette, with a spectrum of multicolored hues, ranges from the red of the model's hair to a blue-green ground. The rendering of the colorful Japanese-style pattern of the purplish shawl against the white chemise shows Henri's technical facility.

Betalo Rubino and Viv posed for numerous portraits during 1915 and 1916. In March 1915, back in New York, Henri painted a striking portrait of Viv. In *Viv (New York)* (cat. 40), he placed the sitter against an imposing decorative pattern, and the symmetry of the frontal pose imbues the portrait with strength and solidity. Viv's strong features are brought into prominence by the light band around the crown of her hat and the white collar protruding from her fur coat.

In the summer of 1915, George and Emma Bellows accompanied the Henris to Ogunquit, Maine, a popular artists' colony. Henri initially expressed reservations about the choice of location and its conduciveness to working:

> *The war and other attendant conditions have driven us to Maine. It is certainly not Spain or Holland but we are making it do . . . . We have had some luck with getting models, but the children have none of the definitive established character that they had in Holland.*[79]

By August, Henri adjusted to the extreme weather, found an encampment of gypsies who served as models, and settled in. Among the gypsies, Henri painted Patience and her three-year-old cousin, Lily. He included bouquets of flowers in a number of portraits of them, including *Village Girl (Lily Cow)* (cat. 39).[80] Writing about Ogunquit a few weeks later, he said, "it appears that after all our coming here will prove a rather good thing for I already have a few things that are very good. Particularly of a gypsy child laughing—I think it is one of my very best in this type of work."[81] The gypsy child, Lily Cooper, known as Lily "Cow," was one of Henri's favorite models that summer and posed for twelve other paintings.[82] Formal issues of color and composition continued to be integral to these compositions of 1915 and 1916. Likely influenced by his exposure to the European Fauves and Expressionists at the Armory Show, Henri's experimentation with unusual and vivid palettes and color combinations reached a climax in the Ogunquit portraits, particularly in the more than twenty canvases of Maine gypsies with the similarly vibrant background colors seen in *Village Girl*.[83]

Among the most important works of Henri's career was a commissioned portrait of the art patron, artist, and philanthropist, Gertrude Vanderbilt Whitney (Mrs. Harry Payne Whitney) (fig. 7). Though extremely wealthy and part of established society, she was also known for her bohemian lifestyle and personal flamboyance. For the portrait, she choose an elaborate, multicolored silk

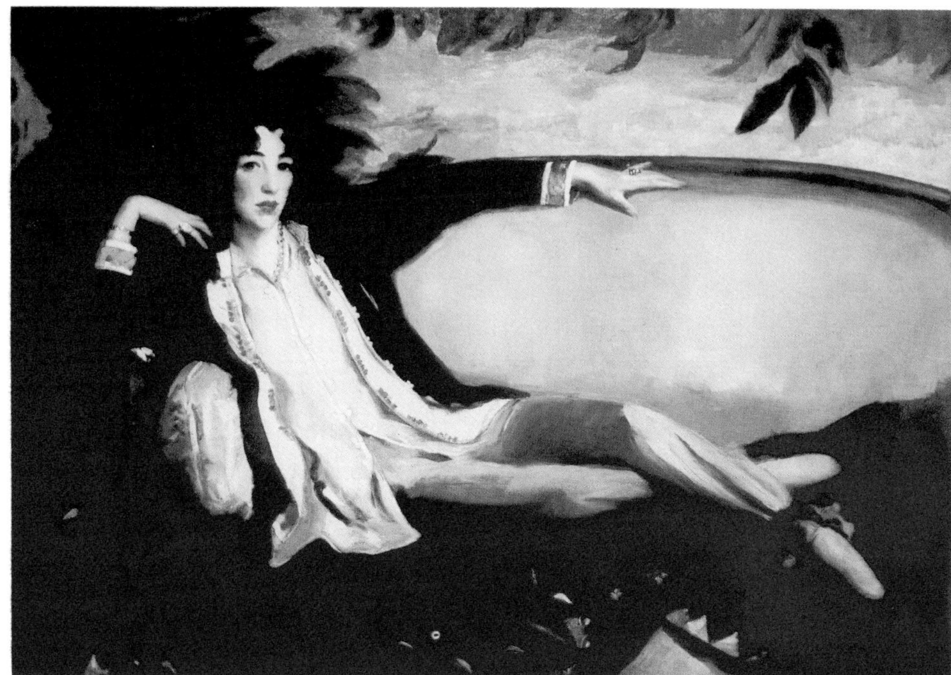

Fig. 7
Gertrude Vanderbilt Whitney, 1916
Oil on canvas, 50 x 72 in.
Whitney Museum of American Art,
Gift of Flora Whitney Miller

pants outfit and an unusual pose, in which she draped herself full length across a sofa, reclining in the classical pose of an odalisque. The portrait, though highly stylized, faithfully captures the subject, as evidenced by photographs of her from the period.[84] Marjorie described the effort:

> *Bob is painting Mrs. H.P. Whitney in a very interesting Japanese costume which she got in San Francisco. It's the usual—coat and trouser effect, only that she wears three coats—all different colors—light blue green, yellow, and dark blue—It's a stunning effect, and the picture is going to be one of his finest.*[85]

A major opus in his career, the portrait of Gertrude Vanderbilt Whitney is one of Henri's most complex endeavors in terms of composition and palette, as well as the most genuine and convincing of his commissioned portraits.

Henri received portrait commissions somewhat regularly once his artistic status was established, though he did not actively cultivate this aspect of his career, preferring to rely on a modest income from teaching. His need for a sympathetic rapport with his portrait subjects often precluded successful results in his commissioned works. And because he could not select models he personally found interesting, the commissioned portraits usually appear lifeless, lacking the distinctive spark of vitality that characterizes his finest efforts.

Besides Gertrude Vanderbilt Whitney, Henri painted a number of other reclining figures, both nude and clothed, during 1916. He most often employed professional models, and the works lean toward figure studies rather than portraiture. One exception is *Betalo Nude* (cat. 41). More resolved than many of his other nudes, this painting is a portrait, thought not, as the title suggests, of Betalo Rubino. The distinctive features are those of Henri's sister-in-law, Violet Organ.[86]

New locations were important for Henri's artistic renewal in the summers, for him the most productive season of the year. In the summer of 1916, Henri first visited Santa Fe, returning the following summer, and again in 1922. Henri's letters from Santa Fe reflect his romanticized view of the spirituality and mystery of Native American culture.[87] Exposed to a diversity of ethnic traditions during his previous visit to California, he immediately rekindled a sympathetic bond he felt with the environment, a bond that translated into the portraits he painted in Santa Fe.

His major picture of 1916 was the stately *Portrait of Dieguito Roybal—Po-Tse-Nu-Tsa* (cat. 42), a Tesuque Indian painted in Santa Fe in September. The structural arrangement of the composition is dominated by a geometrical complex of angles, and the palette hosts a full spectrum of colors. Pleased with the painting of the ceremonial Indian drummer, Henri later gave it to the local Museum of Art and Archeology:

> *I have painted some landscapes and water colors of the pueblos and ceremonial dances as well as some portraits. Among the portraits that of the Tesuque drummer chief Dieguito pleases me as well as some portraits of Indian girls in ceremonial attire . . . .*
> *I have painted them as I felt without regard to fashions old or new. I feel myself a decided modern though not of the modernistic school and am egotist enough to give all my thought to what interests me . . . . Human faces are incentives to clairvoyance.*[88]

The penetrating characterization of the old stately Indian and the faithful detail of his costume endow the portrait with an emotional veracity.

Indian Girl (cat. 43), another portrait painted during his 1916 Santa Fe visit, is a more unadorned composition, streamlined in its simplicity. Clearly constructed with angled divisions of parallel and perpendicular lines, the work is unembellished save for the arrow design on the blanket. With other colors limited, the vivid orange blanket centralizes attention on the face.

In 1917, back in New York, Henri painted a portrait of his friend, the art critic and editor, Mary Fanton Roberts (cat. 44). Roberts, who used the pseudonym Giles Edgerton, was a staunch defender of Henri and the insurgent movement in the early years of the century. She served as editor of *The Craftsmen* and *Touchstone,* journals that lent influential support to Henri. The portrait of her, painted in March 1917,[89] is dignified in pose and more formal than the Indian portraits Henri had been producing. Using contrasting deep and bright hues, the painting exhibits the full spectral range of colors, though is more reserved in approach than the Santa Fe works.

The portraits Henri painted in Santa Fe in the summer of 1917 were experimental and unusually inventive. Though he was unable to move beyond the essential confines of realism, in numerous portraits of this summer he began to assimilate Native decorative elements into the composition and focus more visual attention on the complementary space around the figures. In *Gregorita with the Santa Clara Bowl* (cat. 45), Henri included an example of Native black pottery. Intrigued with the culture and art of the Southwestern people, he also painted a number of portraits that incorporate the abstract ornamental quality of the Native textiles, shown either wrapped around or hanging behind the figures. Among the Native American models he found, Julianita and Gregorita were two he pictured in a number of brightly keyed canvases with Indian blankets in the background (fig. 8). *Pepita* (cat. 46) is a richly colored portrait of a young Hispanic girl named Juanita. The abstract design forming the background of the composition represents an extension of Henri's experimentation with Indian textiles. *Tilly* (cat. 47), painted later that summer in a brilliant palette of complementary colors, portrays another young Mexican girl who made an impression on Henri:

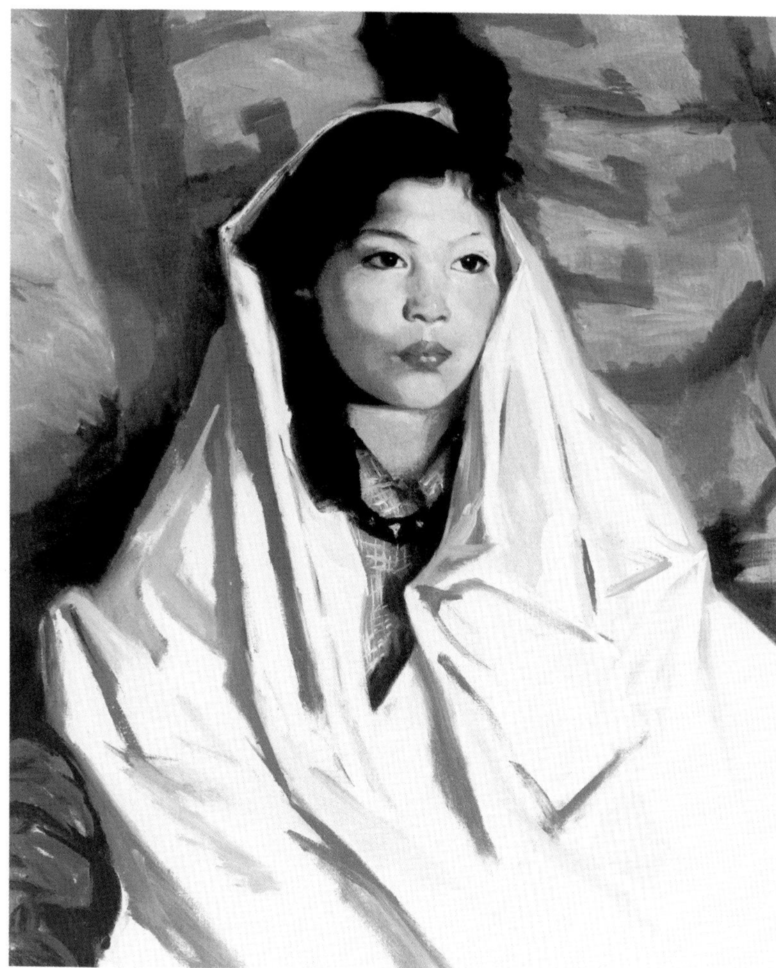

Fig. 8
Gregorita, 1917
Oil on canvas, 36 x 26 in.
Gilcrease Museum, Tulsa, Oklahoma

> *We have a little Mexican girl posing, play the victrola for her and she poses fine. Wild black hair, eyes that have looked into the sun and a face well burned by it. Her name is "Tilly" she speaks only Spanish, but we know enough . . . .*[90]

In this portrait of her, one of nine Henri painted, she is shown leaning against an orange pillow in front of a green wall, and corresponding tones are picked up in her clothing. Similarly, *Bernadita* (cat. 48), painted in October 1922 when Henri again returned to Santa Fe, is a portrait of a Mexican-Indian girl named Berna Escudero, whose elegant, exotic features Henri recorded in eleven portraits.[91] Painted during Henri's last trip to Santa Fe, the work is consistent with the theme and style of portraits he had previously been exploring there, and the work of this last summer forms a coda to the Indian subjects in Henri's oeuvre.

As Henri noted in a letter to his brother, his experimentation with color reached a second peak in 1919:

> *I have done a good deal of new study lately and I believe I will have an advance of considerable importance in my work as a result—richer and more beautiful color and form.*[92]

Though no specific reference defining the development is made, his portraits show a shift in palette and a new opulence. Non-traditional color combinations appear in his canvases of this period, most often characterized by deeper, more intense hues. The unusual tonal innovations, however, led to results that the public and critics did not always perceive as effective. One critic commented on the exhibition of recent work that was touring in 1919:

Color is the distinctive quality of painting . . . and Henri's example in color, his feeling for new, fresh harmonies, is the biggest thing in his art. But nevertheless one is dubious about the success of much of his painting. There are "chords" of color in this gallery that fairly hurt at first glance, and one cannot imagine becoming attuned to them in any length of time.[93]

Monumental works became fewer among Henri's portraits of the late years. However, the masterpiece of his late career is a life-size painting of the dancer Ruth St. Denis (cat. 49) in costume, painted in 1919. Henri's interest in dance as an art form brought him into contact with many noted dancers of the day, including Isadora Duncan, Roshanara (Olive Craddock), and Betalo Rubino, who all had modeled for him. The portrait of Ruth St. Denis engaged Henri's attention throughout the second half of February and the beginning of March. Henri reported the story of the painting and his progress:

I am painting a portrait of Ruth St. Denis, the great dancer. Have had three sittings and am to have 3 more next week—it's a big piece of work getting on very well so far. She is in her dance of the "Peacock." The story is Egyptian princess very proud, etc. whose spirit is confined in a peacock. It is a very wonderful dance and she is very beautiful in it. Costume is naturally in the character and colors of peacock.[94]

Henri made numerous sketches for the painting and lavished attention on every detail. Though he had routinely finished even large works in a few days, he was still refining the portrait in April. He complained that "it's almost done—have a foot to finish without her, which is difficult as it is important—must be *her* foot. No other will do. Have several drawings I made of it but it is difficult nevertheless."[95]

Henri's facination with movement and form reflected a natural affinity for dance. *Ruth St. Denis in the Peacock Dance* shows the dancer in a pose suggesting movement by the fluid sway of her body. The lush palette is of strikingly rich blues and greens, offset by red-purple accents. Following the completion of this portrait, Henri began a painting of another dancer, Roshanara, later that spring. Again the dancer is pictured in an exotic and elaborate costume of multicolored veils and skirts of deep hues. The portrait is most clearly distinguished, however, by the unusual seated pose and the horizontal format.

Henri's perpetual restlessness led him to visit the artists' colony of Woodstock, New York, in the summer of 1921. Woodstock attracted many artists, and George Bellows, Eugene Speicher, and Leon Kroll also went that summer. Henri completed an extensive series of canvases, many of the young local residents: "here I am painting principally children. There is a good crop of them available and some are excellent."[96] Among the subjects that he found intriguing were Jimmie Gerry and the three Sleicher children, Agnes, Hans, and Carl. Of Carl posing for the painting *Carl Sleicher* (cat. 51), Henri said:

The one I had today is a wonder—a little gnome of two and a half—and I think I landed a good one. This is perhaps the reason that I have felt the power to sit down and write. The youngster has light blond hair, dark brown eyes, a jumper of fine gray blue purple with a deep red edging, a white shirt in excellent tone with the rest, he sits on a little sienna

> *colored childs rocker which is mainly covered up with a warm colored back cushion which has a design on it that adds excellent notes of color to the composition. I know you would like the youngster and I believe you would like the painting.*[97]

In the Woodstock portraits, which include six other versions of *Jimmie Gerry* (cat. 50) and numerous portraits of the Sleicher children, color harmony and structural arrangements are intricately interwoven. The works from this summer form a transition to Henri's late period, which is almost exclusively devoted to the subject of children. However, Henri's primary focus in the Woodstock portraits is still the personality of the subjects, whereas in his late Irish portraits, done between 1924 and 1928, formalistic concerns dominate.

In 1923, any financial concerns were dissolved by an inheritance he received from his mother. He formulated plans for a return trip to Europe, visiting Paris before moving on to Madrid, where he spent about eight months. As on his earlier visits to Spain in 1906, 1908 and 1912, he gravitated toward subjects of street people, local peasants, and gypsies. Working in a bold painterly style as he had been in 1912, he now developed an even warmer and richer palette based on earth tones. In reevaluating some of his earlier notions about the intensity and combination of colors, Henri wrote:

> *Derain . . . has done some beautiful work with earth colors. It is not easy to get color with a sober palette, but when it is well done the effect is remarkable. Sometimes it is with earth colors and one bright color that meaningful color schemes can be made . . . .*
> *In reference to the beauty of low toned colors in backgrounds and accessories, the beautiful colors which can be made with red as the basic color should be remembered. These reds keep back but remain strong . . . . Too many bright colors and too many different colors are often the cause of bad color in painting.*[98]

Henri's rethinking of the palette is evident in the red-orange tonalities of *Dorita* (cat. 52), painted in Madrid in January 1924. The luminous warm hues contrast sharply with the cool whiteness and daring brushwork of the dancer's skirt. Dorita was a young café dancer Henri thought to be not more than fifteen. He noted that she

> *came with her father, an ex-bullfighter. The fact that I had seen Mazantinito in the bull ring and therefore himself as picador, made everything all right. I started painting the little dancer on Monday and hope the result will pay for the house I hope to have eventually in Santa Fe.*[99]

He painted several versions of Dorita, experimenting with different costumes and proportions, cutting down the size of the canvases in less successful attempts. Many of the paintings Henri executed on this trip exhibit the same smoldering tonalities, though they are typically characterized by a harsher brush technique that leaves much of the pigment raw and unblended.

Following Madrid, Henri's peripatetic nature took him back to Ireland. There he again went to Achill Island for an extended stay, from April to November 1924. Henri began negotiations for the purchase of Corrymore House, which he had previously rented. Between 1924 and 1928, he returned every spring or summer for extended stays. For his remaining years, the children of the village of Dooagh became Henri's primary portrait subjects. His paintings of the Irish children capture and celebrate the spirited innocence and openness of the young Irish faces.

The late portraits form a distinct and cohesive body of work within Henri's oeuvre. Through repetition of subjects, Henri explored formal and abstract ideas of color and compositional harmonies in a virtual shorthand vocabulary. In these paintings, he used a more limited tonal range, with one or two foundation colors to build the composition. Against rich reds, blues, and greens, he juxtaposed dark earth tones of brown and gray, which comprise the color schemes of many of these portraits.

Henri's portraits document the offspring of many of the Irish village's families, including the Lavelles, O'Donnels, MacNamaras, Burkes, O'Malleys, and Caffertys, all of whom reside in Dooagh, on Achill Island. The portraits record the children's growth, since Henri often returned to paint the same sitters. *Moira (Mary O'Malley)* and *Tom Cafferty* (cats. 53, 54) are among the subjects Henri painted in the fall of 1924.

Traditionally, Henri had carefully documented and supplied accurate titles that reflected the identity of models. However, with the Irish portraits, his titles became notably less accurate.[100] He painted numerous portraits that he titled "Tom Cafferty," though *Tom Cafferty* is actually one of many portraits he painted of a villager named Michael Cafferkey. *The Fisherman's Son: Thomas Cafferty* (cat. 55) is a portrait of a relation of Michael Cafferkey's, Tom Cafferkey.[101] This fact accounts for the physiognomical differences between *Tom Cafferty,* and *The Fisherman's Son: Thomas Cafferty,* which were painted only about one year apart. Stylistically, both works exhibit the painterly abandon and generous fluency of pigment that characterizes the late portraits.

Mary Ann Cafferkey, sister of Michael, was the model for *Young Chevass (Mary Ann Cafferty)* (cat. 56) and appeared in a number of other portraits.[102] In later portraits, she is pictured in a more feminine guise, as in *Mary Ann, with Her Basket,* 1926 (Currier Gallery of Art, Manchester, New Hampshire) and *The Pink Ribbon,* 1927 (Museum of Fine Arts, Boston). However, *Young Chevass (Mary Ann Cafferty)* is distinguished by the complexity of the backdrop: a swirl of colors intimating drapery forms suggests backgrounds Henri had been employing in the teens.

Henri's last important honor during his lifetime was the receipt of the prestigious Temple Gold Medal. The prize, awarded by the Pennsylvania Academy of the Fine Arts in January 1929, was for *The Wee Woman* (cat. 57), painted in October 1927. The painting is notable for its deep coloration and visibly liberated brushwork, and the model, Mary Gallagher, is recognizable by her straw-colored hair and gray-blue eyes.[103]

Henri painted *Wee Annie Lavelle (Pet)* (cat. 59) in 1927; the following summer he used the same model for *Girl in Pink (Anne Lavelle)* (Mt. Holyoke College Art Museum, South Hadley, Massachusetts). According to the model, she was about five years old when she first sat for Henri.[104] The contrast between the two portraits shows the physical changes in the model, as well as the artist's tendency toward increasingly abbreviated allusions to non-essential details in his late portraits.

Thomas Cafferkey and Bridget Lavelle, older sister of Annie Lavelle, were among the most frequently repeated subjects of Henri's late Irish portraits. He wrote in his diary of Bridget Lavelle, "this is the very good looking girl with the oval face . . . ."[105] A cycle of portraits depicting Bridget Lavelle occupied Henri during his last season of painting in 1928, and he painted her intermittently from late July to mid-September. The series forms the final coherent exploration of a single subject in Henri's career.[106] Evident in the late portraits, such as *Blond Bridget Lavelle* (cat. 58) and *Fergus* (cat. 60), is Henri's use of the subject as a suggestive framework, a study of color and form that only focuses on the face. The intellectualized conception of these portraits, these studies in visual harmony, represents Henri's closest proximity to abstraction. The torso and clothing of the models become only minimal painterly intimations made by broad undefined strokes of the paintbrush. The doctrine Henri had advocated to his students is manifested most clearly in his own late work:

> *Gesture expresses through form and color the states of life. Work with great speed . . . . Finish as quickly as you can. There is no virtue in delaying. Get the greatest possibility of expression in the larger masses first . . . . Do it all in one sitting if you can. In one minute if you can . . . . The most vital things in the look of a face . . . endure only for a moment.*[107]

The Irish portraits are defined by Henri's ability to rapidly capture the outward vitality of the model. Critical of the academic polish of such artists as William-Adolphe Bouguereau, he had advised his students:

> *Do not require of your work the finish that anyone may demand of you, but insist on the finish which you demand . . . .*
> *The demand we so often hear for finish is not for finish, but is for the expected. Judging a Manet from the point of view of Bouguereau the Manet has not been finished. Judging a Bouguereau from the point of view of a Manet the Bouguereau has not been begun.*[108]

Though the influences of Hals and Velázquez are no longer apparent in Henri's final portraits, the qualities he admired in their work—their superb technique and ability to reveal so much with so little through economy of brushwork, form a conceptual underpinning for his late portraits.

The late Irish portraits are devoted almost entirely to childen, a theme Henri began to concentrate on in the early 1920s. Echoing in the numerous portraits painted toward the end of his career are his own words:

> *If you paint children you must have no patronizing attitude toward them. Whoever approaches a child without humility, without wonderment, and without infinite respect, misses in his judgement of what is before him . . . . Paint with respect for him . . . He is the great possibility, the independent individual.*[109]

Emblematic of his universal and positive view of humankind, children had a particular spirit and sense of optimism that had a powerful allure for Henri.

By the time of his death, Robert Henri had effected an enduring legacy through his actions and promotion of his ideals, but more importantly by the astonishing body of portraiture he produced. Spanning the transitional period from the dominance of realism to the onset of modernism and abstraction, his portraits appear to occupy a middle ground in an era marked by rapid change. Though by reputation known as an arch-radical and a rebel, from a late twentieth-century perspective Henri's portraiture now appears to fall squarely within the mainstream evolution of realism. The artistic status he acquired was founded on portraiture, his principal mode of expression, which was defined by the candid perceptions of his "people" as revealed through incisive characterizations. Not for some time, if ever, has any artist successfully achieved a comparable rank with portraiture.

Though often technically adventurous, Henri's portraits never depart from representation. He remained more daring in the realm of theoretical and abstract ideas about art, which he passed on through teaching to the next generation. The view of Henri as out-of-step with the art world after the Armory Show has left a shadow over his reputation. Though he had been resistant to contemporary changes in outlook, and was bewildered by the Armory Show, he ventured forward on his own path of artistic inquiry, which involved experimental ideas of color and compositional design.

Eschewing the polished technique of virtuoso painters such as Sargent or Chase, Henri instead featured the subject, sublimating ego and technical prowess in his portraiture. He let the sitter's character eloquently speak through the painting. Every nuance, gesture, and expression of an individual was captured in an attempt to reveal what lay beneath superficial appearances. Through he limited his portraits predominantly to single figures, either life-size or bust-length, that directly confront the viewer, Henri managed to exhibit a wide range of diversity and originality in his work through constant self-analysis, innovation, and the embrace of various stylistic influences.

A strong biographical undercurrent as well as his democratic view of humanity is reflected in Henri's portraiture. He recorded the world in which he lived by painting the individuals he found there, whether intimates, acquaintances, or the exotic "types" he sought in his travels. The psychological empathy he developed for each individual seduced him, and as a result he endowed each portrait with a spark of life and a sense of the subject's uniqueness:

> *I find as I go out, from one land to another seeking "my people," that I have none of that cruel, fearful possession known as patriotism . . . . My love of mankind is individual, not national, and always I find the race expressed in the individual. And so I am "patriotic" only about what I admire, and my devotion to humanity burns up as brightly for [and] . . . just as completely as though each of these people were of my own country . . . . Everywhere I see at times this beautiful expression of the dignity of life to which I respond with a wish to preserve this beauty of humanity.*[110]

NOTES

1. Robert Henri, *The Art Spirit,* comp. Margery Ryerson (1923; reprint, New York: Harper & Row, 1984), p. 91.

2. Guy Pène du Bois, "Robert Henri—Realist and Idealist," *Arts & Decoration,* 2 (April 1912), pp. 214–15.

3. Richard Brilliant, *Portraiture* (Cambridge, Massachusetts: Harvard University Press, 1991), p. 67.

4. Quoted in Bennard B. Perlman, *Robert Henri: His Life and Art* (New York: Dover Publications, 1991), p. 143.

5. Robert Henri, "'My People': By Robert Henri," *The Craftsman,* 26, no. 5 (February 1915), p. 459.

6. Charles De Kay, "Six Impressionists: Startling Works by Red-Hot American Painters," *The New York Times,* January 20, 1904.

7. Henri to his mother, September 4, 1898, Henri Papers, Beinecke Rare Book and Manuscript Library, Yale University.

8. See, for example, Henri to his mother, July 16, 1906, July 9, 1907, and July 15, 1907; and during his first trip to Europe, Henri to Tucker, June 15, 1890; Henri Papers, Beinecke Rare Book and Manuscript Library, Yale University. See also Henri, *The Art Spirit*, passim, for numerous references to these masters.

9. "The Work of Robert Henri," *Philadelphia Ledger,* November 16, 1902.

10. Artist's Record Book, collection of Janet Le Clair.

11. Riter Fitzgerald, "Robert Henri's Works: The Eccentric Artist Improving," *Philadelphia Item,* December 1, 1902.

12. "Notable Specimens of Robert Henri's Brush on Exhibition," *New York American,* November 16, 1902; and Francis J. Ziegler, "News of the Art World: Robert Henri's Pictures on View at the Academy," unidentified 1902 clipping.

13. William B. M'Cormick, "Seventy-Second Exhibition of the Pennsylvania Academy," *New York Press,* January 19, 1903.

14. De Kay, "Six Impressionists."

15. Henri, *The Art Spirit,* p . 41.

16. Artist's Record Book, collection of Janet Le Clair.

17. Artist's Record Book, collection of Janet Le Clair. The family left Nebraska and adopted different names after Henri's father, originally named John Jackson Cozad, was brought up on charges of murder. The parents became Mr. and Mrs. Richard Henry Lee and their sons were referred to as adopted foster brothers and renamed Robert Earle Henri and Frank L. Southrn to disguise their identities. For a thorough recounting of Henri's early life, see "The Early Years," in William Innes Homer, *Robert Henri and His Circle* (1969; reprint, New York: Hacker Art Books, 1988), pp. 7–20. See also Perlman, *Robert Henri: His Life and Art.*

18. De Kay, "Six Impressionists."

19. "Mr. Henri's Canvases Prove to be the Most Magnetic at the Galleries of the National Arts Club," *Standard Union* (Brooklyn, New York), January 24, 1904.

20. Henri diary, January 16, 1906, p. 16, collection of Janet Le Clair.

21. Artist's Record Book, collection of Janet Le Clair. Henri gave Sloan the portrait in April of that year.

22. Artist's Record Book, collection of Janet Le Clair.

23. John E.D. Trask, "Art Exhibitions of the Middle West," *Book News,* December 1905, p. 211.

24. "Glamour About Name of Sargent, Painter: His Work Draws All Eyes at the American Artists' Show Yet Not as Good as Henri's," *New York Press,* March 27, 1904.

25. Samuel Isham, *The History of American Painting,* with supplemental chapters by Royal Cortissoz (1905; reprint, New York: The Macmillan Company, 1936), p. 506.

26. John Sloan, *John Sloan's New York Scene,* ed. Bruce St. John (New York: Harper & Row, 1965), pp. 185–86.

27. Ira Glackens, *William Glackens and the Ashcan Group: The Emergence of Realism in American Art* (New York: Crown Publishers, 1957), p. 151.

28. Ibid., p. 61.

29. Homer, *Robert Henri and His Circle,* p. 238. Homer describes the various influences at work in Henri's early portraiture, using *Portrait of W.J. Glackens* as an example. His discussion focuses on the dominant influence of Velázquez.

30. Artist's Record Book, collection of Janet Le Clair.

31. Henri diary, August 10, 1906, p. 222, collection of Janet Le Clair.

32. Henri to his parents, July 25, 1906, Henri Papers, Beinecke Rare Book and Manuscript Library, Yale University.

33. Henri to his parents, August 7, 1906, Henri Papers, Beinecke Rare Book and Manuscript Library, Yale University.

34. Ibid.

35. The following contemporaneous articles document Henri's break with the Academy: "National Academy Stirred by Mr. Henri's Withdrawal of Pictures," *The Sun* (New York), March 14, 1907; "The Thirty and Mr. Henri: Why the Painter Withdrew His Academy Canvases," *The Evening Post* (New York), March 13, 1907; and "The Henri Hurrah," *American Art News*, 5 (March 23, 1907), p. 4. See also Elizabeth Milroy, *Painters of a New Century: The Eight,* exh. cat. (Milwaukee: Milwaukee Art Museum, 1991).

36. Henri to his parents, September 18, 1906, Henri Papers, Beinecke Rare Book and Manuscript Library, Yale University.

37. Henri diary, September 6, 1906, p. 249, collection of Janet Le Clair.

38. Henri to his parents, September 18, 1906, Henri Papers, Beinecke Rare Book and Manuscript Library, Yale University.

39. Ibid.

40. Henri to his parents, September 23, 1906, Henri Papers, Beinecke Rare Book and Manuscript Library, Yale University.

41. Henri to his mother, July 9, 1907, Henri Papers, Beinecke Rare Book and Manuscript Library, Yale University.

42. Henri to his mother, July 15, 1907, Henri Papers, Beinecke Rare Book and Manuscript Library, Yale University.

43. Henri to his mother, July 28, 1907. Henri Papers, Beinecke Rare Book and Manuscript Library, Yale University.

44. Ibid.

45. Artist's Record Book, collection of Janet Le Clair.

46. Artist's Record Book, collection of Janet Le Clair.

47. Henri to John Sloan, September 3, 1908, Sloan Archive, Helen Farr Sloan Library, Delaware Art Museum, Wilmington.

48. See Alfonso E. Pérez Sánchez and Eleanor A. Sayre, *Goya and the Spirit of Enlightenment,* exh. cat. (Boston: Museum of Fine Arts, 1989), pp. 299–300. Goya's drawing *La Madre Celestina,* c. 1816, which the authors believe is derived from the main character "La Celestina," of Fernando de Rojas' 1499 literary work, *Tragicomedy of Calixto and Melibea* (popularly known as *La Celestina*), may be an antecedent for Henri's painting *Celestina.* Enamored of Spanish culture, Henri may have been familiar with the work, though no definitive proof exists.

49. Henri, *The Art Spirit,* p. 191.

50. Henri, *The Art Spirit,* p. 166.

51. Artist's Record Book, collection of Janet Le Clair. Henri noted other possible titles for the painting, including *¡Venga de Whi!—Come Here!* or *Begin to Dance!*

52. Elisabeth Luther Cary, "Robert Henri," *Bulletin of The Metropolitan Museum of Art,* 26 (March 1931), p. 60.

53. Henri entered the first version of *Salome* in the 1910 Spring Annual at the National Academy of Design, along with two other portraits. Both *Salome* and one of the other works were rejected, motivating Henri to work with Arthur B. Davies, Walt Kuhn, and John Sloan in forming what became the 1910 Exhibition of Independent Artists, in which Henri entered the rejected painting of *Salome.*

54. Sloan, *John Sloan's New York Scene,* p. 311.

55. Ibid., p. 390.

56. Henri diary, June 7, 1909, p. 159, collection of Janet Le Clair.

57. Henri diary, August 21, 1909, p. 233, collection of Janet Le Clair.

58. Sloan, *John Sloan's New York Scene,* pp. 128, 329.

59. Artist's Record Book, collection of Janet Le Clair.

60. See, for example, Whistler's *Caprice in Purple and Gold: The Golden Screen,* 1864, and *Le Princesse du Pays de la Porcelaine,* 1863–64 (Freer Gallery of Art, Washington, D.C.), and Chase's *The Blue Kimono (Girl in Blue Kimono)*, c. 1898 (The Parrish Art Museum, Southampton, New York), and *The Japanese Print,* c. 1888 (Neue Pinakothek, Munich).

61. Artist's Record Book, collection of Janet Le Clair. *The Red Flower* was originally conceived as a 50 x 70-in. composition.

62. Artist's Record Book, collection of Janet Le Clair.

63. John Cournos, "What Is Art? Answered By Henri, Art 'Insurgent,'" *The Philadelphia Record,* December 25, 1910, p. 3.

64. Artist's Record Book, collection of Janet Le Clair.

65. Henri to Col. A.R. Lawton, December 5, 1919, Telfair Academy of Arts and Sciences Archives. I would like to thank Feay Coleman for calling this letter to my attention, and Pamela King for sharing the contents with me.

66. Henri diary, September 19, 1910, and September 23, 1910, collection of Janet Le Clair. On September 20 and 22 Henri worked on the bust portrait. He had started the full-size standing portrait in red on September 19, but on September 23 substituted the pink and green costume.

67. Henri diary, September 25, 1910, collection of Janet Le Clair. Entries from September 15 to September 24 mention working on the various paintings of *La Madrileñita*, and on September 25 Henri writes extensively about exploring the same or similar themes in a number of canvases.

68. Artist's Record Book, collection of Janet Le Clair. Henri notes that Bellows picked up the portrait for the National Academy of Design on November 27. The submission of a portrait of the artist was required to attain the status of Associate in the National Academy of Design. An example of the artist's own work was required to become a full Academician.

69. See George Bellows, "'The Art Spirit,' By Robert Henri," *Arts & Decoration,* 20 (December 1923), pp. 25, 87; Charles Morgan, *George Bellows: Painter of America* (New York: Reynal and Co., 1965), p. 37.

70. Henri to his mother, August 9, 1912, Henri Papers, Beinecke Rare Book and Manuscript Library, Yale University.

71. Royal Cortissoz, *American Artists* (New York: Charles Scribner's Sons, 1923), p. 180.

72. Henri to his mother, undated 1913 letter, p. 3, Henri Papers, Beinecke Rare Book and Manuscript Library, Yale University.

73. Violet Organ, "Robert Henri," unpublished manuscript, p. 99, collection of Janet Le Clair.

74. Henri, "'My People,'" pp. 462, 467.

75. Artist's Record Book, collection of Janet Le Clair.

76. Ibid.

77. "Henri's La Jolla Portraits," unidentified Los Angeles newspaper, September 20, 1914.

78. William B. M'Cormick, "Mastery of Medium Shown in Henri's Exhibit of Far Western Types at Macbeth's," *New York Press,* November 22, 1914.

79. Henri to Helen Niles, July 17, 1915, Henri Papers, Beinecke Rare Book and Manuscript Library, Yale University.

80. Organ, "Robert Henri," p. 109.

81. Henri to his mother, August 19, 1915, Henri Papers, Beinecke Rare Book and Manuscript Library, Yale University.

82. Artist's Record Book, collection of Janet Le Clair; also Janet Le Clair to the author, August 3, 1992. *Village Girl* was painted on August 16, 1915. In Henri's Record Book, nine of the thirteen portraits of Lily were marked "destroyed" by Violet Organ. Upon Marjorie Henri's death, Organ became the executor of the Henri estate, and in her zeal to portray Henri in the best light, she destroyed many portraits of a variety of subjects she believed to be duplications or of inferior quality.

83. Artist's Record Book, collection of Janet Le Clair. See also catalogue entry on *Village Girl (Lily Cow)* in *Catalogue of the Collection* (St. Petersburg, Florida: Museum of Fine Arts, 1994), pp. 164–65.

84. B.H. Friedman, *Gertrude Vanderbilt Whitney* (Garden City, New York: Doubleday & Company, 1978), pp. 174–75. Mrs. Whitney commissioned the portrait, paying the artist a fee of $2,500.

85. Majorie Henri to Helen Niles, 1916, undated, Henri Papers, Beinecke Rare Book and Manuscript Library, Yale University.

86. Artist's Record Book, collection of Janet Le Clair. It has been suggested by Janet Le Clair that Henri's mistitling of the painting derived from his sense of propriety. Another reclining nude portrait, *Betalo Nude (Pink and White),* 1916 (Collection of Janet Le Clair, Estate of Robert Henri), painted shortly before *Betalo Nude,* also depicts Violet Organ, and Henri's Record Book shows that he had done a number of other reclining studies of her prior to this painting.

87. Henri to his mother, August 3, 1917, August 11, 1917, and August 19, 1917, Henri Papers, Beinecke Rare Book and Manuscript Library, Yale University.

88. Henri to Mary and Bill Roberts, undated letter, quoted in Homer, *Robert Henri and His Circle*, pp. 203, 205.

89. Artist's Record Book, collection of Janet Le Clair. The portrait was given to Mary Fanton Roberts the following month.

90. Henri to his mother, August 19, 1917, Henri Papers, Beinecke Rare Book and Manuscript Library, Yale University.

91. Artist's Record Book, collection of Janet Le Clair.

92. Henri to Frank Southrn, January 27, 1919, Henri Papers, Beinecke Rare Book and Manuscript Library, Yale University.

93. Leonard Lanson Cline, "Paintings by Henri at the Art Museum: Color and Candor Shocking, But Underneath Evidence of Notable Rebel," *Detroit News,* July 11, 1919.

94. Henri to his mother, February 15, 1919, Henri Papers, Beinecke Rare Book and Manuscript Library, Yale University.

95. Henri to Helen Niles, April 9, 1919, Henri Papers, Beinecke Rare Book and Manuscript Library, Yale University. The Artist's Record Book additionally notes that he again repainted the foot on February 13, 1922.

96. Henri to Helen Niles, August 8, 1921, Henri Papers, Beinecke Rare Book and Manuscript Library, Yale University.

97. Ibid. This painting was Henri's sixth essay of Carl.

98. Organ, "Robert Henri," p. 123.

99. Henri to John Sloan, quoted in Organ, "Robert Henri," p. 124.

100. Henri to his mother, August 28, 1913, Henri Papers, Beinecke Rare Book and Manuscript Library, Yale University. Henri wrote that Irish given names were excessively redundant, though no reason is known for his actual mistitling of the portraits.

101. Thomas McNamara to the author, June 22, 1994.

102. Ibid. "Chevass" is a pet name, according to Thomas McNamara.

103. Ibid.

104. Anne Lavelle Fell to Ellen Simak, undated; Anne Lavelle Fell to Ellen Simak, February 24, 1993; and Anne Lavelle Fell to Thomas McNamara, undated, Archive, Hunter Museum of Art, Chattanooga, Tennessee. The model recalled that she had initially been afraid of the artist. Each time she came to pose, Henri gave her a box of sweets and paid her for posing.

105. Henri diary, July 28, 1928, collection of Janet Le Clair.

106. Henri diary, August 17, 1928, collection of Janet Le Clair. The entry also makes reference to the fact that there is a second Bridget Lavelle who has dark hair whom he refers to as "Black Bridget Lavelle." He believes that the two Bridgets are not related to each other, and that dark-haired Bridget Lavelle is a niece of the O'Malleys.

107. Henri, *The Art Spirit,* p. 26–27.

108. Ibid., pp. 181–82.

109. Ibid., pp. 237–38, 246.

110. Henri, "'My People,'" p. 459.

Robert Henri: Theory and Practice

MICHAEL QUICK

Manuscripts in Robert Henri's own hand,[1] in addition to the testimony of fellow artists such as John Sloan and George Bellows,[2] reveal Henri to have been an exceptionally deep and thorough student of color theory and to a lesser extent of compositional systems. A born leader, he was able to transmit these interests to those in his immediate circle and organize group efforts to resolve theoretical questions. Although Henri's theoretical work has been discussed in the literature,[3] it still may seem surprising that such complicated theorizing could lie behind such natural-looking portraits. A closer look at his writings in relation to the portraits will help to close the apparent gap between his theory and his practice.

During the period 1891–93, following his return from his first, extended stay in Paris, where he was strongly impressed by an exhibition of recent paintings by Claude Monet, Henri painted a number of pictures in a style of strong, divided color, which were among the clearest examples of late Impressionism by any American artist in those years. He thus early manifested a sensuous enjoyment of color and evidenced at least some knowledge of color theory.[4] On subsequent trips abroad, in 1895–97 and in 1898–1900, however, Henri was exposed to other artistic currents, which led him away from Impressionism's pure and exultant color.

From at least his return to Paris in 1898, Henri's art was a highly self-conscious and austere one. He developed rapidly in that hothouse of turn-of-the-century aestheticism, painting city views in which he arranged and composed the elements in an "artistic" way, with a strongly geometrical structure based upon the Golden Section, with a decorative surface, and with a muted palette and dim lighting meant to convey a mood. In his *Night, Fourteenth of July* (fig. 9), for instance, Henri boldly announced his organizing principle by arranging the three largest flagpoles according to the golden-section ratio.[5] The top row of lights along the eaves of the tent likewise align with the golden- section division of the canvas from top to bottom. The top of the light area at bottom center is set at the golden-section division of the distance between the bottom of the painting and the row of lights. Further golden-section divisions determine the placement of other elements in the painting, contributing to its measured, stable feeling. Instead of colorful beach scenes, full of sunshine, Henri now painted Whistlerian nocturnes, dim and in muted color. His paintings were based upon reality but freely modified in terms of composition and color. This would continue to be his approach. After his return to New York in 1900, Henri painted what can be termed Tonalist landscapes and cityscapes, in which a strong mood is established by a pervasive, dominant color.

Henri's portraits of the first decade of the century likewise are limited in color. Drawing inspiration from Spanish painters of the Baroque period, Henri portrayed sitters enveloped in surrounding darkness. The figures seem to glow dimly, being painted in the soft yellow, tan, and

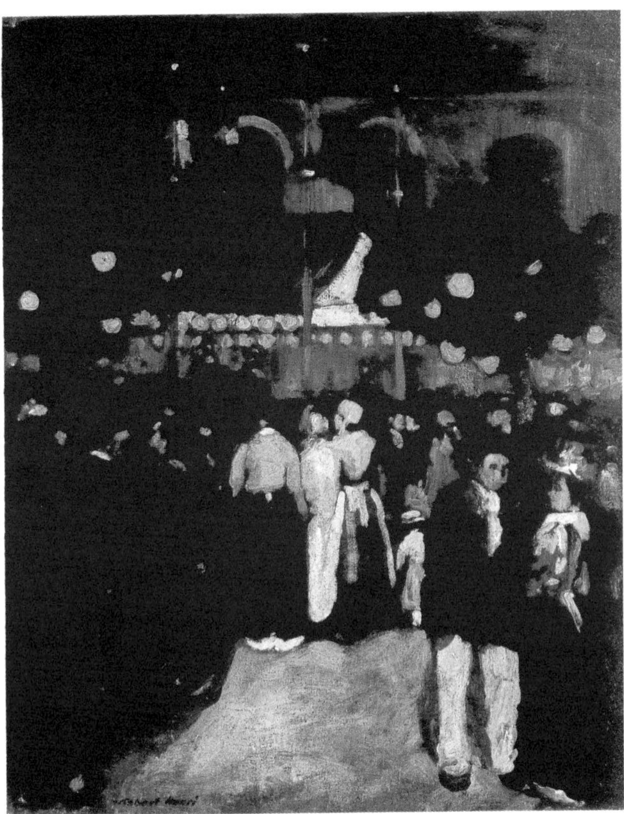

Fig. 9.
Robert Henri
Night, Fourteenth of July, c. 1897
Oil on canvas, 32 x 25 3/4 in.
Nebraska Art Association,
Nelle Cochrane Woods Collection,
Sheldon Memorial Art Gallery,
University of Nebraska-Lincoln.

dull orange of the traditional earth colors, the umbers, ochers, and siennas. The portraits are dramatic and mysterious at the same time, implying that much is hidden by the limited lighting. Henri's use, at this time, of subdued color was a deliberate choice in pursuit of certain aesthetic objectives. This style, while elegant, evocative, and often forceful, offered little scope for Henri to develop his gifts as a colorist.

Henri almost certainly would have encountered some form of color theory in Paris, but his active participation in this theoretical field apparently dates from March 29, 1909, when he entered in his diary a fateful moment that profoundly changed the direction of his style: "Interview with Mr. Maratta who demonstrated his 'Color Law.'"[6] Henri began related color experiments that June and July, but it was the autumn of 1910 before he began working closely with Maratta. On November 27, 1910, Henri and Maratta gave a paint demonstration at the Henri School of Art, with Henri also painting and talking all day. Their close study together continued through most of 1911, with Maratta sometimes coming almost every day.

Earlier in his career an artist, Hardesty Gillmore Maratta (1864–1924) was a color theorist with the brilliant idea of manufacturing and packaging paint in the colors of the spectrum.[7] Although we take this approach for granted today, at the time it was an innovation that put color theory into the hands of the working artist. Traditional artists' pigments were derived from mineral, vegetable, and animal sources. In addition to the oldest pigments, including the earth colors, such as the siennas and umbers (oxides and hydrates of iron), a large number of newer pigments had been produced by the chemical industry that developed in the nineteenth century, such as the cadmium colors. All had a character expressive of their chemical makeup, in that they worked in mixtures with differing amounts of body and strength or could not easily or safely be mixed with other colors. What is more, few of these colors corresponded directly to colors of the spectrum. Generally, the artist had to mix paints from different tubes in order to obtain spectral color, never sure of mixing exactly the same shade each time. For instance, to obtain the red of the spectrum, the artist might mix rose madder and vermilion. A true yellow could be produced by the mixture of aureolin with a bit of vert emeraude. There was an immense gap between the pure color of theory and the material colors in the artist's paint box.

Maratta put the artist's use of color on an entirely different basis by offering a set of pigments that were mixed to be the named colors of the spectrum and to be equally spaced from one another along the spectrum. As mixtures, they were not as brilliant as their component chemical paints, but what they lost in intensity they made up for in greater harmony. Maratta offered the three primary colors, red, yellow, and blue; and the secondary colors between these three, formed by mixtures of the three—orange, green, and purple. (He furnished formulas for mixing the six tertiary colors between these six primary and secondary colors: red-orange, orange-yellow, yellow-green, green-blue, blue-purple, and purple-red. This made a total of twelve colors.) In addition, Maratta offered as part of his set of paints a series of equally neutralized shades of all six of these primary and secondary colors (called, in Maratta's and Henri's terminology, "hues"). Within the set of paints, the artist had a uniform series of colors corresponding directly to the color names of theory.

The written records of Henri's palettes that survive for some later years are largely missing before 1915, but a letter of April 6, 1911, in which Henri describes two palettes, affords a glimpse of his early use of the new paints.[8] Henri's purpose in these early palettes was to establish what Maratta called "analogies" or dominant colors. In one, for instance, Henri used only the colors purple-red, red, and red-orange (i.e., red and the two colors closest to it) in full strength, while using the more neutralized "hues" for yellow, green, and blue.[9] At the back of his diary for 1910, Henri wrote in a chart of analogies, in which he selected related colors on this principle. In his diary on February 22, 1911, Henri recorded painting a portrait of Mrs. Bernstein as an orange analogy and on March 18, 1911, noted painting a portrait of Violet Organ as a blue analogy. This approach parallels the work of 1911 by Henri's pupil and close friend, George Bellows, who likewise painted with dominant colors and extensive use of the muted "hues." This is virtually a formula for a Tonalist painting, of course, a continuation of the paintings of mood both artists had been producing. Henri's initial interest in the new paints was in the harmony and subtlety they afforded him.

The Maratta system set Henri thinking actively about color and color relationships. The impact of this new concept of color can be seen in the portraits Henri painted toward the end of 1910, as his confidence in Maratta's system allowed him to use color more boldly. In the smaller version of *La Madrilenita* (cat. 27), painted in Spain during the summer of 1910, Henri limited his color choices to green, red, and yellow (plus black and white), adding white to the red for the pink ribbons and yellow to this for the orange of the darker ruffles. This restricted choice of color, however, has the additional power of concentrated force. Even though limited in area, the color dominates the painting in a new way. This is still a transitional painting, however, with the color shining amidst darkness, as in the earlier *Marjorie in a Yellow Shawl* (cat. 23) of 1909.

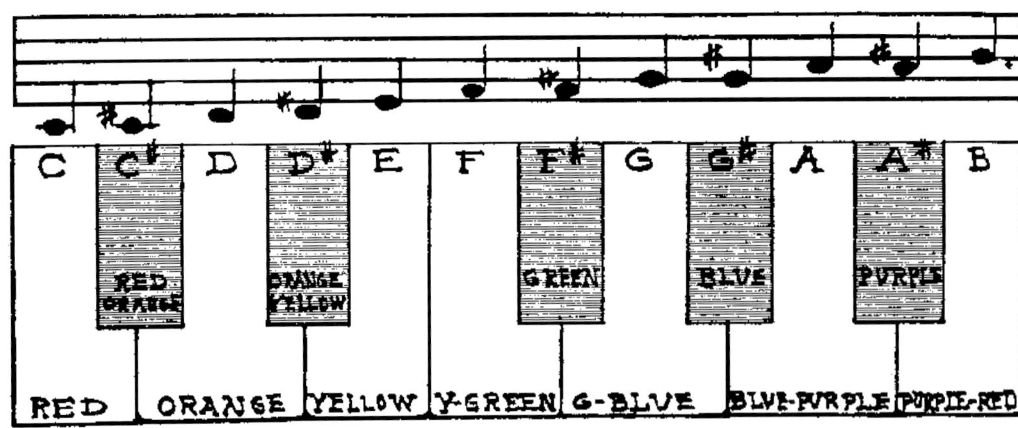

Fig. 10
Musical scale of colors from H.G. Maratta, *H.G. Maratta Artists' Oil Pigments* (advertising circular), 1913, p. 2.

A more radical change resulting from Henri's increased interest in color can be seen in his portrait of Betalo Rubino, *Girl with Fan* (cat. 26), painted in December 1910, after the joint demonstration of Maratta's color theories in Henri's class. The painting is an example of a yellow analogy. Developing the theme of the yellow dress, Henri painted the largest part of the background in a neutralized yellow. Rare up to this point, such light, colored backgrounds henceforth would be the rule for Henri's portraits and dark backgrounds the exception, more often used for male portraits. Color now becomes a more active, assertive element in his paintings.

Maratta described his paints as a tuned "instrument," through which the artist could apply color theory directly to his work, dealing with color considerations separately and rationally. From the autumn of 1910, it would appear to have been a rare occasion when Henri did not plan the selection of colors he would use in a given painting. In another sense, as well, Maratta's colors were a tuned instrument, because Maratta worked out a systematic approach to the musical correspondence to color, a topic very much in the air around the turn of the century. It was central to his theory and one of its strongest selling points. Because the twelve colors were like the twelve notes (naturals and accidentals) in a musical octave, Maratta proposed assigning each color a musical note (fig. 10), which would enable the painter to choose harmonious triads of color corresponding to agreeable musical chords. For instance, the color red frequently was chosen to correspond to the musical note C. The next color, red-orange, then corresponds to the note C#, the color orange to D, and so on, along the spectrum and up the scale to purple-red as B. With his scale of colors before him, the artist now could reproduce the harmonies of music. The tonic chord in the key of C-major (the notes C-E-G) would translate into the three colors, red, yellow, and green-blue. Triads of colors corresponding to the dominant (the notes F-G-B-D) and sub-dominant (the notes F-A-C) chords in the key of C-major might also be employed to agreeable effect in another painting or even together in the same painting. It was thought that a picture painted with the four colors (yellow-green, green-blue, purple-red, and orange) corresponding to the dominant chord in the key of C-major would have the tense mystery of that musical chord, yearning for resolution.

Using the three or four colors of his chord as his primary colors, instead of the normal red, yellow, and blue, the artist created intermixtures for secondary colors, and so on, until he had a full set of twelve colors, but with a different flavor. Just as a composer could set a piece in the key he

	Scale Tones									Tonic			Sub Dominant			Dominant		
Signature	Key	I	II	III	IV	V	VI	VII	VIII	I	III	V	IV	VI	VIII	V	VII	IX or II
1 Flat	F	F	G	A	B♭	C	D	E	F	Y	B	RP	BP	RO	Y	RP	YO	G
2 "	B♭	B♭	C	D	E♭	F	G	A	B♭	BP	RO	Y	O	G	BP	Y	B	RP
3 "	E♭	E♭	F	G	A♭	B♭	C	D	E♭	O	G	BP	BG	RP	O	BP	RO	Y
4 "	A♭	A♭	B♭	C	D♭	E♭	F	G	A♭	BG	RP	O	R	Y	BG	O	G	BP
5 "	D♭	D♭	E	F	G	A	B	C	D	R	Y	BG	G	P	RO	BG	RP	O
6 "	G♭	A♭	B♭	G	D♭	E♭	F	G♭	A♭	G	P	RO	R	Y	BG	R	Y	BG
7 "	C♭	D♭	E♭	F♭	G♭	A♭	B♭	C♭	D♭	R	Y	BG	YG	BP	R	G	P	RO

RP	R	RO	O	YO	Y	YG	G	BG	B	BP	P	
C	D♭	D	E♭	E	F	G♭	G	A♭	A	B♭	B	C

Fig. 11
Robert Henri, *Chart of Color Scales and Chords,* c. 1913, Henri Papers, Beinecke Rare Book and Manuscript Library, Yale University.

felt appropriate to its mood, the painter could choose a palette with the right feeling for his interpretation of a subject. So far, this example has been based on the key of C-major. Maratta's tuned instrument offered the choice of no fewer than twelve major and twelve minor keys, each with a different flavor in its harmonies (fig. 11). Profoundly influenced by the concept of Maratta's musical correspondences, Henri worked in these terms mostly from 1911 to 1913, but continued to respect and use the concept. In 1920 he distributed to his class charts of the Maratta Chord Palettes,[10] and as late as 1928, the year before his death, still painted pictures with triads of colors.

Another concept of Maratta's that captivated Henri, particularly during the early period, 1910–13, was Maratta's theory of composition, his "Science of Form." Henri's friend and fellow artist, John Sloan, recorded in his diary for July 3, 1911:

> *He [Henri] is deep with Maratta in the geometrical problem of rhythm in construction and design of pictures and form. There is a great deal he is sure and so am I. Maratta claims that it was well understood by the ancient Greeks and Egyptians, etc. Henri says that of course most of "them" would call him crazy to experiment in this line. He goes into the thing with his usual thoroughness. He has a large full length shape black board cloth on canvas stretcher ruled with scratches in the geometric triangulations, dividers, compasses, T squares, etc.*[11]

Henri's own diaries first record a discussion with Maratta of his geometrical system on October 22, 1910, the very day he resumed his contact with Maratta, for whom the laws of color and of form alike were derived from the study of music. Harmony and proportion were the key to all three. Maratta claimed that the five regular solids (the cube [earth], octahedron [air], tetrahedron [fire], icosahedron [water], and dodecahedron [aether]) represented the five elements to the Greeks and were the sources of their harmonious designs.[12] Henri worked with Maratta on fire and star compositions, probably based on these solids.[13] The only one of Maratta's compositional systems

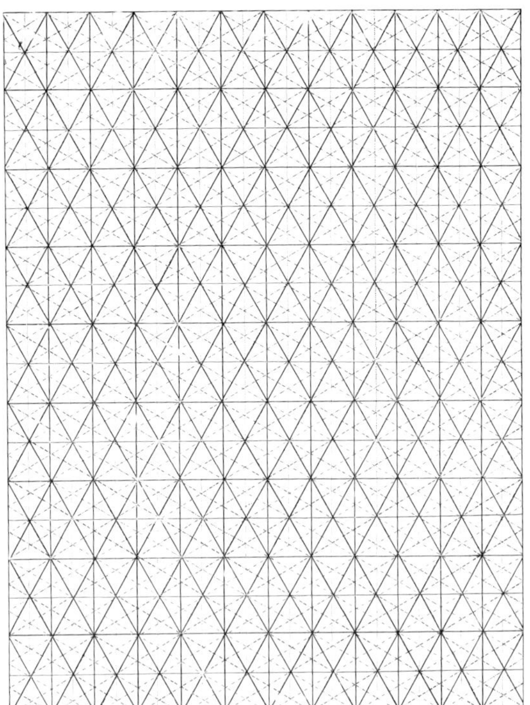

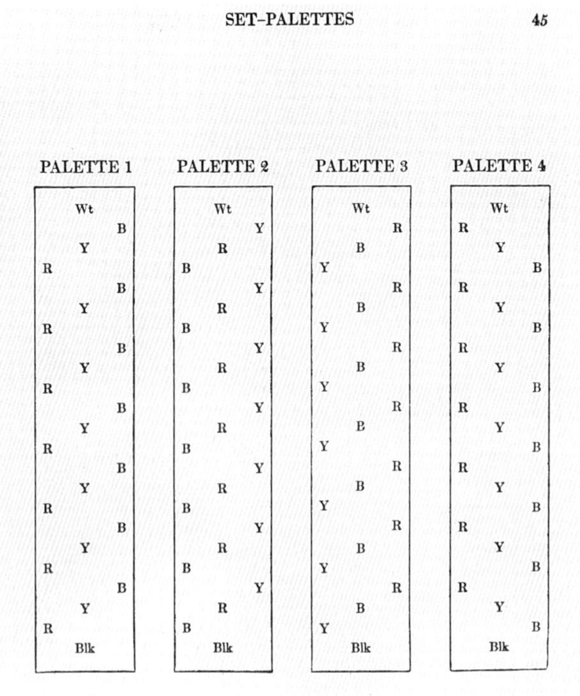
SET-PALETTES 45

PALETTE 1	PALETTE 2	PALETTE 3	PALETTE 4
Wt	Wt	Wt	Wt
B	Y	R	R
Y	R	B	Y
R	B	Y	B
B	Y	R	R
Y	R	B	Y
R	B	Y	B
B	Y	R	R
Y	R	B	Y
R	B	Y	B
B	Y	R	R
Y	R	B	Y
R	B	Y	B
B	Y	R	R
Y	R	B	Y
R	B	Y	B
B	Y	R	R
Y	R	B	Y
R	B	Y	B
B	Y	R	R
Y	R	B	Y
R	B	Y	B
Blk	Blk	Blk	Blk

to be published, and apparently the fundamental system, was based upon the equilateral triangle (and thus the tetrahedron). In 1915 Maratta published this design (fig. 12), which shows a network, or "web," of interlocking triangles and other geometrical forms. Its purpose was to provide a framework for proportionate and harmonious designs. There is no observable physical evidence that Henri used Maratta's compositional systems as the basis of his portraits during this period, but some of the portraits of 1912 do look different, compositionally.[14] *The Green Fan (Girl of Toledo, Spain)* (cat. 31), with its frontality, symmetry, and large, triangular shapes, easily could be derived from the web of equilateral triangles. The same compositional characteristics are found in *The Guide to Croaghan (Brien O'Malley)* (cat. 33). Maratta's system seems to have encouraged in Henri a taste for large, simple, regular forms, for stability, and for surface tension. Both figures fill the canvas and function equally well as two-dimensional designs.

Maratta's influence upon Henri and his circle was profound, especially during the period 1910 to 1913, and Henri remained in close touch professionally and socially, until his friend's death in 1924. Over time, however, Henri incorporated other influences into his approach to color and composition. Beginning apparently in 1914, a strong influence was the Harvard lecturer and author of books on design, Denman Waldo Ross, whose major work, *On Drawing and Painting,* appeared in 1912.[15] The key concept Henri learned from Ross was the "set palette" (fig. 13). Believing that the full range of available colors could confuse the artist, Ross advocated a limited palette, or selection of colors. Before beginning his painting, the artist was to analyze the colors in the subject and select just the colors required. As the diagrams indicate, these selected colors were mixed with white or black to make them lighter or darker in distinct steps, the seven registers of value Ross recognized as high light, light, low light, medium, high dark, dark, and low dark. (The term "value" is used to refer to a color's lightness or darkness.) The paints in each register of value would be used together in a different plane or lighting condition in the painting.

COLOR CHART AS IT WAS ESTABLISHED AT THE MEETING (1915) IN WINTER'S STUDIO.
CH. WINTER, HG MARATTA, JOHN SLOAN, G BELLOWS, R. DAVEY, H.
The sign + indicates repeat of the color in decreasing intensity. —The HUE USED.

13												YG^{c}	
11	G^{c}	GB^{c}								OY^{c}	Y^{c}	+	G^{c}
9	+	+	COBALT + M. GB^{c}				R^{c}	RO^{c}	O^{c}	+	+	+	+
7	+	+	B^{c}	BP^{c}		PR^{c}	+	+	+	+	+	+	+
5	+	+	+	+	P^{c}	+	+	+	+	+	+	+	+
3	+	+	B^{H}	+	P^{H}	+	R^{H}	+	+	+	+	+	+
1	G^{H}	GB^{H}	B^{H} O^{c}	BP^{H}	P^{H} Y^{H} Y^{c}	PR^{H}	R^{H} GB^{c}	RO^{H}	O^{H}	OY^{H}	Y^{H}	YG^{H}	G^{H}
S	G^{H} R^{c}		B^{H} O^{c}	BP^{H} OY^{c}	P^{H} Y^{H} Y^{c}	PR^{H} YG^{c}	R^{H} GB^{c}	RO^{H} GB^{c}	O^{H} P^{H} P^{c}	OY^{H} BP^{c}	Y^{H} P^{c}	YG^{H} P^{c}	G^{H} R^{c}

There were some slight changes — but the chart remained practically thus during its life. The mixtures indicated for the 1 and S. lines were those which seemed the most practical. The fixing of the higher intensity of each color was difficult. It was rather surprising that YG should be thought the most "intense." There evidently was some confounding of "value" with "intensity." Evidence of this may be found in the great step between P. and YG. This P. while very dark proved itself to be a very powerful (intense) pigment when mixed with white.

Fig. 12 (opposite, left)
Web of Equilateral Triangles and Certain Rectangles: For Designers (New York: H.G. Maratta, 1915). John Sloan Archives, Delaware Art Museum, Wilmington.

Fig. 13 (opposite, right)
Set-Palettes. From Denman Waldo Ross, *On Drawing and Painting* (1912), p. 45.

14. (left)
Color Chart, 1915. Henri Papers, Beinecke Rare Book and Manuscript Library, Yale University.

The emphasis on Ross' system of set palettes was on value. Henri accordingly mixed for himself a set of paints with varying amounts of white and put each of them into tubes marked with both the color and the value of the paint.[16] On October 29, 1915, Henri wrote a didactic letter to his class at the Art Students League, describing a palette organized in terms of the seven registers of value.[17] This represented a shift from Maratta's system, which did not concern itself with value. As a result of this new organizing principle, Henri's portraits of 1914 and 1915 can display greatly increased contrast, as in *Viv in Blue Stripe* (cat. 35) and in *Edna* (cat. 38); the latter ranges from excessively light flesh and linens to the deep shadows of the folds of the patterned drapery. Ross-influenced portraits of these years also can be painted in exceptionally pale colors from the top of the palette, as in *Tam Gan* (cat. 36) and *Jim Lee (The Vegetable Man)* (cat. 37). Ross' set palettes lent themselves to effects of very strong daylight that blanched colors. It actually was a system better suited to the needs of American Impressionists of the period.

According to today's terminology, which was coming into use during the first quarter of the century, three terms are used to describe a color: "hue," meaning its position along the spectrum, as red or orange; "value," meaning its relative lightness or darkness, as a pale red or dark red; and "intensity," meaning its relative strength (purity, saturation) or neutralization, as a brilliant red or a dull red.[18] Maratta had been concerned mainly with hue and Ross mainly with value. Although Maratta offered a set of neutralized colors and Ross touched on the question of intensity, neither had presented an organized approach to the third component of color, intensity. Henri gathered his like-minded friends about him and produced his own system of color intensity, codified in a chart (fig. 14). For each of the twelve primary, secondary, and tertiary colors, the chart recognizes a range of intensity, from the most intense, purest color at a rating of as high as 13, all the way down the scale of increasing neutralization to the lowest rating, "s," in which each color was almost completely neutralized (by mixing it with its complementary color, as mixing green with red to produce gray).

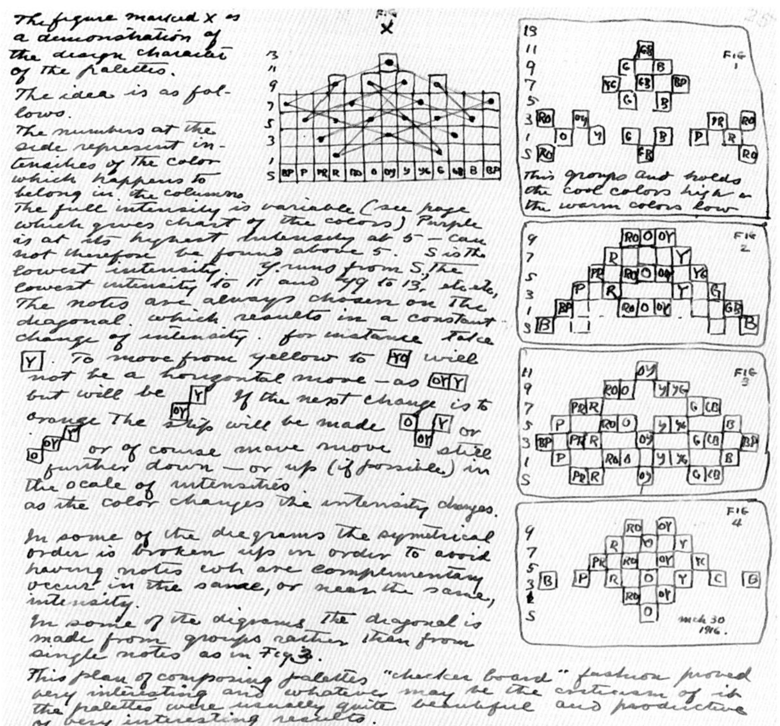
The figure marked X is a demonstration of the design character of the palettes.
The idea is as follows.
The numbers at the side represent intensities of the color which happens to belong in the columns
The full intensity is variable (see page which gives chart of the colors) Purple is at its highest intensity at 5 — can not therefore be found above 5. S is the lowest intensity. Y. runs from S, the lowest intensity to 11 and YG to 13, etc etc,
The notes are always chosen on the diagonal. which results in a constant change of intensity. for instance take Y. To move from yellow to YO will not be a horizontal move — as OY Y but will be OY Y If the next change is to orange the step will be made O OY Y or O OY Y or of course move move still further down — or up (if possible) in the scale of intensities.
as the color changes the intensity changes.
In some of the diagrams the symmetrical order is broken up in order to avoid having notes wh are complementary occur in the same, or near the same, intensity.
In some of the digrams the diagonal is made from groups rather than from single notes as in Fig 3.
This plan of composing palettes "checker board" fashion proved very interesting and whatever may be the criticism of it the palettes were usually quite beautiful and productive of very interesting results.

Fig. 15.
Demonstration of Palettes Based on the Chart of Color Intensities, 1916. Henri Papers, Beinecke Rare Book and Manuscript Library, Yale University.

It is not clear exactly when in 1915 the group produced the chart of intensities. Already in March of that year, when he painted *Edna,* Henri was using intense color, and on May 5 he wrote this note to himself: "Paint as near full intensity of colors as possible, i.e., in flesh in the lowest value possible to get the quality of the subject's color so that the canvas will be intense in color—not neutralized by much white."[19] On May 28 he mixed for himself new paints in terms of intensity and put them up in tubes.[20] On August 26, 1915, when he painted *Village Girl (Lily Cow)* (cat. 39), he noted its colors in his record book in terms of both color initials and numbers from the chart of color intensities.[21] For instance, the yellow-green of the background at 13 and the red of the jacket at 9 both were at their highest intensities, while the patch of blue by her elbow, at 5, was duller.

By December 12, 1915, Henri, perhaps with his associates, had developed a new system for arranging set palettes on the basis of intensity of color.[22] His explanation of the system (fig. 15) shows that it combines elements from both his earlier systems. From Maratta's method Henri took the concept of the dominance of a color, three adjacent colors (an analogy), or a chord of colors. From Denman Ross' set palettes he took the principle of diagonal arrangement intended to establish this dominance, and of course the concept of the set palette. He applied these principles to the chart of color intensities. The diagram shows how Henri began with the color, orange-yellow, in its highest intensity, establishing its dominance. He then moved in descending diagonals on the chart of color intensities (fig. 14) to choose colors at lesser intensities, specifically blue-purple, red, orange, yellow, and green. In the process, he reinforced the dominance of orange-yellow by creating an analogy with its adjacent colors (yellow, orange-yellow, and orange). From the entire secondary group of colors he again moved in descending diagonals to choose lower intensities of all the remaining colors. The resulting palettes are very rich, with the same color often occurring in two or three intensities. They usually included, in some intensity, nearly all twelve colors. The color plate shows how one such palette contained twenty- two color notes, with white added to most to produce three values of each note, offering the artist a rich chromatic range, as

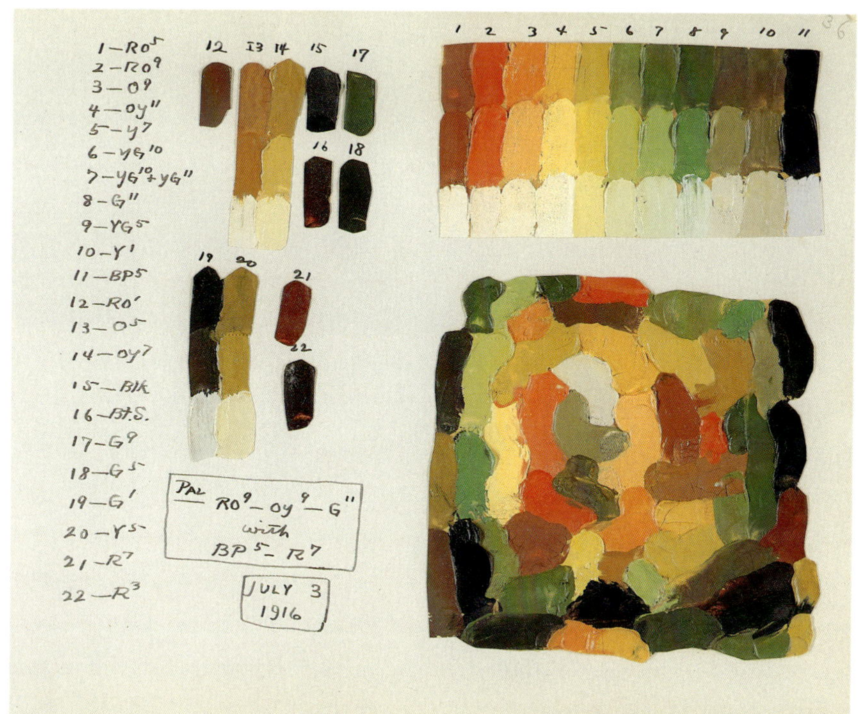

Robert Henri, *Palette of July 3, 1916.* Henri Papers, Beinecke Rare Book and Manuscript Library, Yale University.

explored in the abstract color study. Reflecting this new fullness in Henri's palette, the portraits of 1916 and 1917 contain some of the artist's most opulent color, as for example in *Pepita* (cat. 46). Henri's approach was to devise a palette, create some abstract color studies to try the combinations, and then to paint a series of paintings with that same palette, before modifying it in some way and beginning another series of paintings with that modified palette. He named each palette after either the date or the notebook page on which it was first recorded. Henri noted on September 25, 1916, in Sante Fe, "This [palette] has been used with some modifications through summer. It is related to 104 . . . ."[23] In a change from Denman Ross' set palettes, which usually were specific to a subject, these new set palettes were meant to be used routinely, until they were improved through modification. Being more complex than Ross' set palettes, they were more flexible and thus more broadly applicable.

During the period 1914–17, Henri used intermittently Maratta's web, or spatial grid, and his older, golden-section approach to compositional design. In 1915 Henri received the gift of a gadget that made work with the golden section much easier, eliminating most of the calculations.[24] Then in November 1917 Henri received word from George Bellows about a new compositional system, dynamic symmetry, which was to fascinate both artists during the next several years.[25] Not yet available in published form, dynamic symmetry became known to Henri through a series of lectures delivered in 1918 by the system's inventor (or re-discoverer) Jay Hambidge.[26] Henri took careful notes and prepared an elaborate manuscript that could have been a proposal for a publication.[27] Like Maratta, Hambidge claimed that his design system had shaped the masterpieces of the Golden Age of Greece and then had been forgotten until Hambidge uncovered it. But unlike Maratta's system, with its extreme simplicity, Hambidge's dynamic symmetry was bewilderingly complex. It nevertheless was adopted by a significant number of American artists working the 1920s, and versions of it are still in print and used by some artists even today.

Because dynamic symmetry offered the artist so many, many options in developing a design, and because each option involved at least several indirect steps, it is nearly impossible to unravel the process in analyzing a painting. Either one of two general characteristics, however, affected almost all designs. One aspect of dynamic symmetry stressed diagonals, often to the corners of the canvas. Examples of this approach might be *Bernadita* (cat. 48) and *Tom Cafferty* (cat. 54), with their pronounced diagonals. Once one is aware of this principle, it is striking how artfully arranged many of Henri's portraits of this period actually are. The second major approach of dynamic symmetry is the subdivision of the design surface into smaller geometrical components. Henri's diagram (fig. 16) shows how such subdivisions are made and how the artist then tries to contain elements of the design within these units. The location and proportion of a subject's head in a portrait might be determined in this manner, and then other parts of the figure aligned with the geometry. This application of dynamic symmetry is less conspicuous than the other one based on diagonals, but sometimes can be sensed in portraits in which the figure is oddly placed within the rectangle of the canvas, as in the portrait of *Jimmie Gerry* (cat. 50). A special case, which should be mentioned in addition to these two general characteristics, is the increasingly curved, logarithmic spiral, the geometrical shape at the theoretical heart of dynamic symmetry, which appears to have been used several times in the design of *Ruth St. Denis in the Peacock Dance* (cat. 49).

During the years 1918 through 1922, several currents at times intermingled in Henri's application of color theory. It had been the overall pattern that his theory became increasingly complex as he incorporated additional elements. Henri continued to work with Maratta and Denman Ross and received suggestions from his circle of artists, especially from Charles Winter and John Sloan. During the summer of 1918, Henri took up again one of Denman Ross' set palettes, the "Rubens palette" he had used in 1914, which was the most complex of Ross' published palettes.[28] During 1919 he worked with Ross on a new approach, set palettes organized into groups of hot colors and cold colors. This effort culminated in the "Palette IV HC-Denman Ross," dated October 2, 1919, with which he worked into 1920.[29] At the same time, John Sloan described to Henri a triangular system for choosing a set palette[30] (fig. 17). Arranged in the traditional manner, with the three primary colors at the points of the triangle, it was marked with symbols of the secondary and tertiary colors around the outside of the large triangle. All colors on this outer triangle were meant to be at full intensity, which Sloan indicated with the number 7. Spaces for all the colors on the two inner triangles indicated these colors at progressively more neutralization, denoted by the numbers 5 and 3. The center, representing near-complete neutralization, connects complementary colors: there is a straight line, through the center, between red and green. Across the bottom is a band with Denman Ross' abbreviations for his registers of value between white and black; the artist was to choose a value for each of the colors he selected. In this case, white has been added to yellow-orange, yellow-green, and blue-green to put them into the "L," or light register. Other colors are medium or dark. The triangular palette thus addressed all three issues about color, hue (also acknowledging complementaries), intensity, and value. The concept of this palette was that the artist included no white on his palette. Instead, he used the light colors, or "lighteners," for the

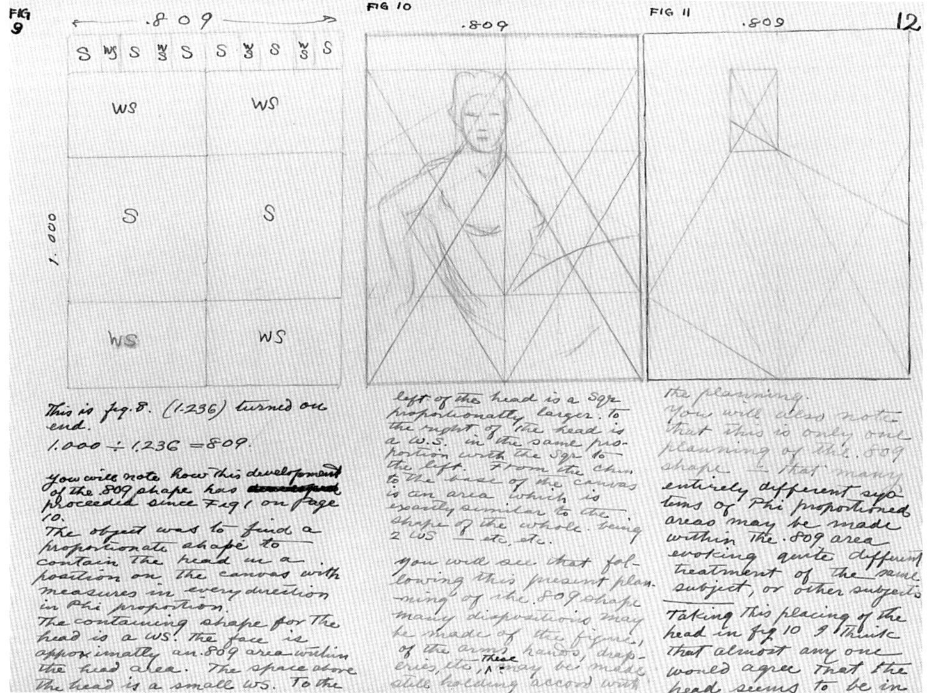

Fig. 16
Robert Henri, *Division of the Rectangle .809*, 1918.
Henri Papers, Beinecke Rare Book and Manuscript Library, Yale University.
The letter "s" signifies a square and the letters "ws" indicate one type of rectangle.

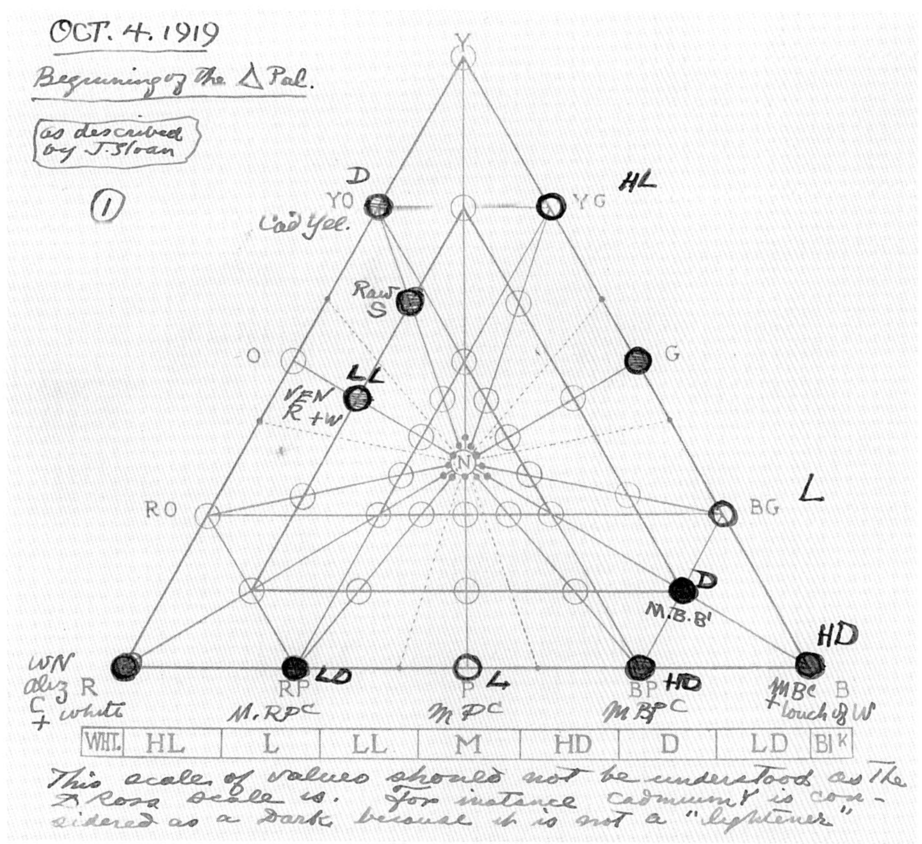

Fig. 17
The Beginning of the Triangular Palette, as Described by J. Sloan, 1919.
Henri Papers, Beinecke Rare Book and Manuscript Library, Yale University.

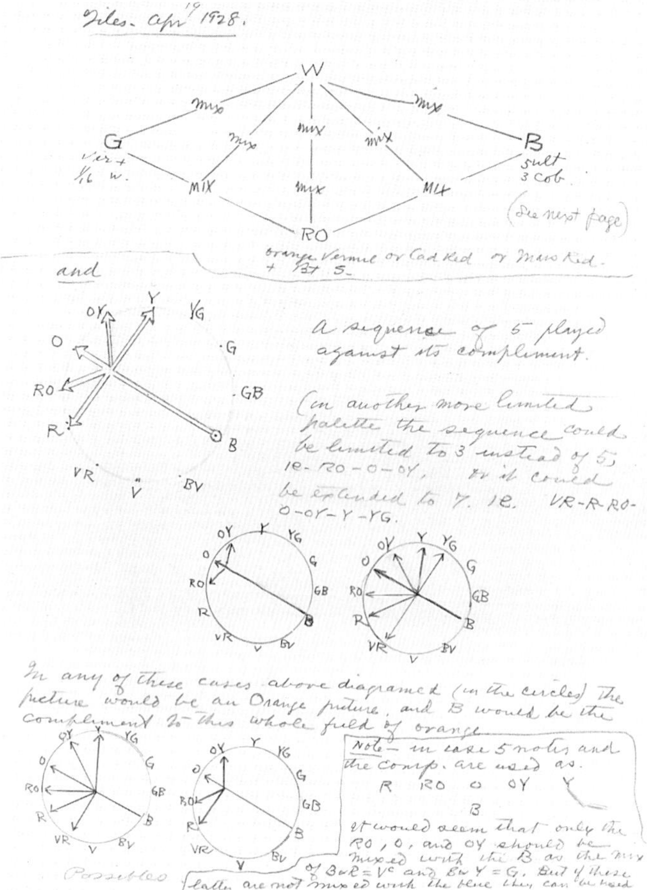

Fig. 18
Robert Henri, *A Sequence of 5 Played Against Its Complement,* 1928. Henri Papers, Beinecke Rare Book and Manuscript Library, Yale University.

purpose of lightening any of the other colors as necessary. Henri worked with the triangular palette at least during the final quarter of 1919 and may have incorporated some of its concepts into his selection of palettes after that, but did not adopt it as his basic approach, as Sloan had done.[31]

Further complicating one's understanding of Henri's color theory during the period 1918–22 are two more technical matters. The first is that in about 1918 Henri began to experiment with the Old Master technique of indirect painting. As Henri understood it,[32] this involved dividing the painting process into two phases. The artist first painted his subject in monochrome, in terms of light and dark. After this had dried well, the artist used transparent paints to glaze areas with their appropriate color. This approach had the effect of separating value (first step) from color and intensity (second step), which may have been appropriate to Henri's attempts at a more sculptural style during this period. Henri also sometimes glazed over backgrounds to make them richer and more atmospheric. The second technical matter that had an impact on Henri's color theory at this time had to do with Henri's study of pigments, prompted by problems with the manufacture of Maratta's paints and Henri's concern about obtaining the best materials for the short- lived League of American Artists. Henri went to great lengths to classify chemically the various pigments, determine which were most permanent, and note which could not be combined because of chemical interaction.[33] Beginning in about 1919 and increasingly after 1920, his notations of his own palettes are in terms of traditional pigments, rather than in the more abstract color names of the spectrum.

It is characteristic of Henri's approach to color theory that he made it into a group activity. The most thorough of theorists, he nevertheless needed the fresh ideas and momentum of a shared effort. With Maratta's death in 1924 and that of Bellows at the beginning of 1925, with the gradual dissolution of his circle, and with his own advancing age, Henri's involvement in color theory slowed. He seems to have used simpler palettes after 1925 and by 1928 was again using the color triads, the chords he had worked with in 1913. A collaborator from about 1926 to 1928 was the artist Howard Giles, a disciple of both Jay Hambidge and Denman Ross.[34] The palettes Henri and Giles organized appear to consist of pairs of complementary colors. In Henri's portraits of this period, 1926–28, one sees how a painting is enlivened by a strong, complementary accent color as in *Wee Annie Lavelle (Pet)* (cat. 59) and *Fergus* (cat. 60). A variation (fig. 18), pairing five colors in a sequence with the group's complementary color, can also be seen in some portraits of 1928.

Henri had so trained his sense of color by this point that he could achieve wonderful effects with the simplest of palettes. To the end, his portraits are about color—color that works. The years of experimentation had been driven by a belief that knowledge of color laws and geometry would yield practical results, in terms of skills.

In *The Art Spirit,* Henri wrote in defense of his use of color and compositional systems:

> *If a man has the soul of an artist he needs a mastery of all the means of expression so that he may command them, for with his soul in activity he has much to say. If he refuses to use his brain to find the way to signify the meaningful depth of nature on his flat canvas with his colors, he should also refuse to use his hands and his brushes and his colors, and the canvas itself. However, all these, the canvas, paints, brushes, hands and brains are but tools to be guided by the soul of man . . . . The whole fact is that art and science are so close together that they might very well be lumped together. They certainly are necessary to each other and the delights of either pursuit should satisfy any man.*[35]

Art and science may indeed be necessary to each other, but they are different things, operating according to different principles. Systems and theories are necessary to bridge the differences, so that the truths of science can be applied to the creation of art. Each of these systems, however, inevitably contains a relative emphasis on one or more aspects of the whole, leading to some degree of distortion. Henri's application of science was mediated by a series of systems, each of which left its stamp upon his work. Maratta's system, which Henri applied during the period 1910–13, emphasized harmony of color, at the risk of a certain sweetness. Denman Ross' system, emphasizing value, gives the paintings of 1914 and early 1915 a dramatic range from very dark to extremely light passages. The intensity-based system Henri used during 1915–17 encouraged him to use more emphatic, brilliant color than ever before. Henri's change from one system to the next directly affected the appearance of the paintings he produced by directing attention to a particular aspect of color, which he then fully mastered and made part of his personal method. Each of the theories gave him the impetus and the courage to boldly explore a new dimension of his craft. Certainly affected, but seldom carried away by theory, he monitored his efforts for approaches that worked. In the process, he discovered his special gifts for color that could bring his portraits to life.

NOTES

1. I would like to thank Janet Le Clair for her courtesy and helpfulness in allowing me access to the Henri manuscripts in her possession. The other large group of Henri documents is held by the Beinecke Rare Book and Manuscript Library, Yale University. Although references to his work with color theory occasionally appear in his personal diaries and his record books of completed paintings, Henri mostly recorded these efforts in separate notebooks, which might be called palette diaries. One of these, covering the period 1915–16, is in the collection of Janet Le Clair. The other surviving volumes are among the uncatalogued manuscripts in the Henri Papers at the Beinecke Rare Book and Manuscript Library, filed in the box Notebooks and Miscellaneous Writings. They are in folders labeled as follows: Notebook: Artists' Pigments II (containing material dated 1913, 1915, 1916, 1917, 1918, and 1919); Notebook: Paint 3 (October 4, 1919–December 13, 1920); Notebook: Paint 4 (January 2–November 1921); Notebook: Paint 5 (apparently December 1926–June 1928).

2. See Michael Quick, "Technique and Theory: The Evolution of Bellow's Painting Style," in Michael Quick and Jane Myers, *The Paintings of George Bellows*, exh. cat. (Fort Worth: Amon Carter Museum; Los Angeles: Los Angeles County Museum of Art, 1992), pp. 9–95. Bellows' application of color and composition theories closely follows that of his mentor and friend, Robert Henri, but with interesting differences, because Bellows was far more likely to pursue the abstract implications of the theories they shared.

3. William Innes Homer, *Robert Henri and His Circle* (1969; reprint, New York: Hacker Art Books, 1988), pp. 184–94.

4. Henri later wrote: "Signac's book *Neo-Impressionism* is a book that should interest any student . . . . It is an argument in favor of the total division of color in painting, but that does not matter. In making his argument he tells in a simple way many valuable things;" Robert Henri, *The Art Spirit*, comp. Margery Ryerson (1923; reprint, New York: Harper & Row, 1984), pp. 60–61.

5. The Golden Section, a concept of fascination and mystical association since Ancient times, enjoyed new attention in Paris in the 1890s. It is a ratio in geometry best represented numerically by the ratio 1.000/.618. In this example, the distance between the right flagpole and the center flagpole is .618 of the distance between the center flagpole and the left flagpole. The distance between the center flagpole and the left flagpole is .618 of the entire distance between the right flagpole and the left flagpole. The Golden Section is set at a point at which the two ratios are the same.

6. Henri's diary, collection of Janet Le Clair. The diaries are available on microfilm through the Archives of American Art, Smithsonian Institution. Diaries relating to this topic, available on Roll 886, cover the following periods: January 1, 1908–December 21, 1912; April 28–December 16, 1915; June 2, 1924–July 8, 1926; and January 1–October 20, 1928.

7. See Elizabeth Armstrong Handy, "H.G. Maratta's Color Theory and Its Influence of the Painters—Robert Henri, John Sloan, and George Bellows," M.A. thesis (Newark: University of Delaware, 1969). Maratta himself published very little on his color theories—only two advertising circulars for his paints and two articles: "The Maratta System of Color," *Scientific American Supplement No. 1767* (November 13, 1909), p. 311; and "Colors and Paints," *Touchstone*, 7 (June 1920), pp. 249–50.

8. Henri to Helen Niles, April 6, 1911, Henri Papers, Beinecke Rare Book and Manuscript Library, Yale University. I am grateful to Valerie Leeds for kindly bringing this letter to my attention.

9. An alternative method of establishing the dominance of a color is to mix that color into all the other colors.

10. "*The Maratta Chord Palettes*, May 11, 1920. On this date I gave to the [Art Students] League students a copy of my own diagrams of the chord palettes. These are to be copied and marked with Maratta's name"; Notebook: Paint 3, p. 49, Henri Papers, Beinecke Rare Book and Manuscript Library, Yale University. In the same collection (Notebook: Artists' Pigments II, p. 1) is a mimeographed chart of color scales and chords. It shows only minor scales, so presumably there was at least one more sheet.

11. John Sloan, *John Sloan's New York Scene*, ed. Bruce St. John (New York: Harper & Row, 1965), p. 548.

12. Hardesty G. Maratta, "A Rediscovery of the Principles of Form Measurement," *Arts & Decoration*, 4 (April 1914), pp. 230–32. Henri drew illustrations of the solids and

wrote out an explanation of this theory; Notebook: Artists' Pigments II, two unnumbered sheets, Henri Papers, Beinecke Rare Book and Manuscript Library, Yale University.

13. References to the fire and star compositions and celluloids occur in Henri's diaries on November 1 and 2, 1910.

14. I could not see any physical evidence of the system in the one painting I was able to examine, *The Guide to Croaghan* (cat. 33). It would be interesting to examine paintings of 1912 with infrared reflectography, to determine whether Henri drew the grid upon the canvas before beginning his painting.

15. Other books by Denman Ross also available to Henri were *A Theory of Pure Design: Harmony, Balance, Rhythm*, 1907, and *The Painter's Palette*, 1919. Because Henri's diaries for 1913, 1914, and early 1915 are lacking, there is no direct evidence of his personal contact with Ross. On May 6, 1915, Henri recorded, "M[aratta] has just returned from his visit to Denman Ross—they are in great agreement."

16. Recorded in an entry dated May 13, 1915, on p. 37 of Henri's Palette Diary/Notebook, collection of Janet Le Clair.

17. The typewritten letter is in the box labeled Lecture Notes, among the uncatalogued Henri Papers, Beinecke Rare Book and Manuscript Library, Yale University. Portions of this letter were incorporated into a longer discussion with a different emphasis in *The Art Spirit*, pp. 34–37. *The Art Spirit*, pp. 59–60, quotes another earlier but undated manuscript: "If you have not read and studied, for here again you must dig, the works of Denman Ross, get them by all means, for you must want to get the wisdom and the practical advice they contain, and what they suggest."

18. The standard text on the description of color is Arthur Pope, *An Introduction to the Language of Drawing and Painting*, (Cambridge, Massachusetts: Harvard University Press, 1922).

19. Palette Diary/Notebook, 1915–19, p. 35, collection of Janet Le Clair.

20. Ibid., p. 47.

21. Artist's Record Book, collection of Janet Le Clair.

22. The diagram, dated December 12, 1915, is found on p. 66 of Henri's Palette Diary/Notebook, 1915–19, collection of Janet Le Clair. In Henri's Notebook: Artist's Pigments II, the first similar diagram, on p. 25, bears the date December 13, 1915, Henri Papers, Beinecke Rare Book and Manuscript Library, Yale University.

23. Palette Diary/Notebook, 1915–19, p. 107, collection of Janet Le Clair. The palette on p. 104 is dated July 16, 1916.

24. Henri recorded in his diary on May 27, 1915: "Recd from [Manuel] Komroff present of a golden-point compass (proportional compass)." It probably was the "Golden Compass" then manufactured in Germany, a kind of pantograph device. The artist extended the compass to the length of a line, and the device automatically marked the golden-section division of the line.

25. Bellows to Henri, November 16, 1917, Henri Papers, Beinecke Rare Book and Manuscript Library, Yale University. The earliest mention of dynamic symmetry in Henri's own hand is an entry dated December 15, 1917, Palette Diary/Notebook, p. 128, collection of Janet Le Clair. It is not clear from documents just how long after that Henri continued to design his paintings using the system. Unlike Bellows, who made a number of preparatory drawings indicating the dynamic-symmetry design of major paintings, Henri left no evidence of his use of the system in his paintings.

26. Aside from his work in the field of archaeology, Hambidge published little before his early death in January 1924. His principle exposition of the theory of dynamic symmetry was as editor of the *Diagonal*, published monthly by Yale University from November 1919 to October 1920; the texts were later excerpted in the posthumous book *The Elements of Dynamic Symmetry* (New York: Brentano's, 1926). In 1920 Hambidge also published *Dynamic Symmetry: The Greek Vase* (New Haven: Yale University Press), with an archaeological focus, which was of less use to artists. In 1923 he published the thin volume, *Dynamic Symmetry in Composition As Used by the Artists* (Cambridge, Massachusetts: Privately printed), which illustrates dynamic-symmetry designs by George Bellows and discusses its use by Robert Henri and others. On pp. 77 and 78 are a letter of endorsement from Henri and a description of Henri as an eager student of dynamic symmetry.

27. Among the uncatalogued Henri Papers at the Beinecke Rare Book and Manuscript Library, Yale University, are two albums, one marked on its cover with a basic dynamic-symmetry design and the words, "Mss made for Mr. . . . ," the other marked on its cover "Hambidge lectures 1918," with an index of its contents. Several mentions of Maratta in the second album suggest that Henri worked out some of the proofs with Maratta.

28. The Rubens palette, thought by Denman Ross to approximate the palette used by Rubens, Titian, and other Old Masters, is diagrammed as Palette 10 on p. 35 of *On Drawing and Painting*. Henri recorded on June 23, 1918: "The Rubens Pal. above mentioned is the one I made and used in 1914." He emended the entry with the sentence: "see later notes for correct D. Ross Rub. Pal. [no. 10] as set for me by his pupil, Moulton, June 28, 1918"; Notebook: Artists' Pigments II, p. 46, Henri Papers, Beinecke Rare Book and Manuscript Library, Yale University.

29. Henri apparently worked with this palette from October 2, 1919, to at least February 16, 1920; Notebook: Paint 3, pp. 25–38, Henri Papers, Beinecke Rare Book and Manuscript Library, Yale University.

30. Sloan explained his triangular system in *Gist of Art* (New York: Dover Publications, 1977), pp. 119–24. I would like to thank Helen Farr Sloan for her helpfulness in explaining numerous matters relating to her late husband's use of the Maratta system.

31. The sheets of paper printed with the triangular palette were inexpensive and available by the hundreds to be torn off of gummed pads. The marked sheets are found in great numbers among the John Sloan Papers at the Delaware Art Museum, Wilmington. The fact that they are not found among the Henri Papers suggests that Henri did not long use the system.

32. Henri described this method in *The Art Spirit*, p. 62. He may have learned about indirect painting from *The Secret of the Old Masters* (1906) by Albert Abendschein, which he recommended to his students.

33. Henri relied upon three recent publications: Maximillian Toch, *Materials for Permanent Painting* (New York, 1911); A.P. Laurie, *The Pigments and Mediums of the Old Masters* (London, 1914); and Arthur H. Church, *The Chemistry of Paints and Painting* (London, 1915). Henri also was in touch with Hamilton Easter Field, who was the author of *The Techniques of Oil Painting and Other Essays* (Brooklyn, 1913).

34. Giles began as a follower of Hambidge and, probably through him, later investigated color theory with Denman Ross. It is interesting that Ross himself was a strong advocate of dynamic symmetry.

35. Henri, *The Art Spirit*, pp. 53–54.

CATALOGUE

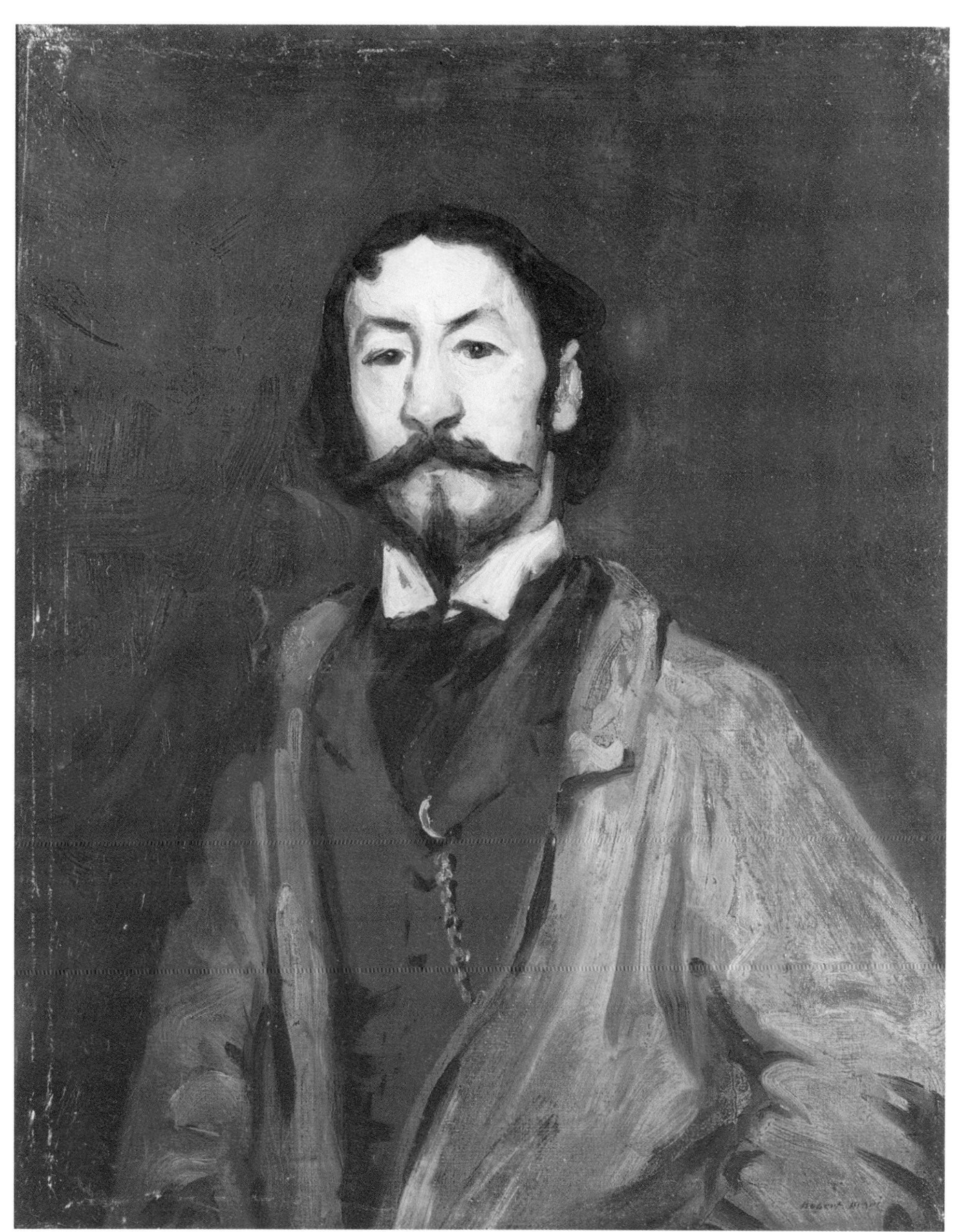

1.
THE MAN WHO POSED AS RICHELIEU, 1898
Oil on canvas, 32⅛ x 25¾ in.
Signed lower right: Robert Henri
The Brooklyn Museum, New York, Gift of Roy Neuberger

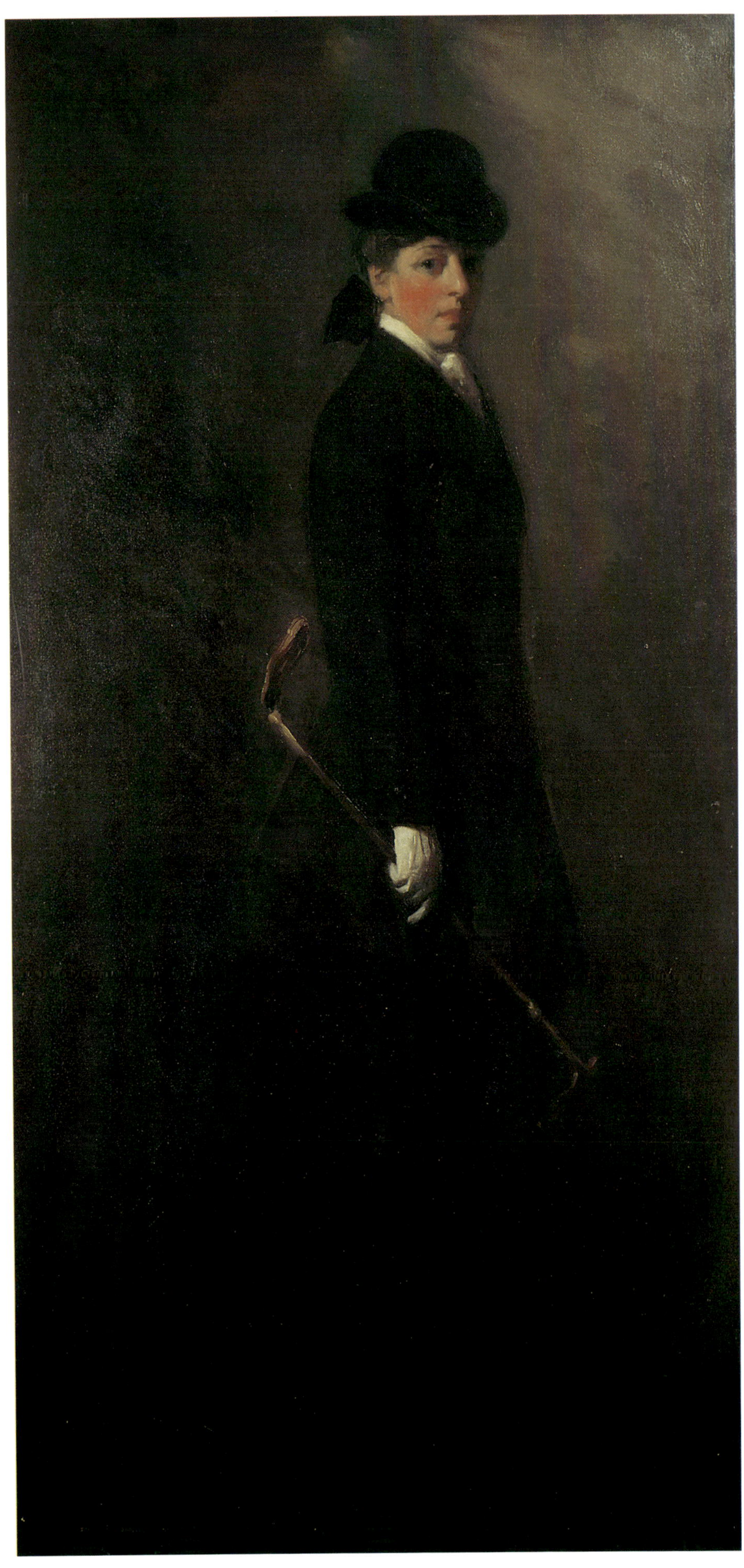

2.
PORTRAIT OF
MISS LEORA M. DRYER IN
RIDING COSTUME, 1902

Oil on canvas, 77 x 35¼ in.
Signed lower left: Robert Henri
Collection of Janet Le Clair,
Estate of Robert Henri

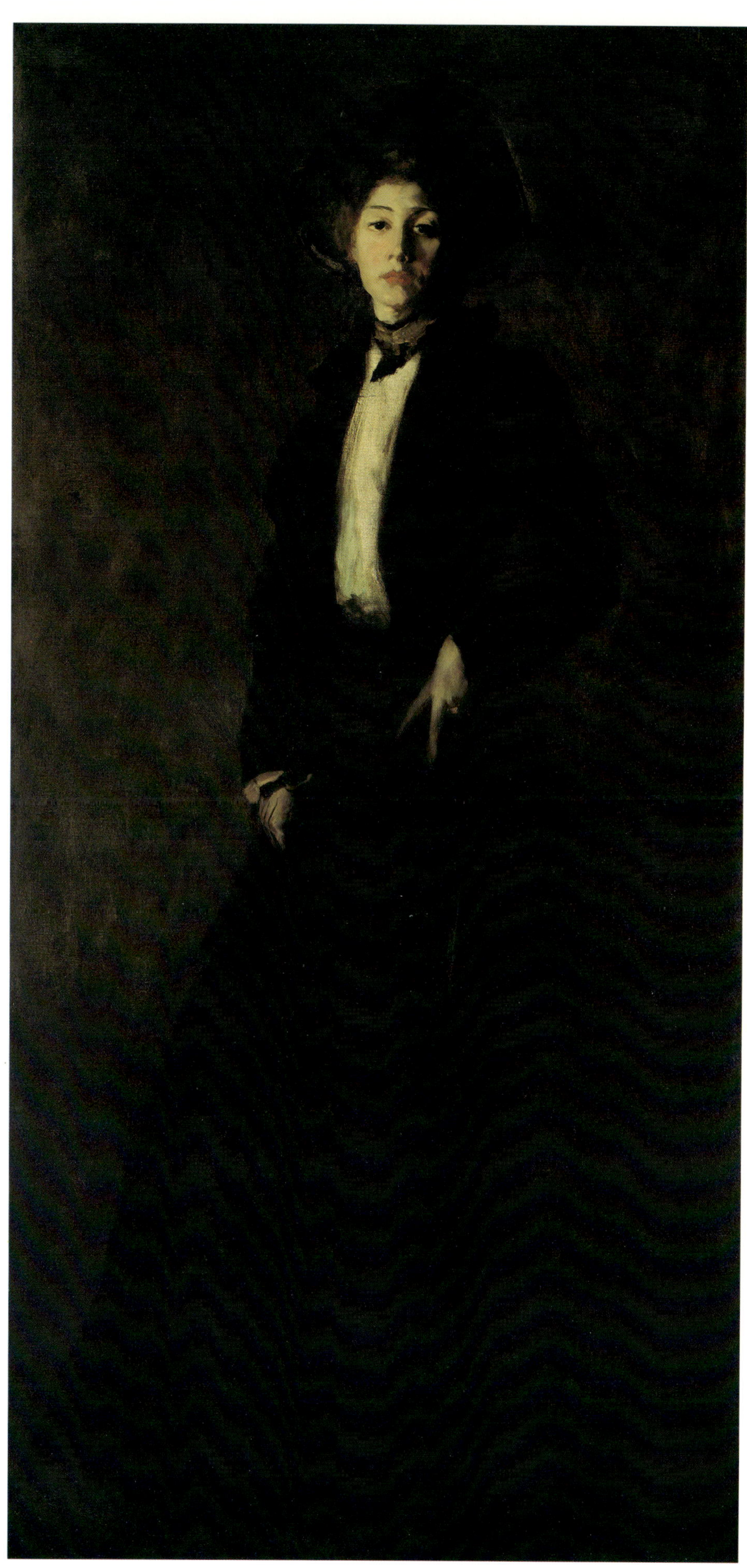

3.
YOUNG WOMAN
IN BLACK, 1902

Oil on canvas, 77 x 38 in.
Signed lower right: Robert Henri
The Art Institute of Chicago,
Friends of American Art
Collection

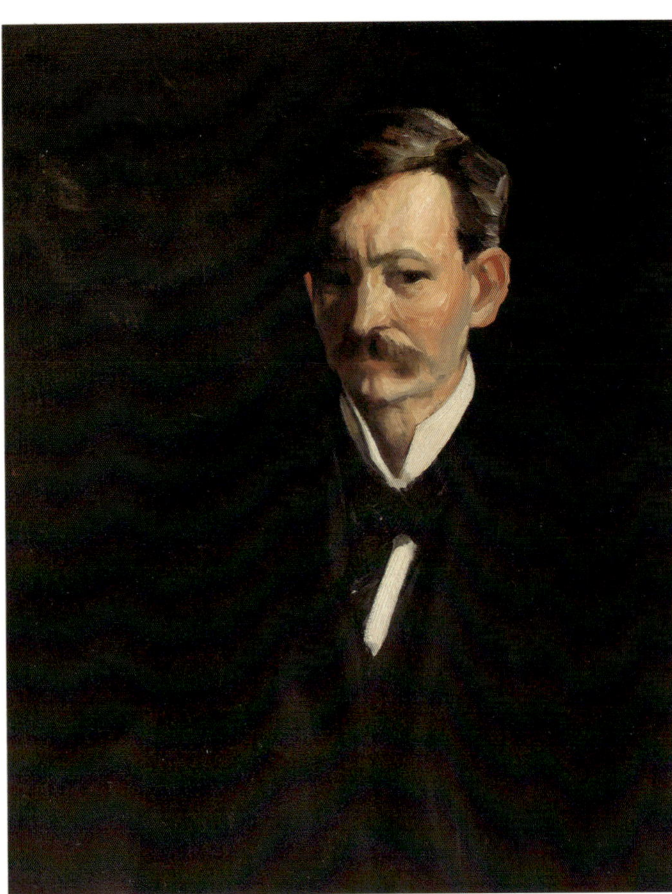

4.
SELF-PORTRAIT, 1903
Oil on canvas, 32 x 26 in.
Signed and dated lower center: Robert Henri 1903
Sheldon Memorial Art Gallery, University of Nebraska-Lincoln, Gift of Mrs. Olga N. Sheldon

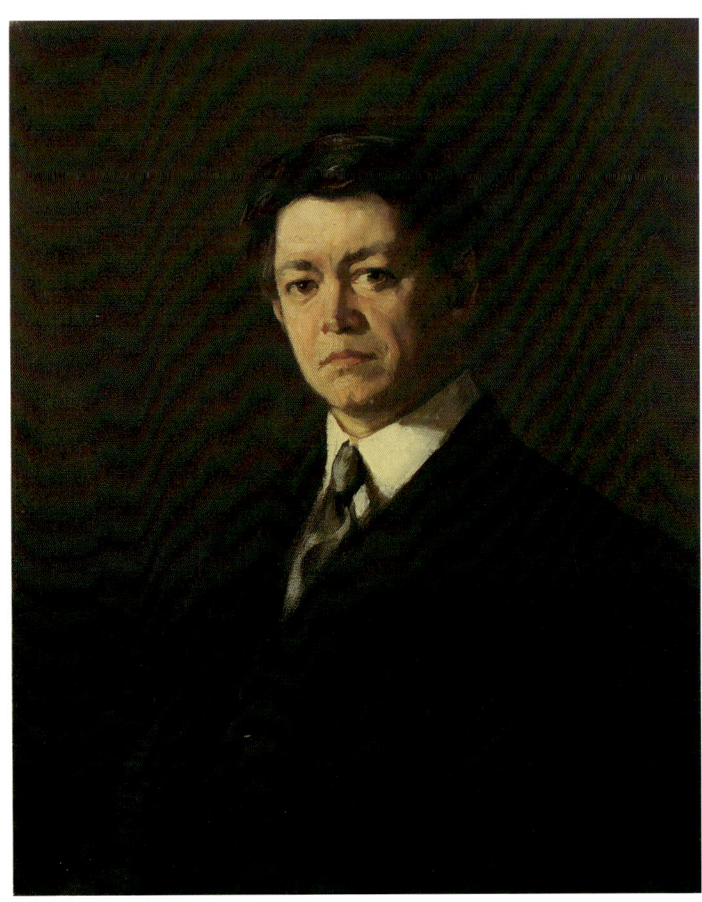

5.
PORTRAIT OF FRANK L. SOUTHRN, M.D., 1904
Oil on canvas, 32 x 26 in.
Signed lower right: Robert Henri
Sheldon Memorial Art Gallery, University of Nebraska-Lincoln, Gift of Mrs. Olga N. Sheldon

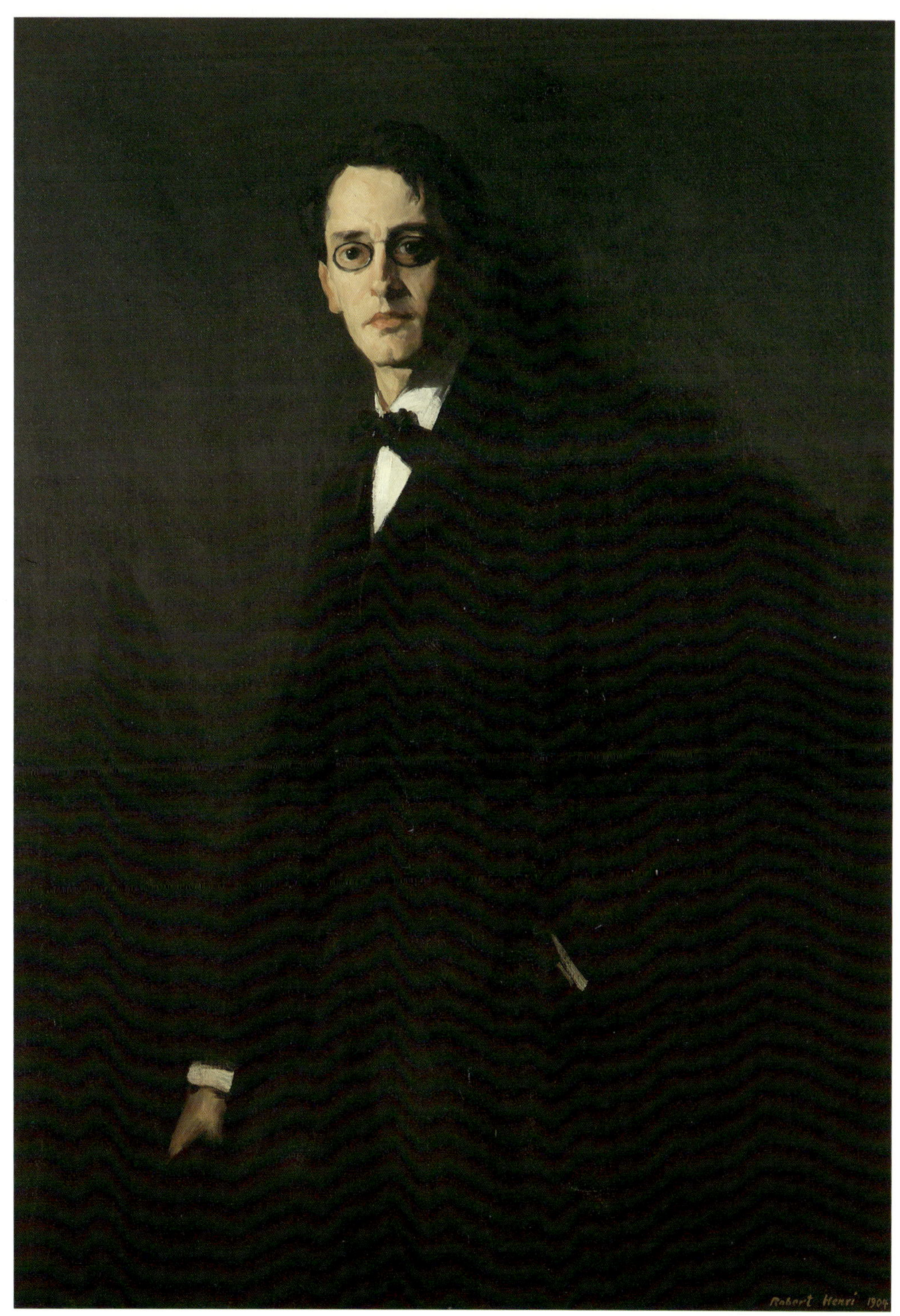

6.
PORTRAIT OF JOHN SLOAN, 1904

Oil on canvas, 56⅝ x 41⅛ in.
Signed lower right: Robert Henri
The Corcoran Gallery of Art, Washington, D.C.,
Gift of Mr. and Mrs. John Sloan

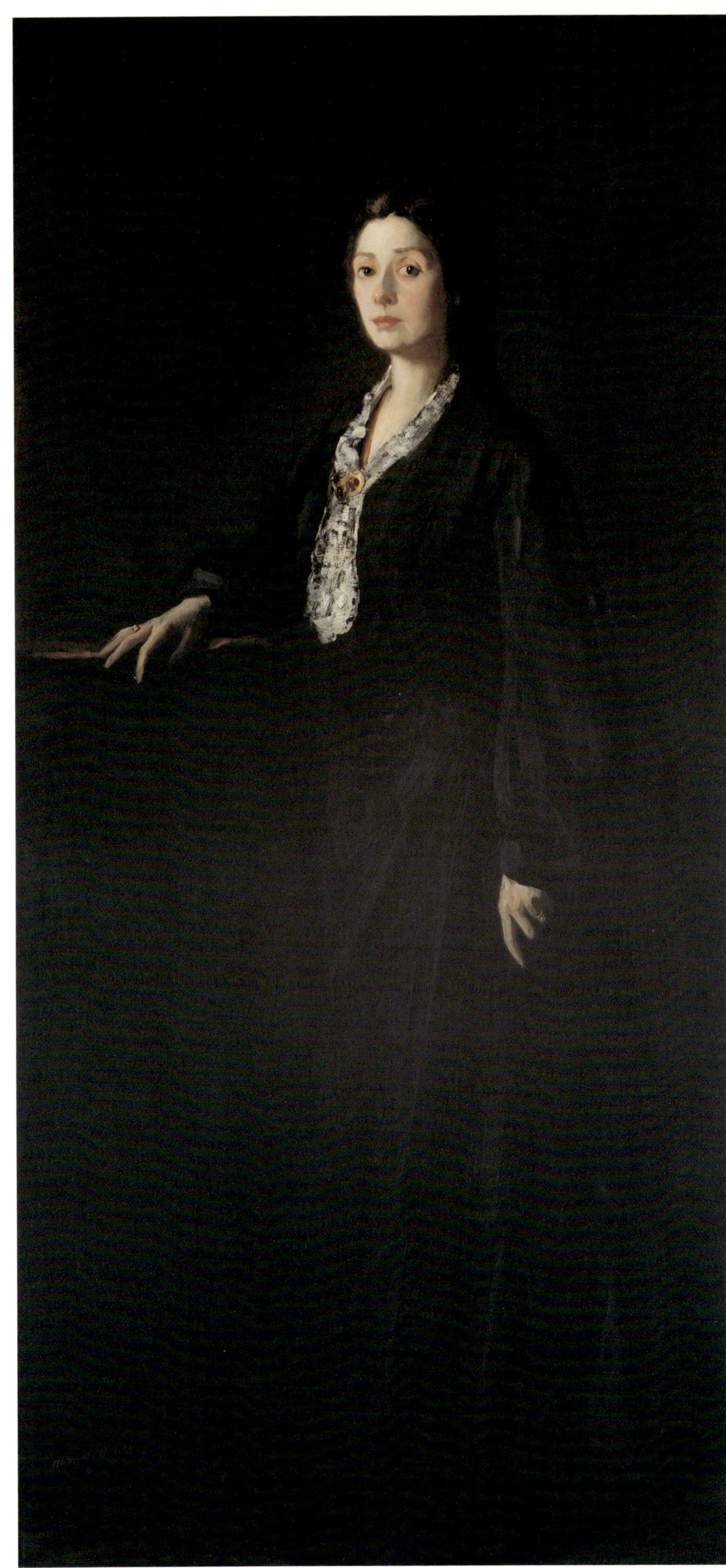

7.
LADY IN BLACK
(MRS. ROBERT HENRI), 1904

Oil on canvas, 78 x 38 in.
Signed lower left: Robert Henri
The Parrish Art Museum,
Southampton, New York,
Gift of Paul Peralta-Ramos

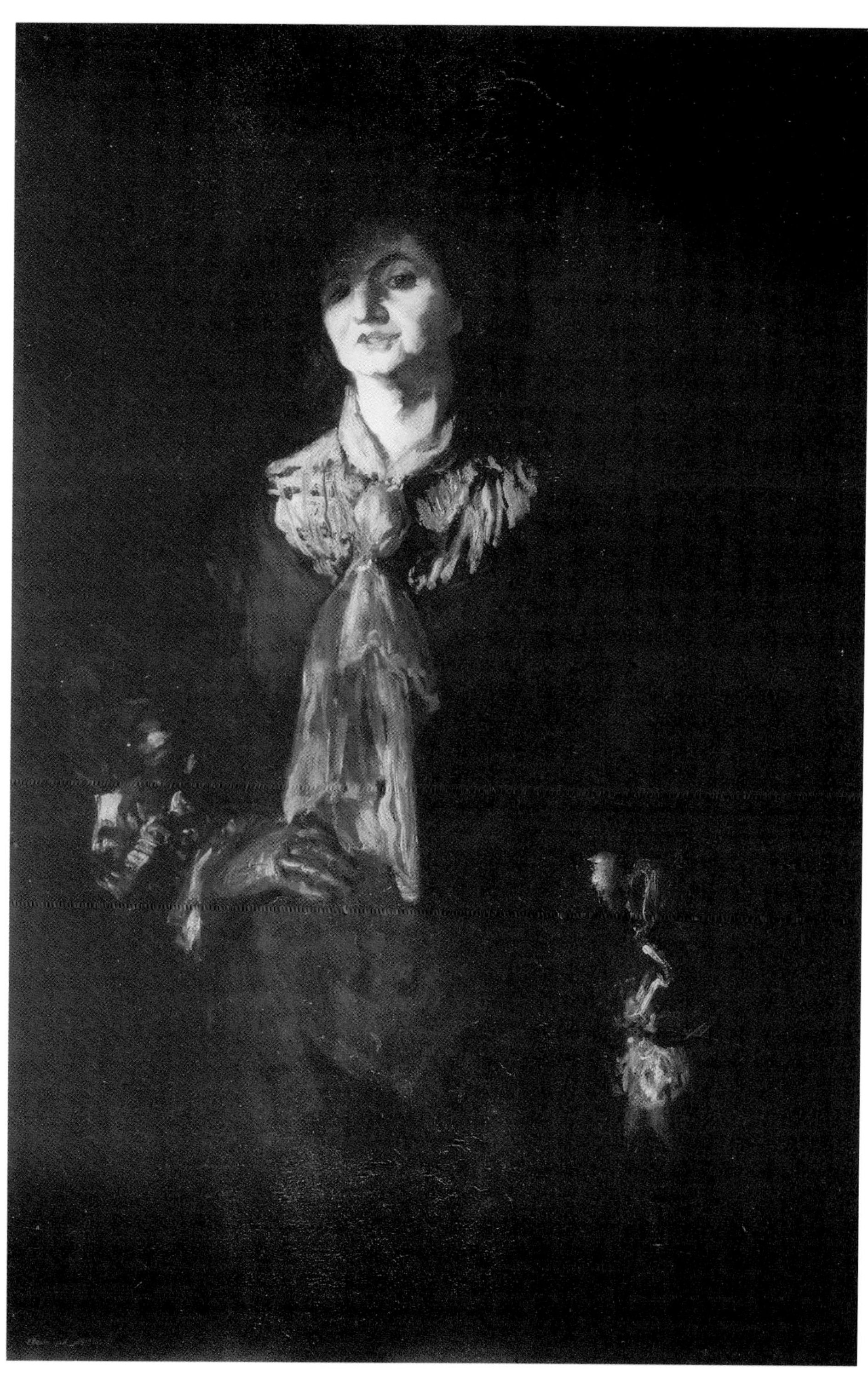

8.
ZENKA (PORTRAIT OF EUGENIE STEIN), 1904
Oil on canvas, 57 x 38 in.
Signed lower left: Robert Henri
Collection of Janet Le Clair, Estate of Robert Henri

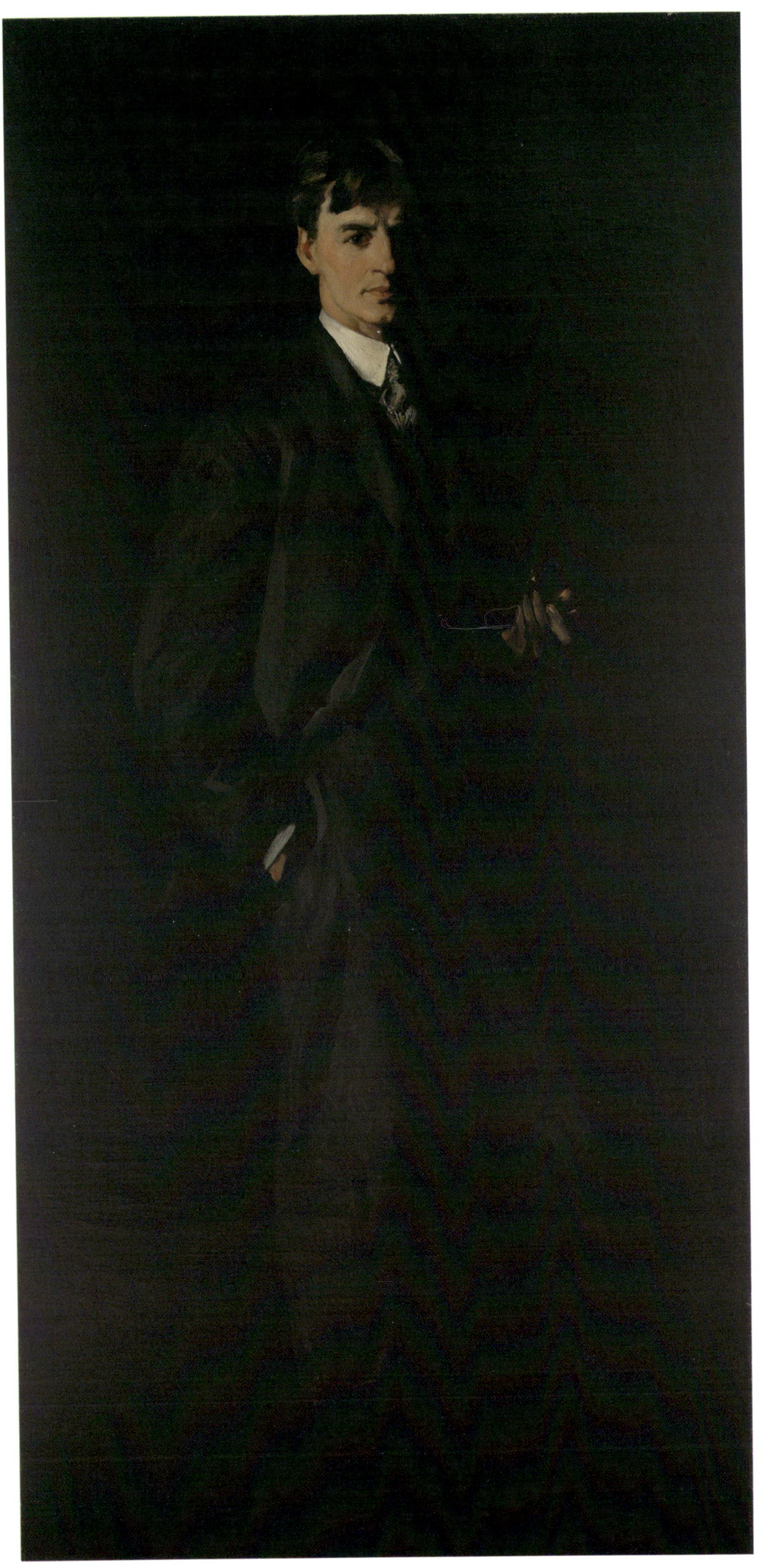

9.
PORTRAIT OF
JAMES PRESTON, 1904

Oil on canvas, 78 x 38 in.
Signed lower left: Robert Henri
On extended loan to the
Orlando Museum of Art,
Courtesy of Mrs. Martin
Andersen

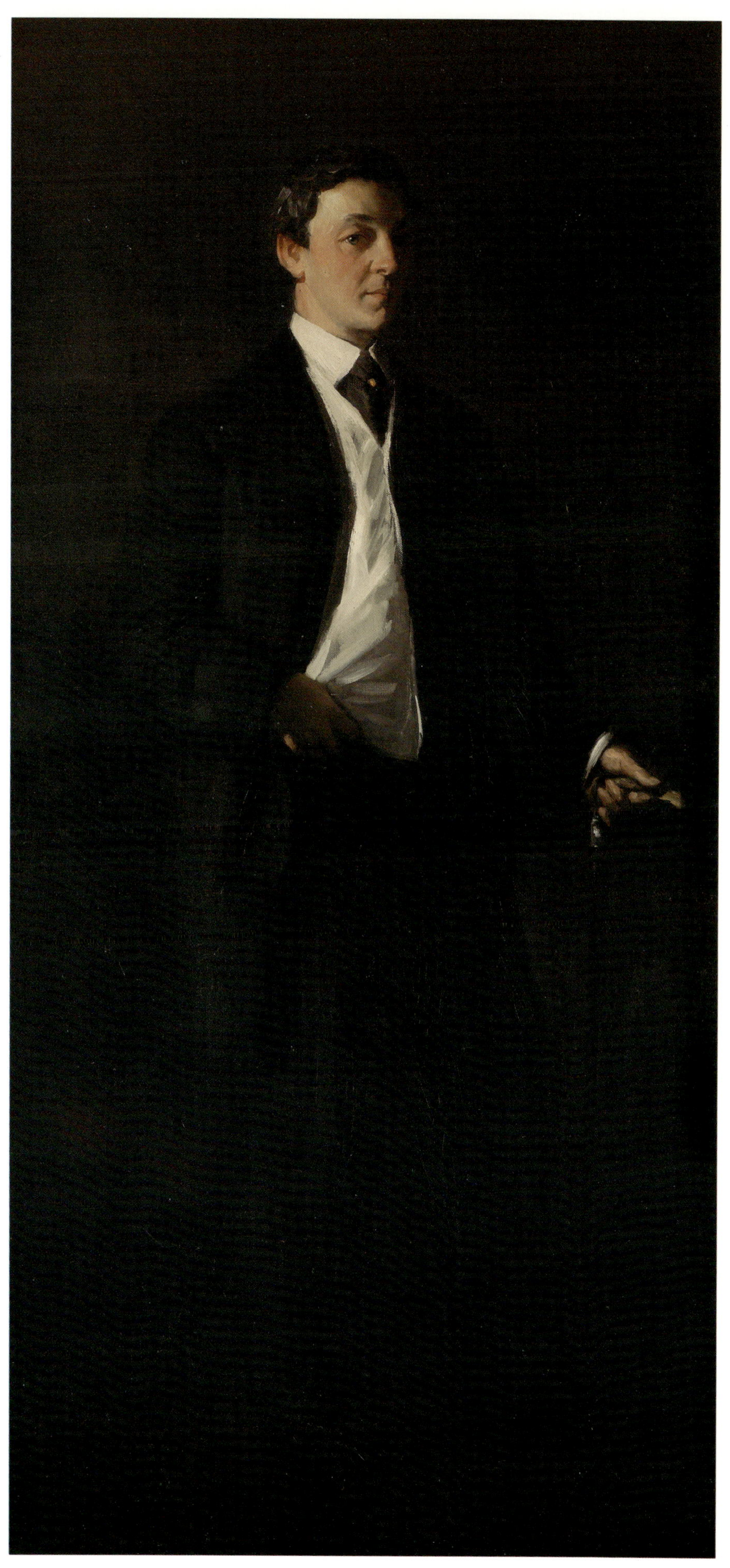

10.
PORTRAIT OF W.J. GLACKENS, 1904
Oil on canvas, 78 x 38 in.
Signed lower left: Robert Henri
Sheldon Memorial Art Gallery,
University of Nebraska-Lincoln,
Nebraska Art Association Collection,
Thomas C. Woods Memorial

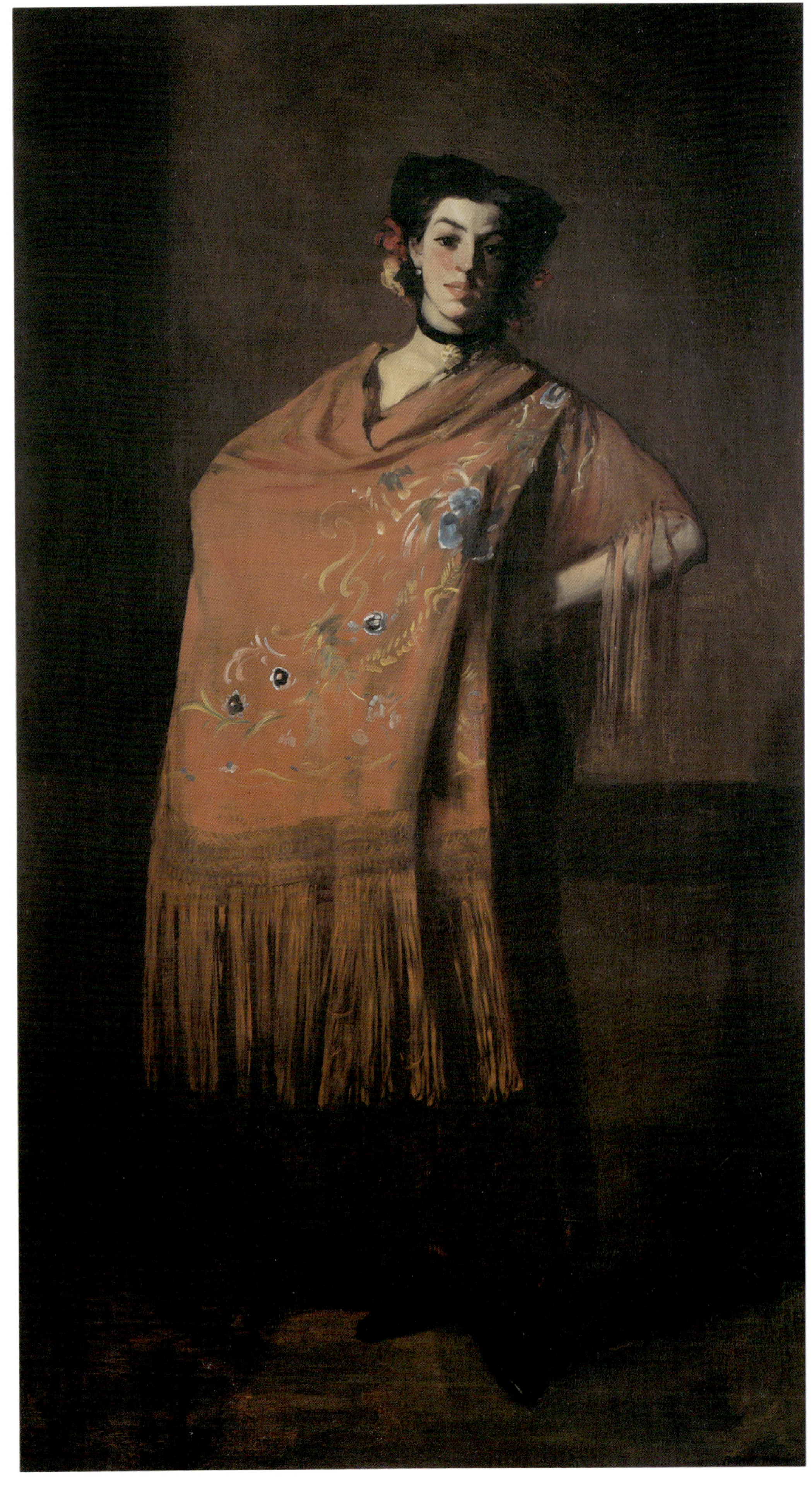

11. (Opposite)
SPANISH DANCING GIRL, 1904

Oil on canvas, 85 x 49 in.
Signed lower right:
Robert Henri.
Collection of Janet Le Clair,
Estate of Robert Henri

12.
MODISTE OF MADRID, 1906

Oil on canvas, 78 x 38½ in.
Signed lower left: Robert Henri
Minnesota Museum of
American Art, St. Paul,
Collections Fund

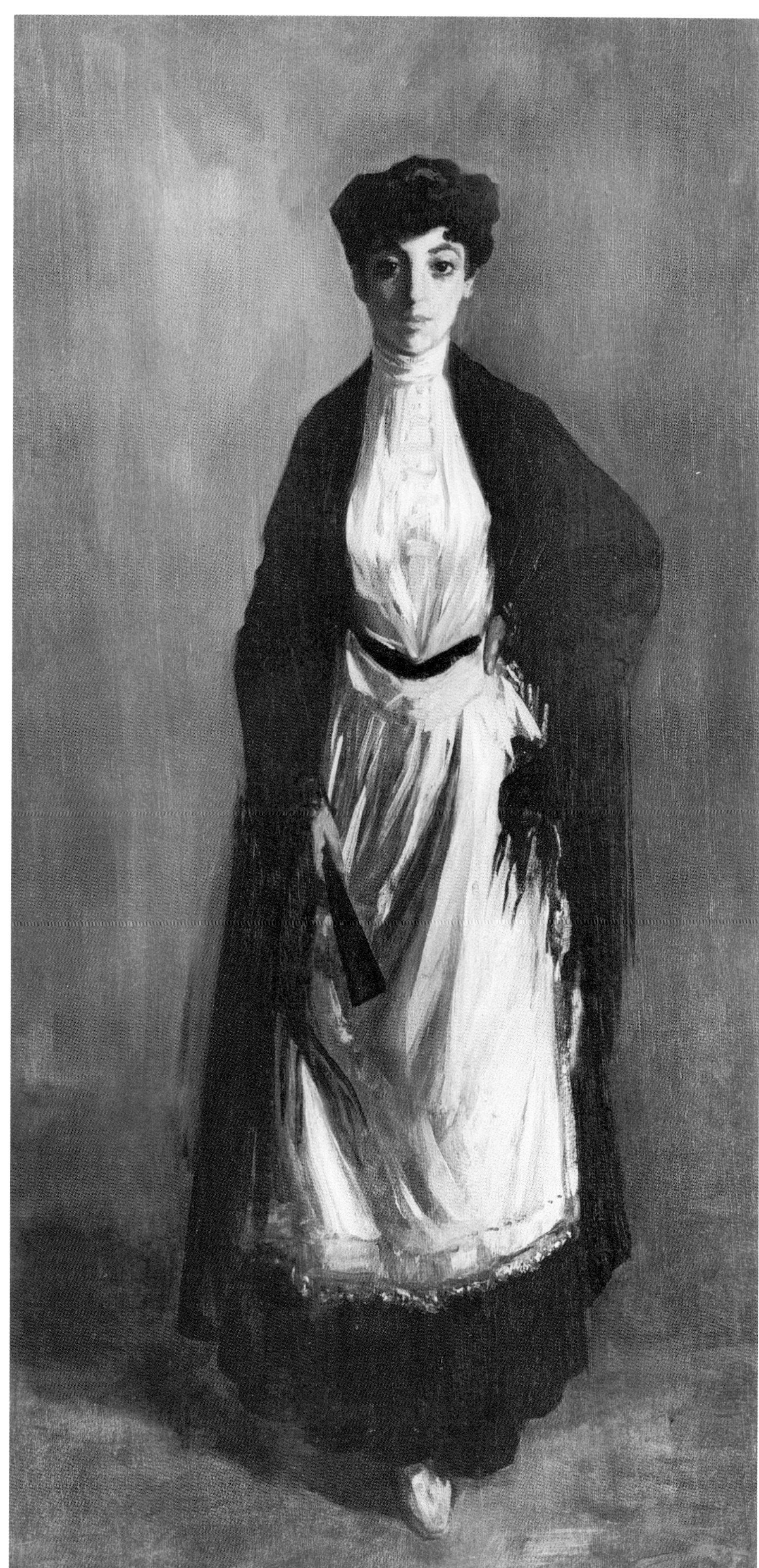

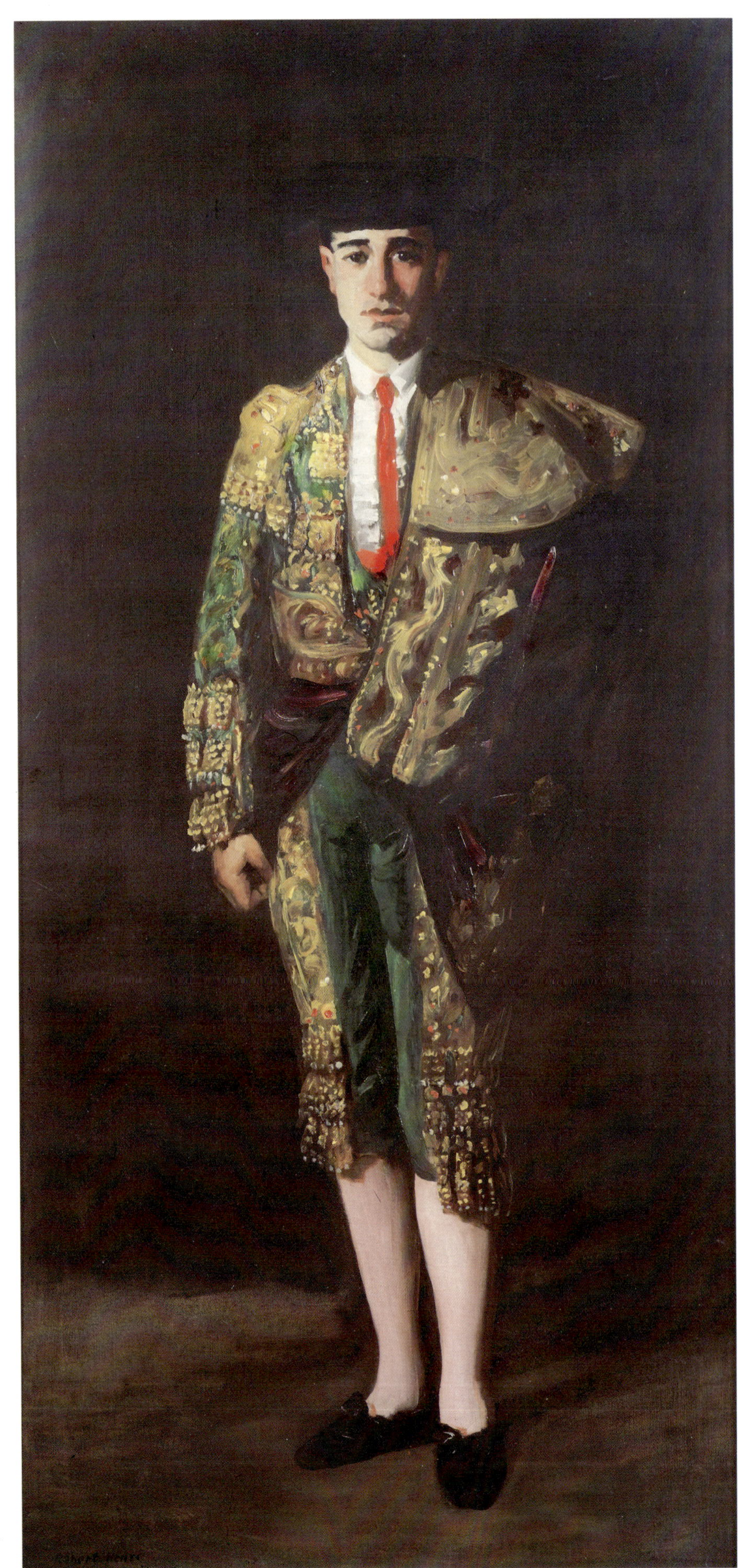

13.
PORTRAIT OF
EL MATADOR
FELIX ASIEGO, 1906

Oil on canvas, 77 x 36 in.
Signed lower left:
Robert Henri
Collection of Janet Le Clair,
Estate of Robert Henri

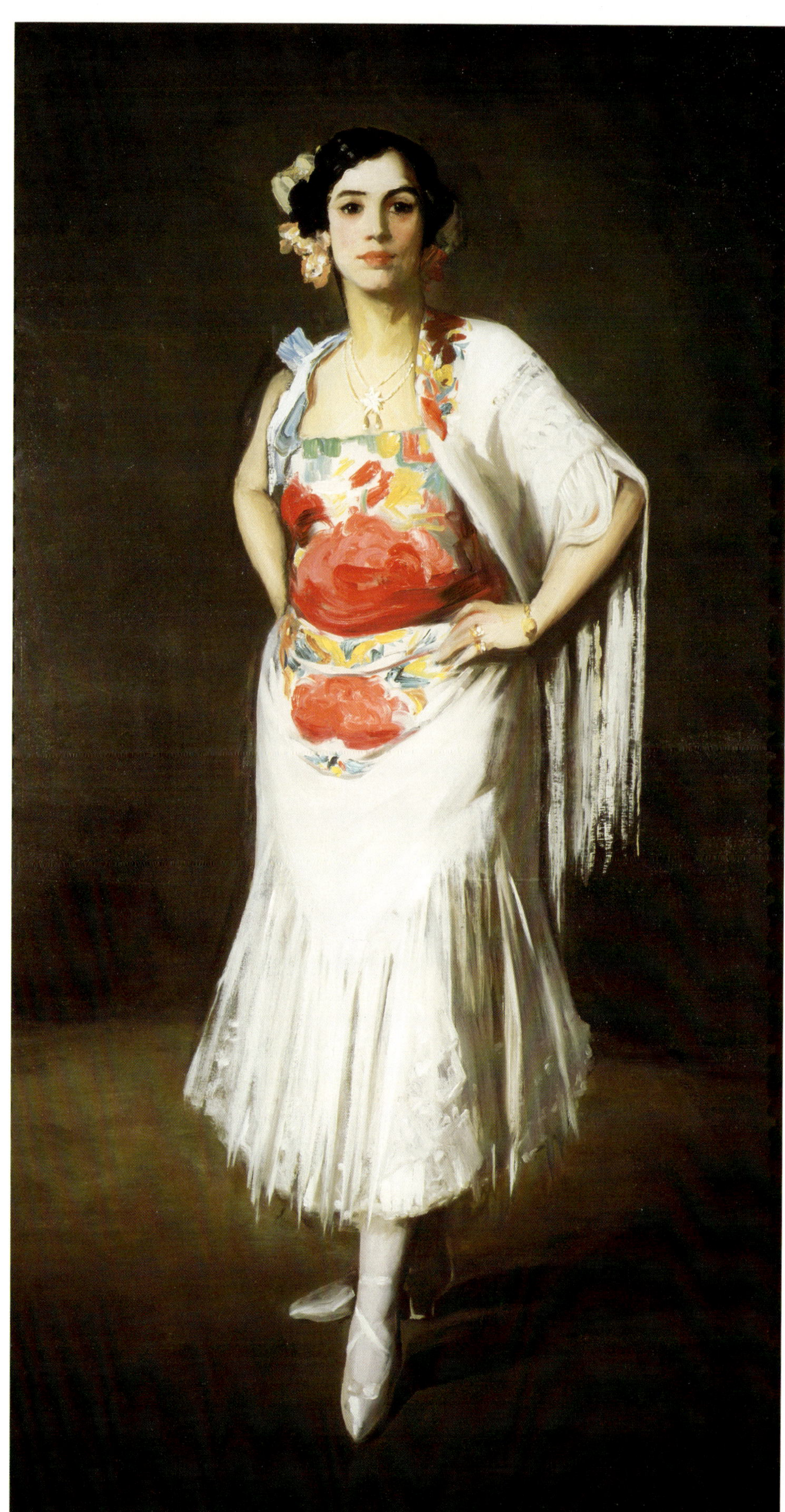

14.
LA REINA MORA, 1906
Oil on canvas, 78 x 42 1/16
Signed lower right:
Robert Henri
Titled lower left:
La Reina Mora
Colby College Museum of Art, Waterville, Maine,
Museum purchase from the Jere Abbott Acquisitions Fund

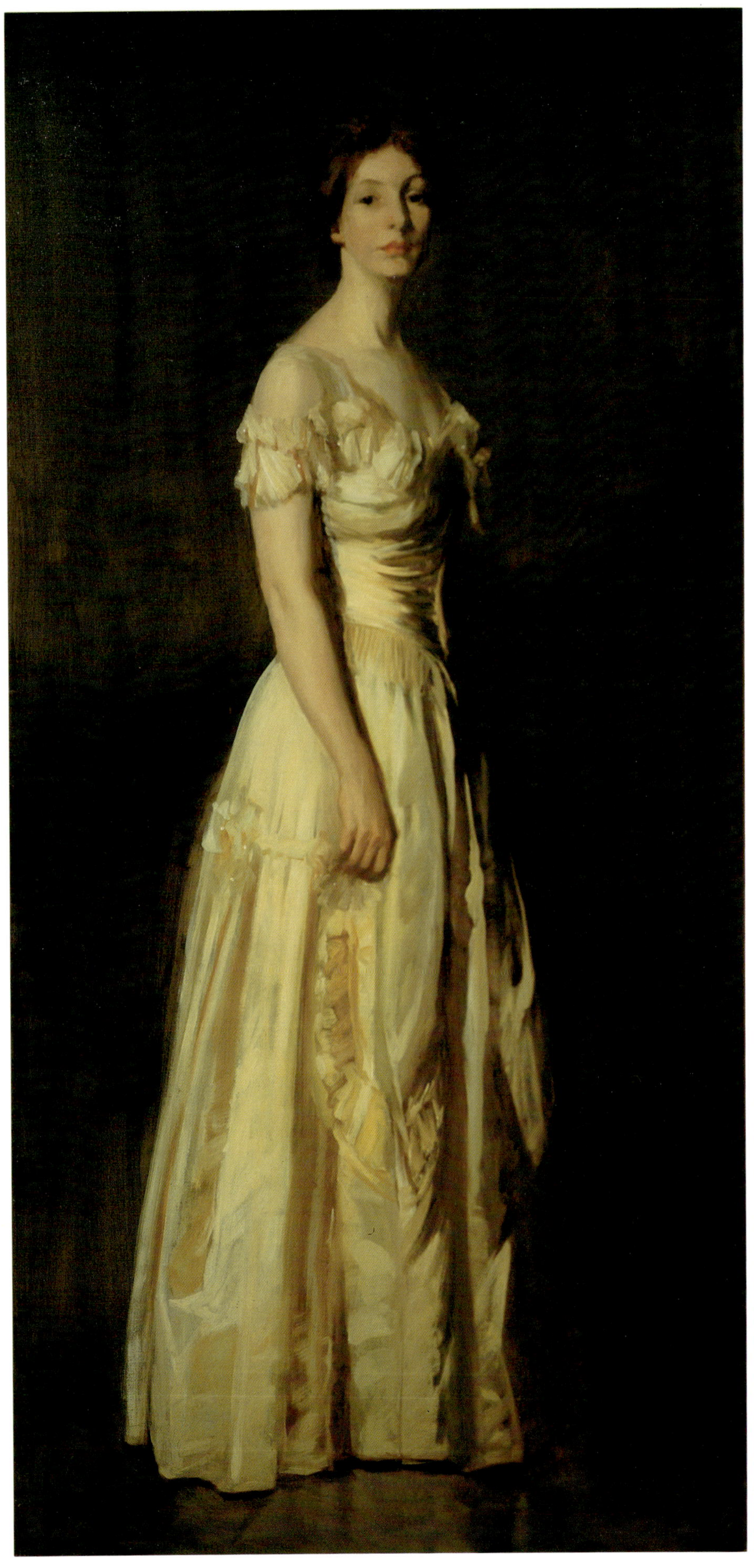

15.
YOUNG WOMAN IN
YELLOW SATIN, 1907

Oil on canvas, 77 x 37 in.
Signed lower left: Robert Henri
Mississippi Museum of Art,
Jackson, Gift of Mr. and Mrs.
Lyle Cashion, Jr.

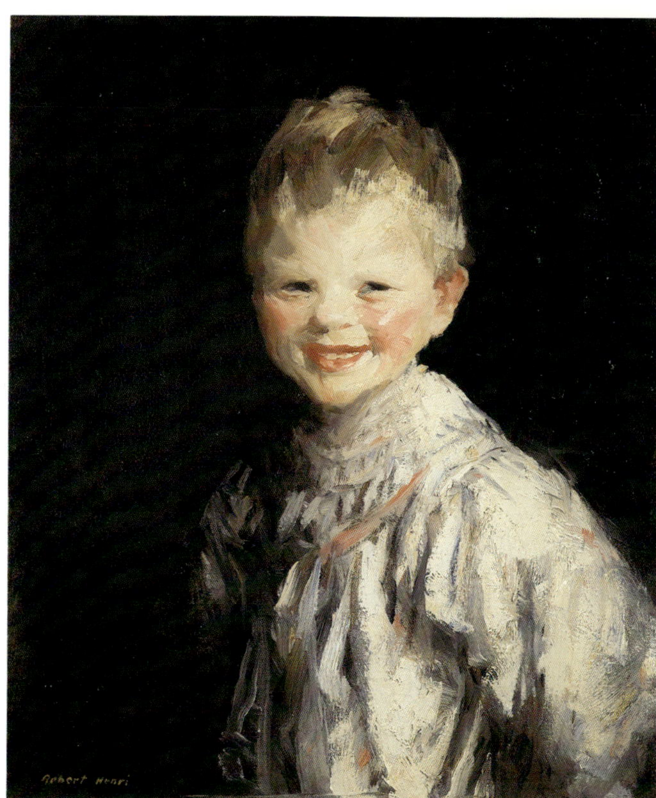

16.
LAUGHING CHILD, 1907
Oil on canvas, 24 x 20 in.
Signed lower left: Robert Henri
Whitney Museum of American Art, New York,
Gift of Gertrude Vanderbilt Whitney

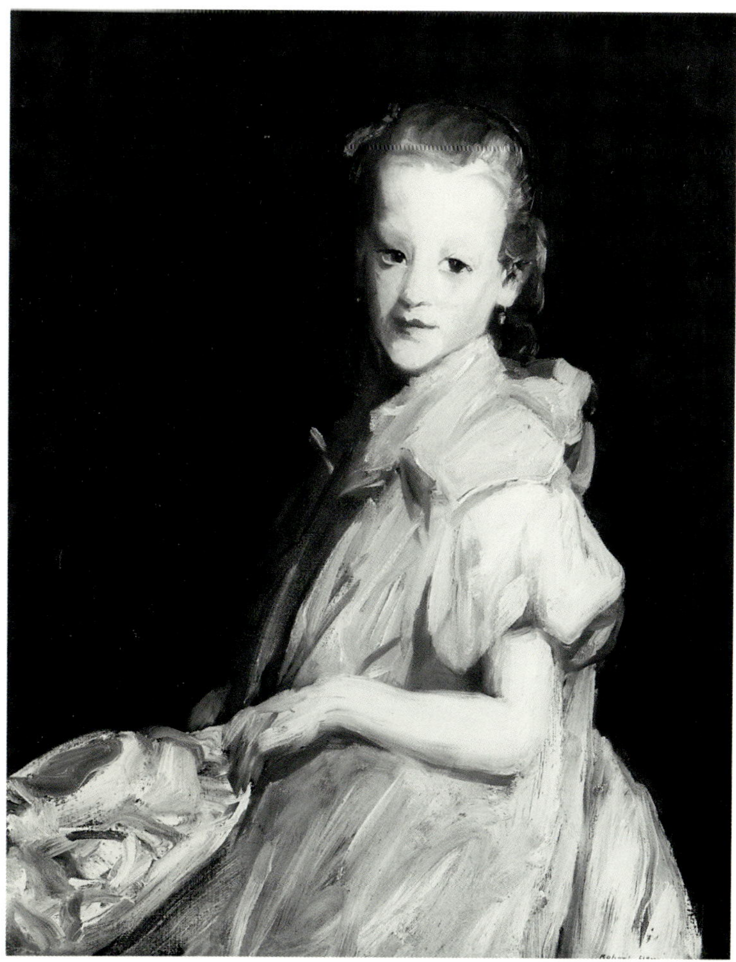

17.
MARTCHE WITH HAT, 1907
Oil on canvas, 32 x 26 in.
Signed lower right: Robert Henri
Virginia Museum of Fine Arts, Richmond,
The Williams Fund

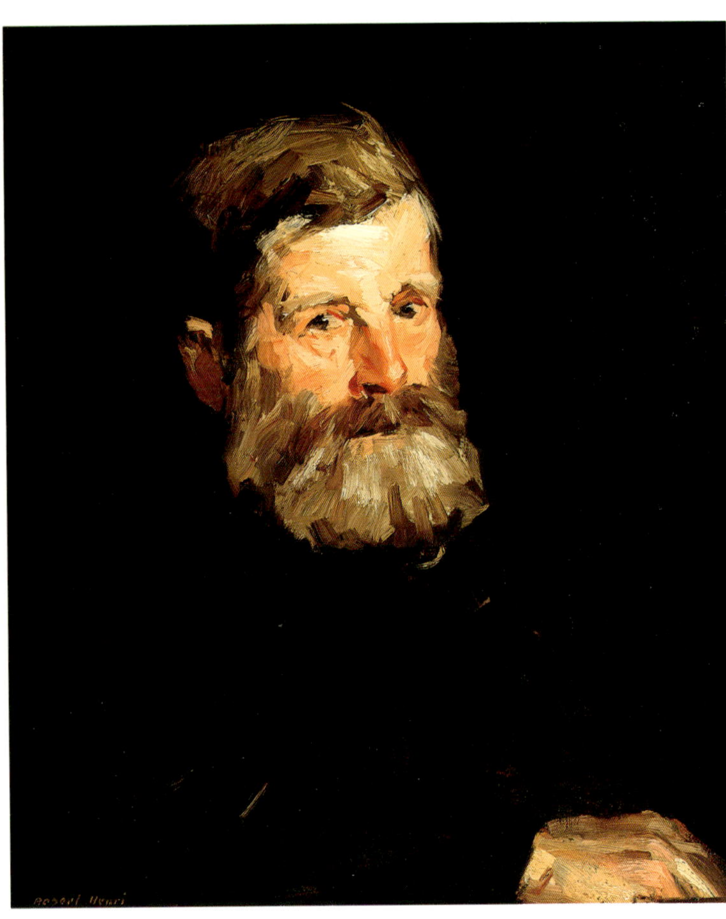

18.
DUTCH FISHERMAN, 1907

Oil on canvas, 24 x 20 in.
Signed lower left: Robert Henri
Westmoreland Museum of Art, Greensburg, Pennsylvania, Gift of Mr. and Mrs. Norman Hirschl

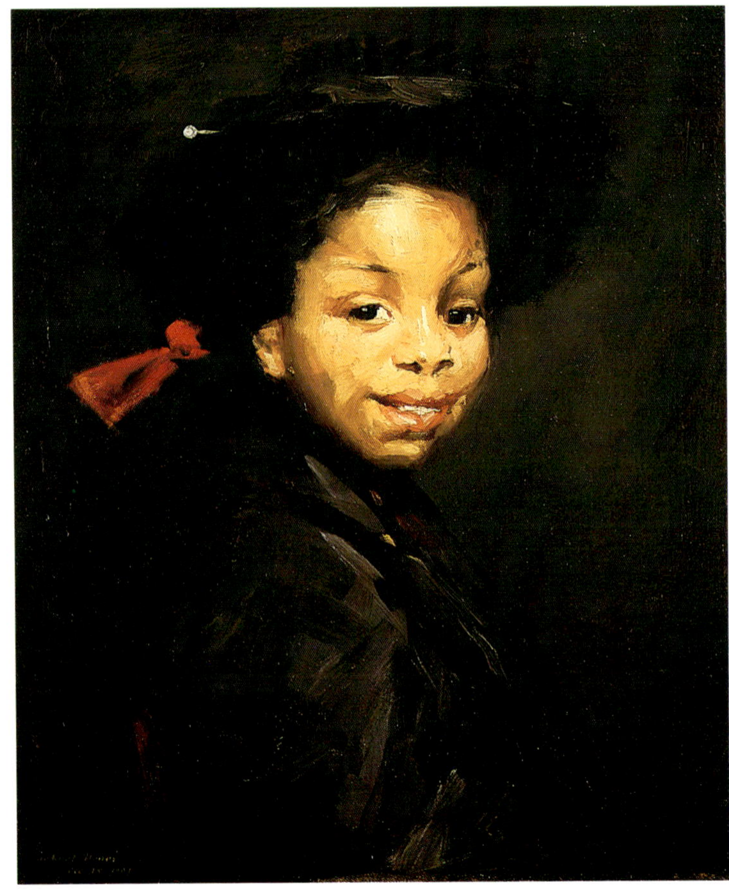

19.
EVA GREEN, 1907

Oil on canvas, 24⅛ x 20¼ in.
Signed and dated lower left:
Robert Henri, December 25, 1907
Wichita Art Museum, Kansas, the Roland P. Murdock Collection

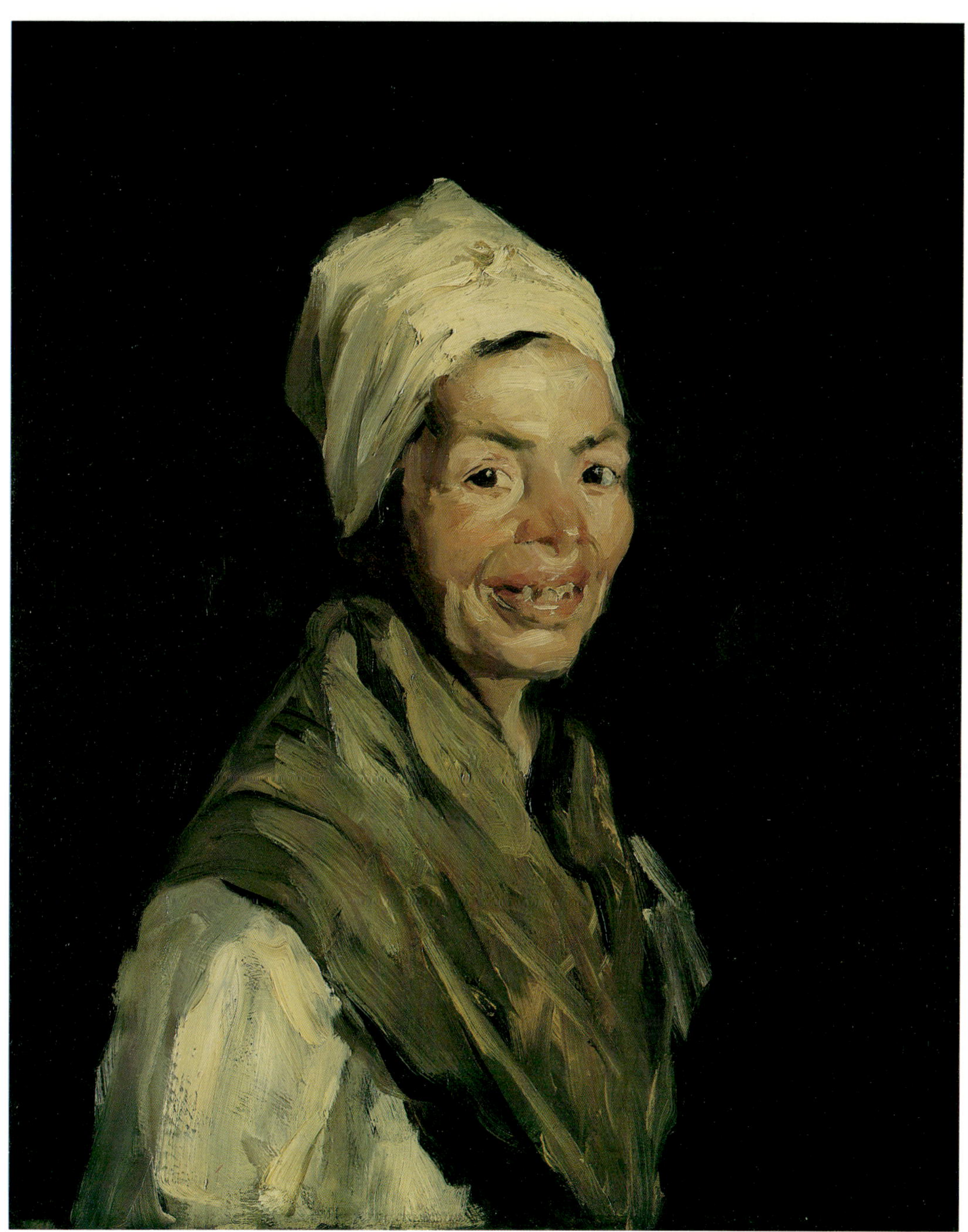

20.
CELESTINA, 1908

Oil on canvas, 24½ x 20 in.
Hirshhorn Museum and Sculpture Garden,
Smithsonian Institution, Washington, D.C.,
Gift of Joseph H. Hirshhorn

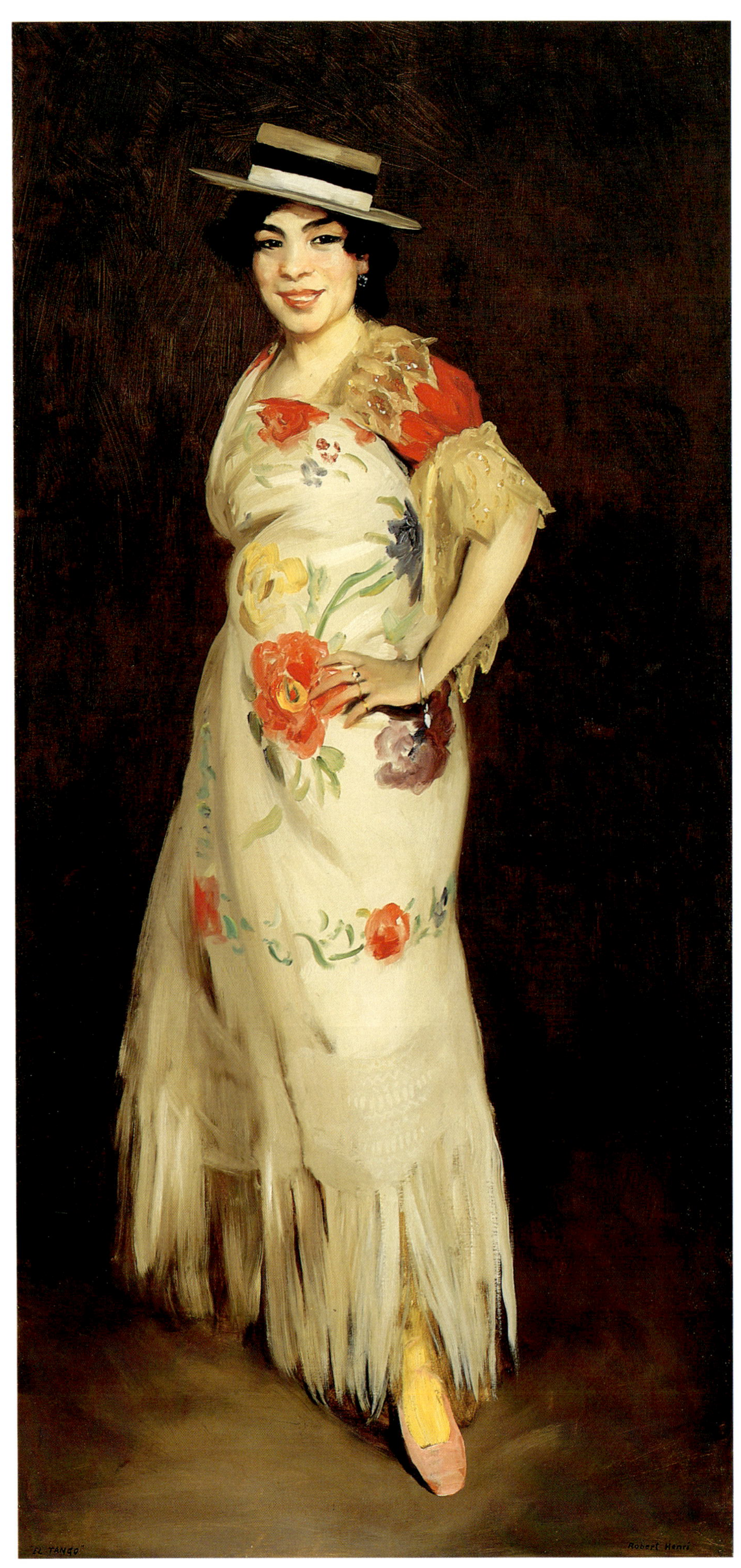

21.
EL TANGO, 1908

Oil on canvas, 77 x 37 ⅛ in.
Signed lower right: Robert Henri
San Antonio Museum of Art, Texas

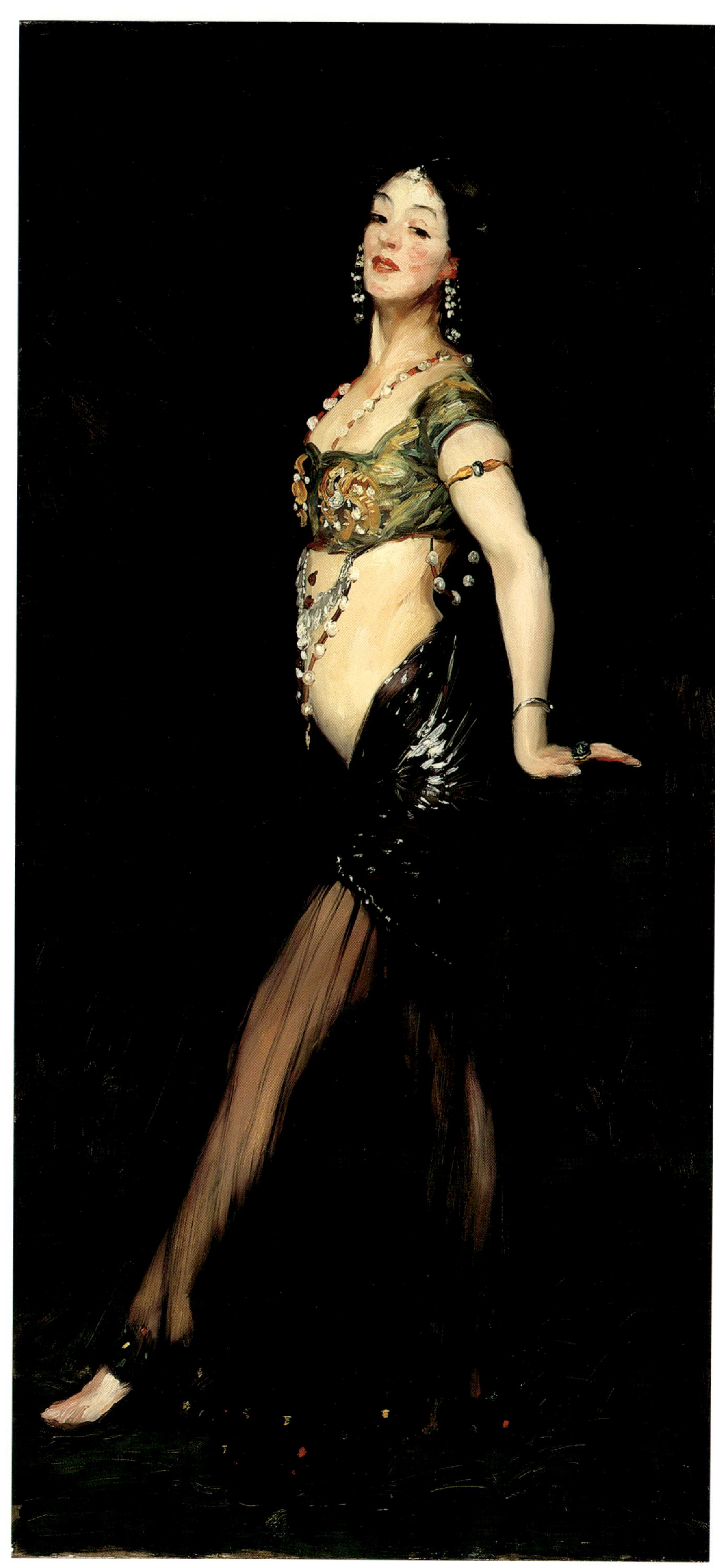

22.
SALOME (NO. 2), 1909

Oil on canvas, 77 ½ x 37 in.
The John and Mable Ringling Museum of Art, Sarasota, Florida, Purchase 1974

[exhibited at Orlando Museum of Art only]

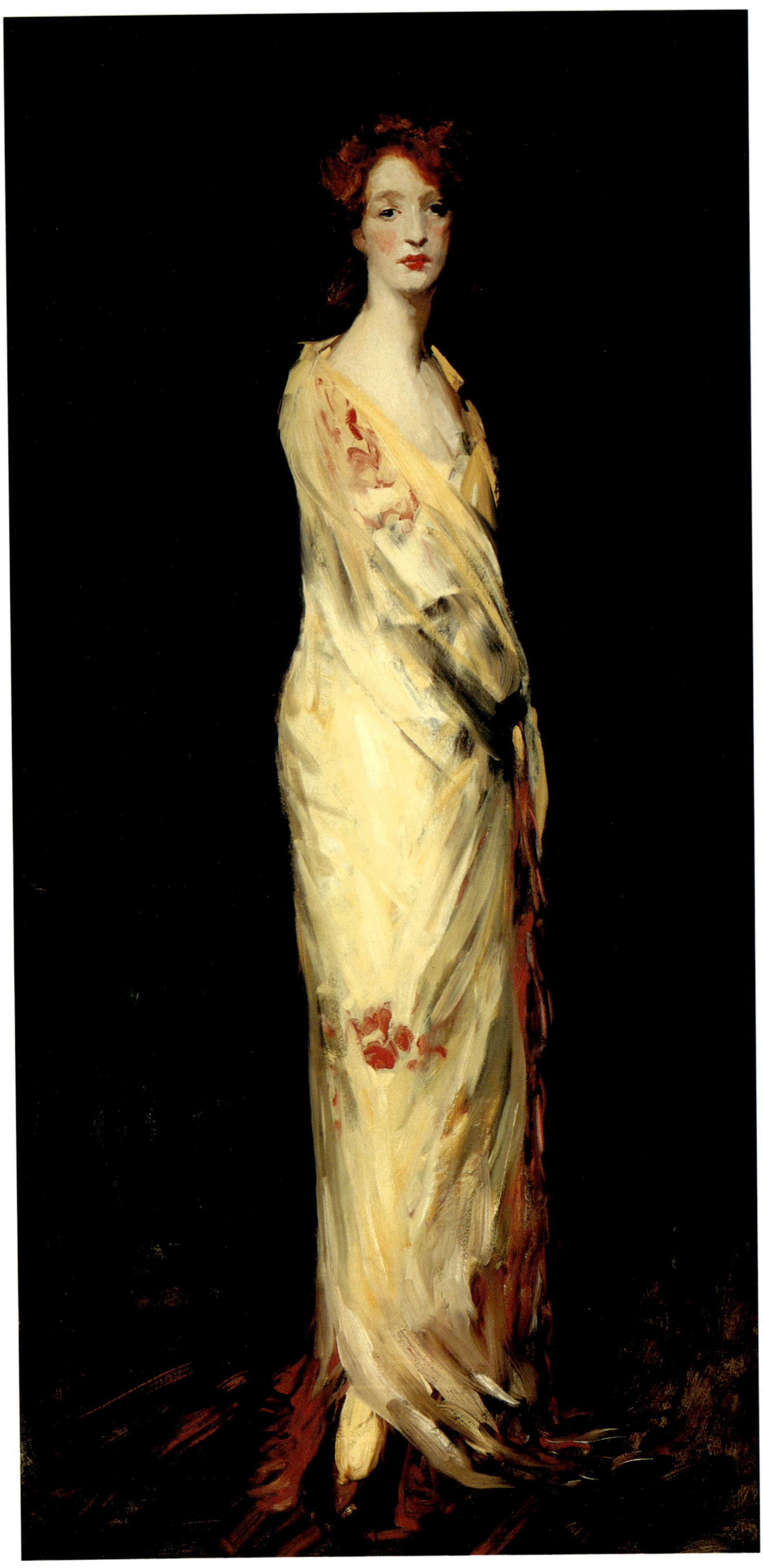

23.
MARJORIE IN A YELLOW SHAWL, 1909

Oil on canvas, 77 x 38 in.
Signed and dated on verso:
Robert Henri, 1909
The Warner Collection of
Gulf States Paper Corporation,
Tuscaloosa, Alabama

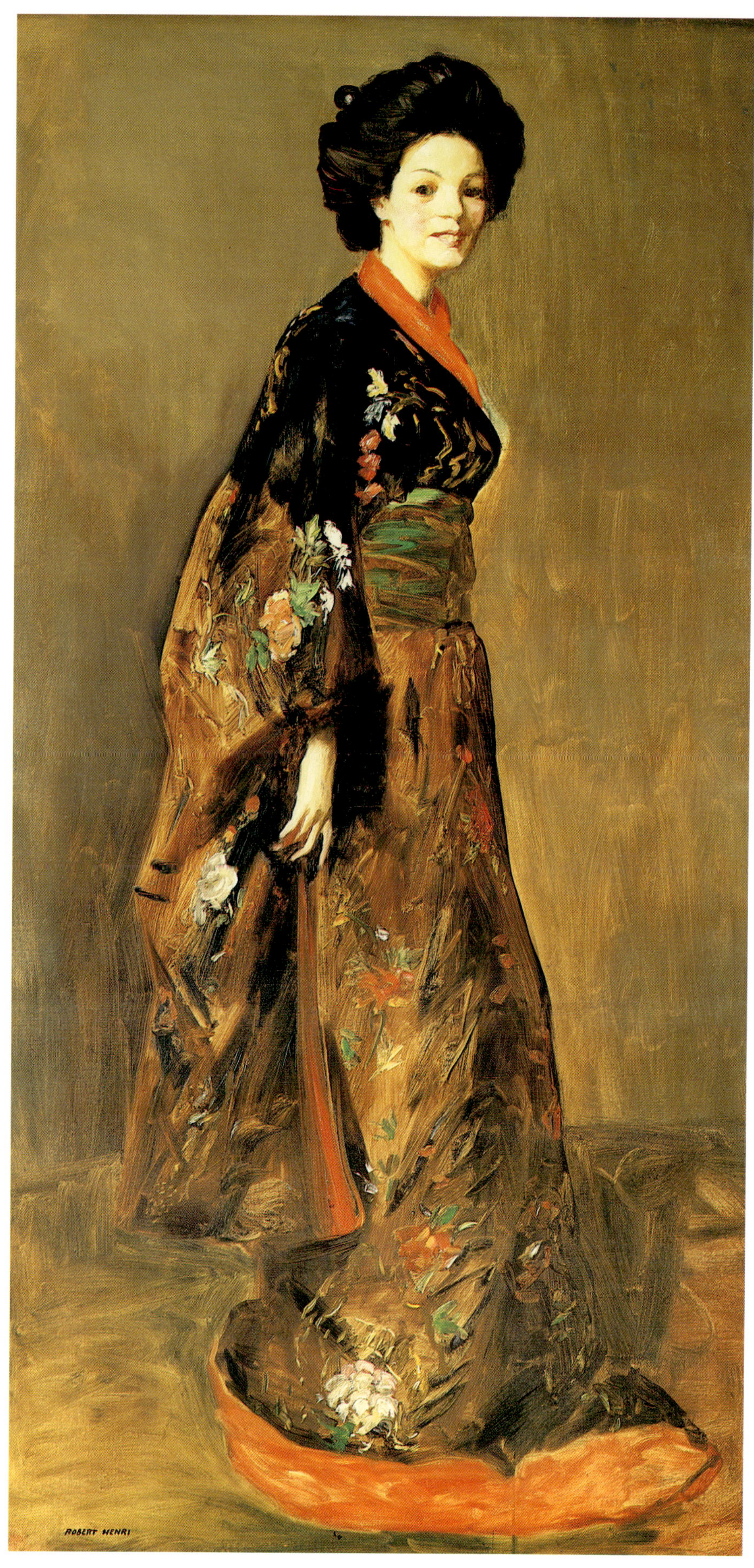

24.
THE BLUE KIMONA, 1909
Oil on canvas, 77 x 37 in.
Signed lower left: Robert Henri
New Orleans Museum of Art,
Louisiana

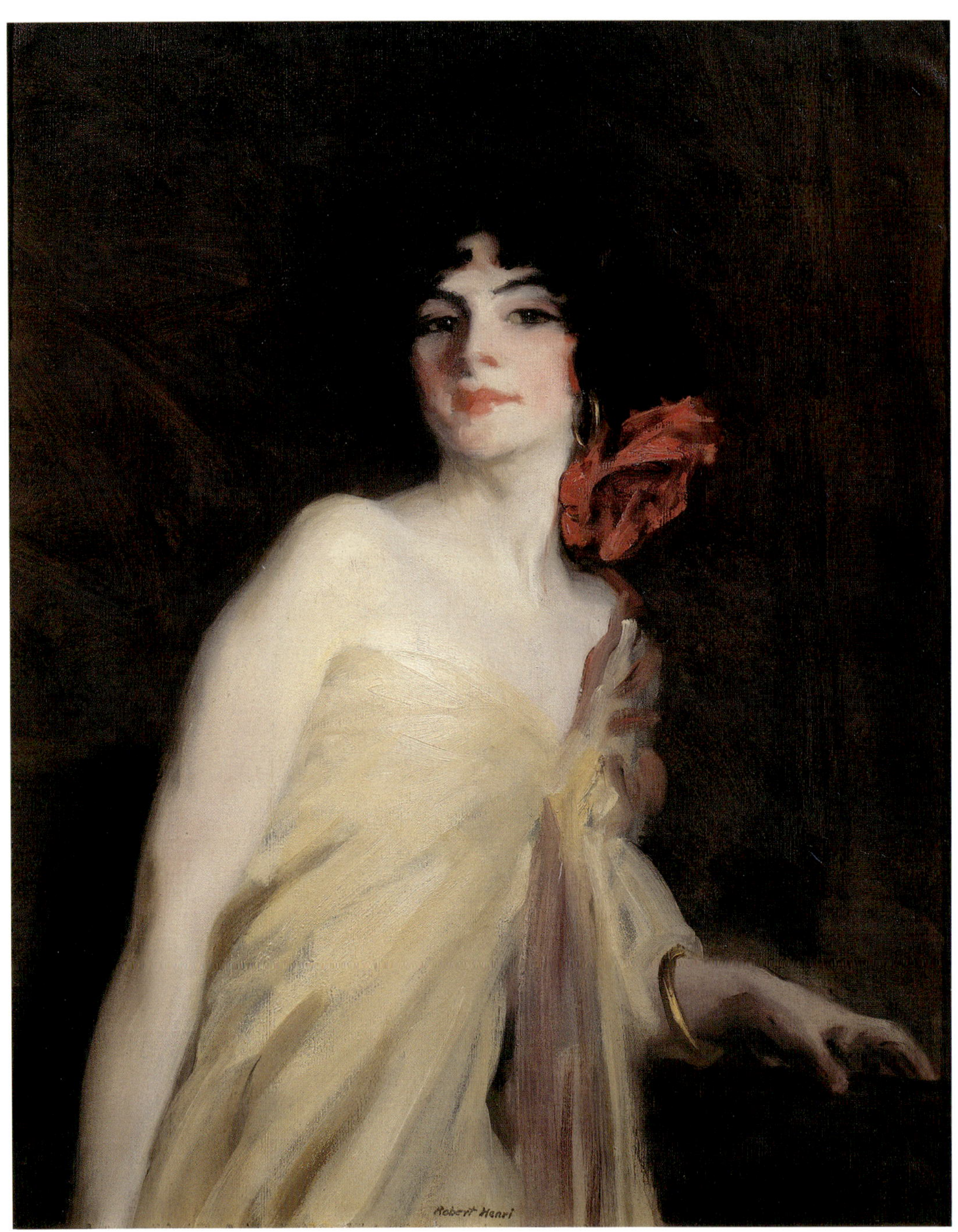

25.
THE RED FLOWER (BETALO IN A SPANISH CHAIR), 1910

Oil on canvas, 32 x 26 in.
Signed lower center: Robert Henri
Collection of Janet Le Clair, Estate of Robert Henri

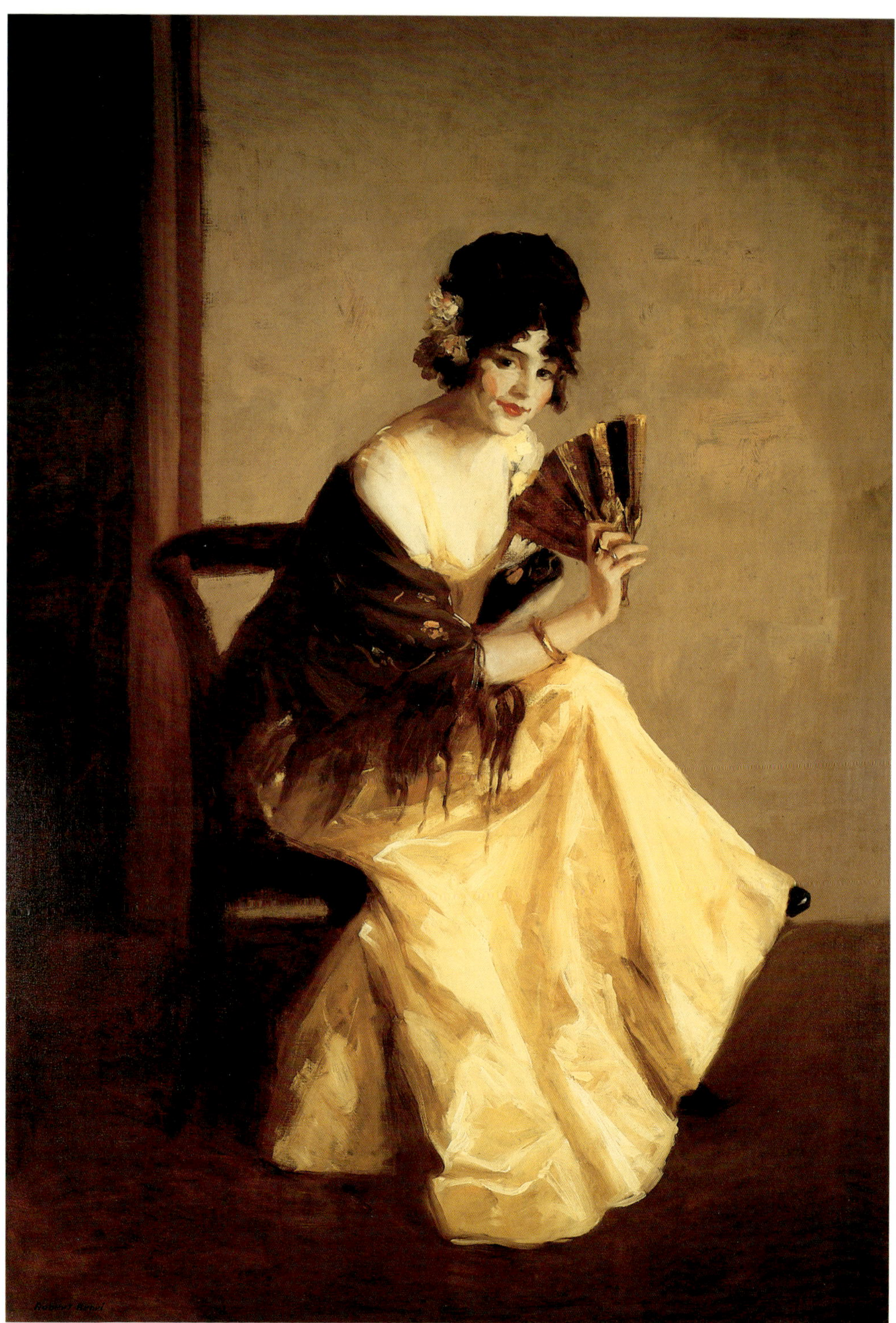

26.
GIRL WITH FAN, 1910

Oil on canvas, 72 x 49½ in.
Signed lower center: Robert Henri
Pennsylvania Academy of the Fine Arts,
Philadelphia, Joseph E. Temple Fund
Signed lower center: Robert Henri

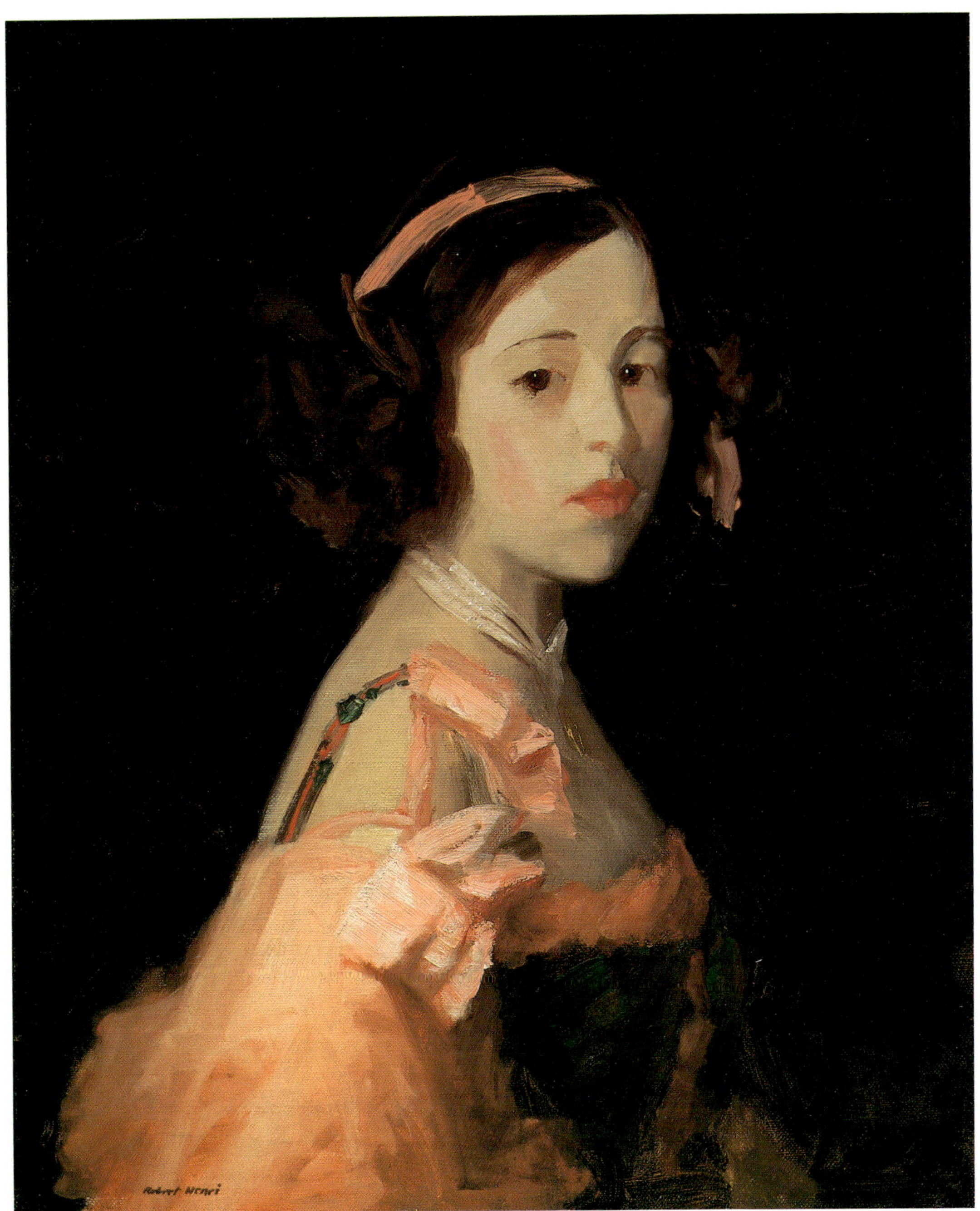

27.
LA MADRILEÑITA, 1910

Oil on canvas, 24 x 20 in.
Signed lower left: Robert Henri
Private collection

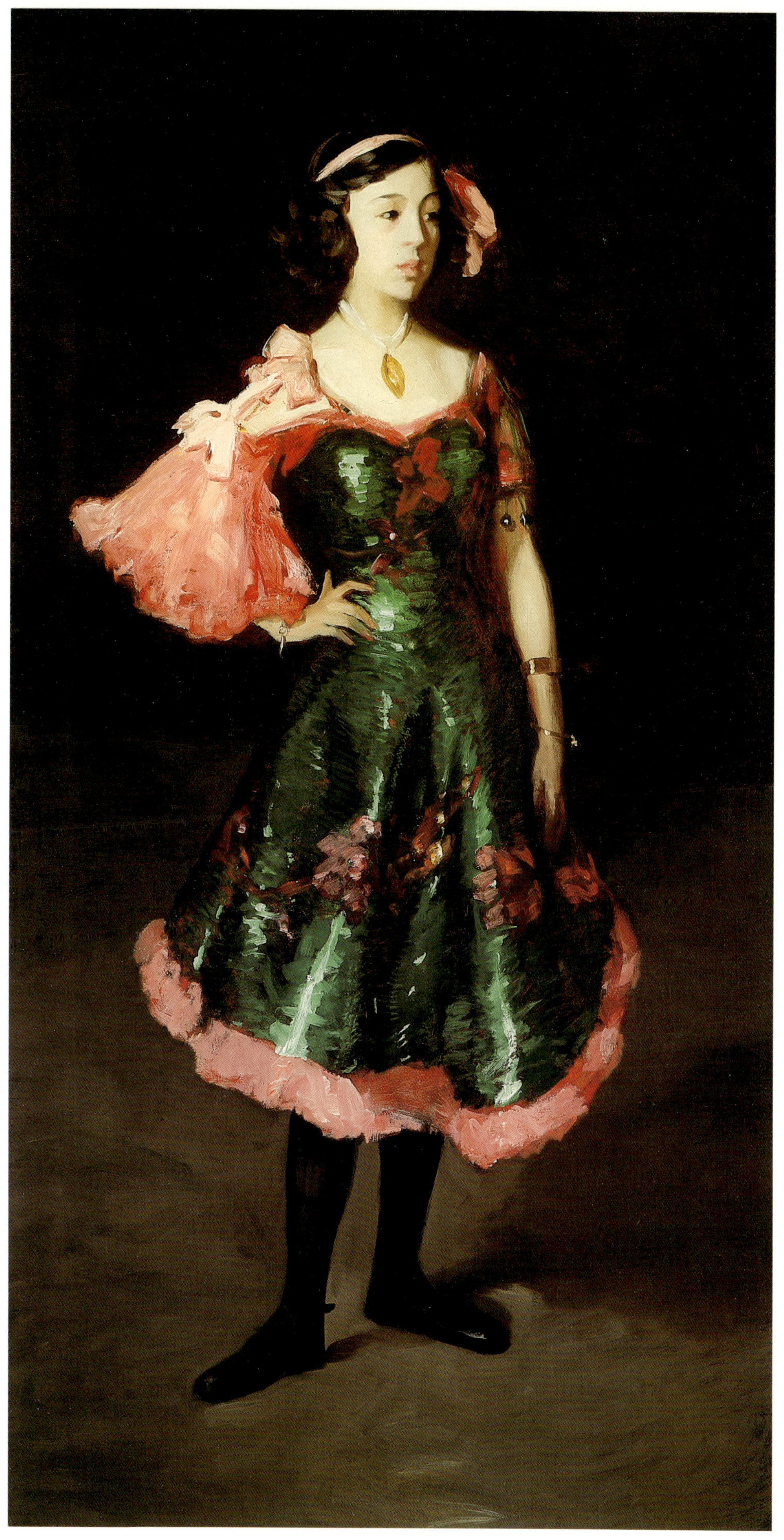

28.
LA MADRILEÑITA, 1910
Oil on canvas, 73 x 37 in.
Collection of Mr. and Mrs.
Terry Stent

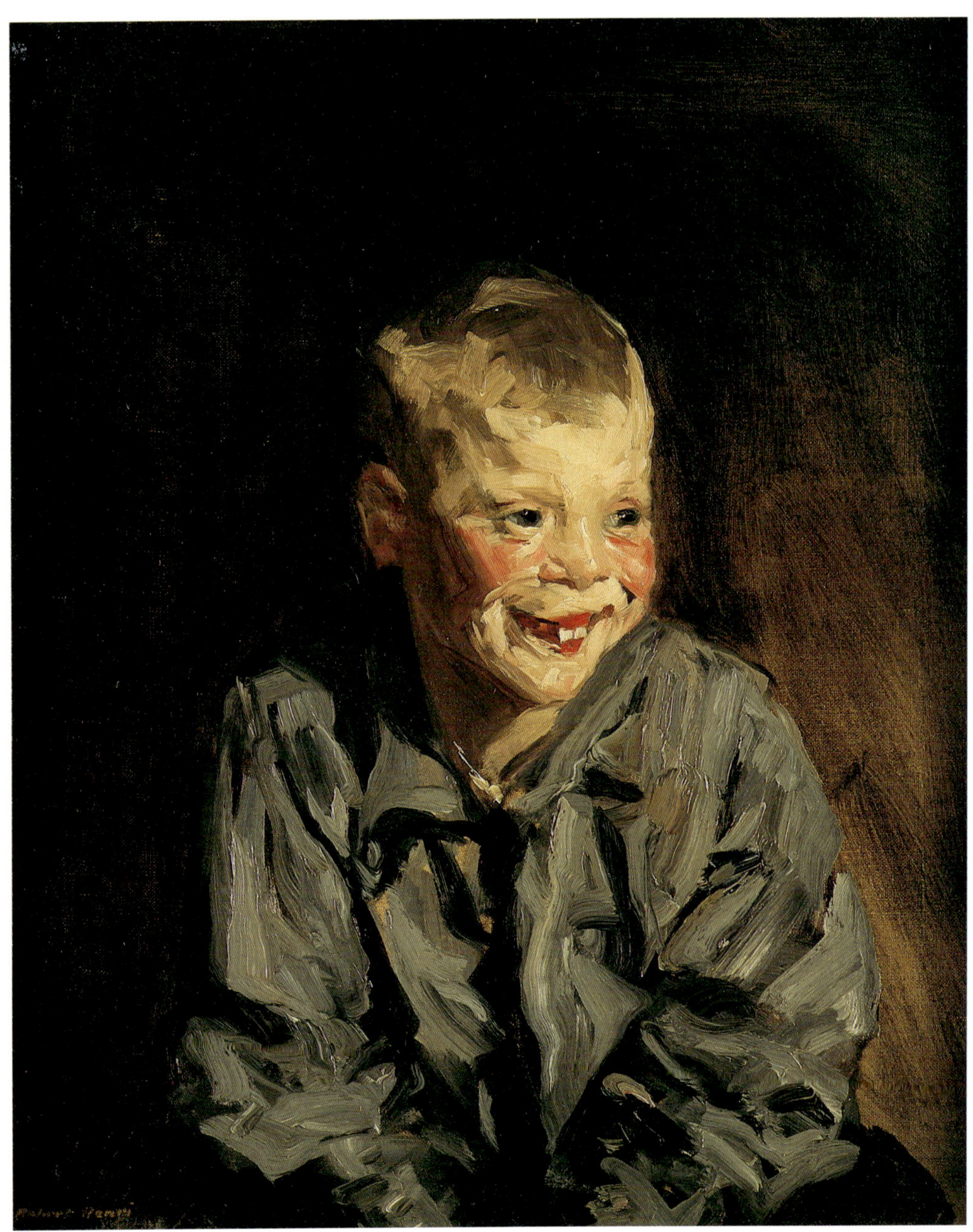

29.
DUTCH JOE (JOPIE VAN SLOUTEN), 1910

Oil on canvas, 24 x 20 in.
Signed lower left: Robert Henri
Milwaukee Art Museum, Wisconsin,
Gift of Samuel O. Buckner

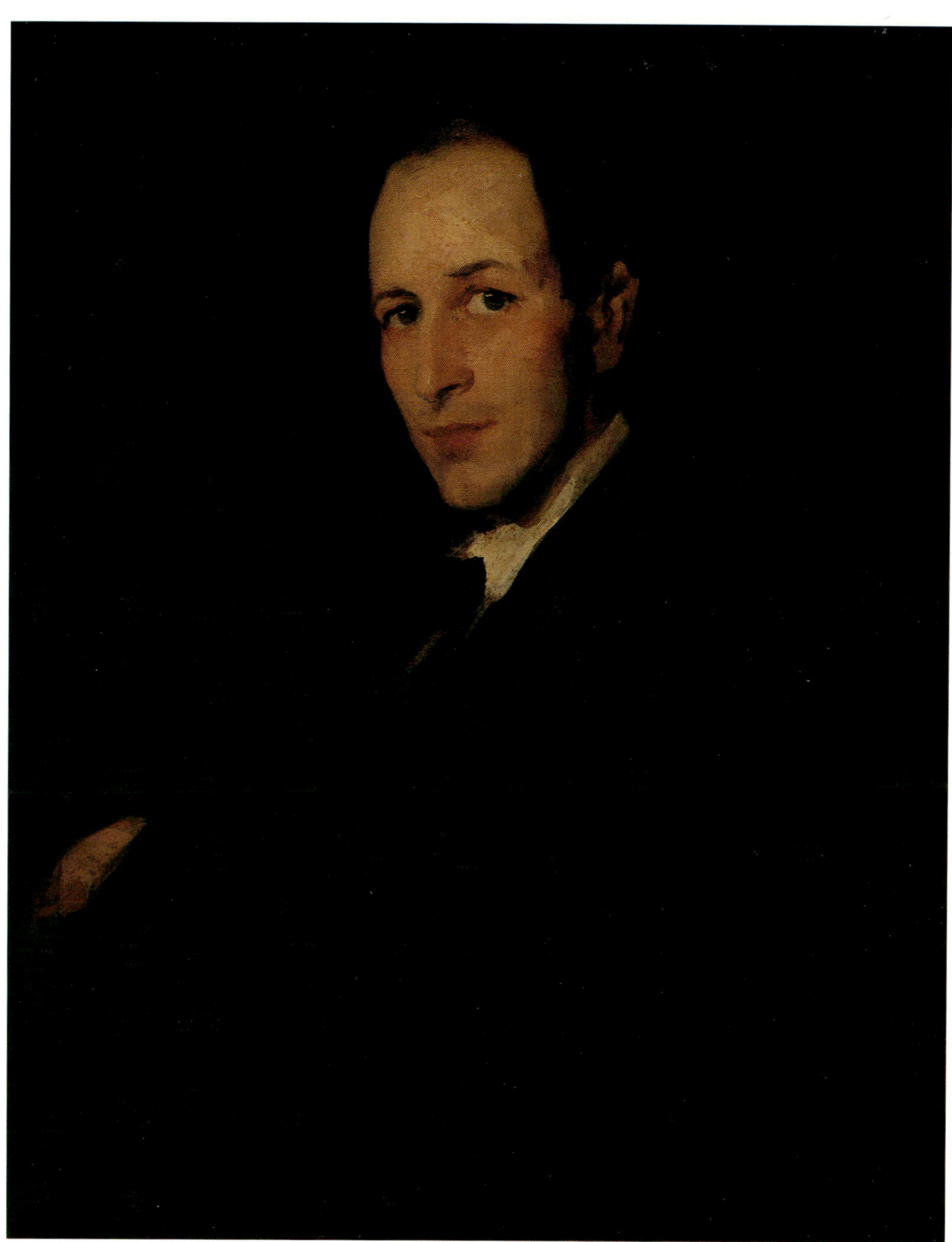

30.
GEORGE BELLOWS, 1911

Oil on canvas, 32 x 26 in.
Signed and dated on verso:
Portrait of George W. Bellows ANA
New York, Nov. 1911 by Robert Henri
National Academy of Design, New York

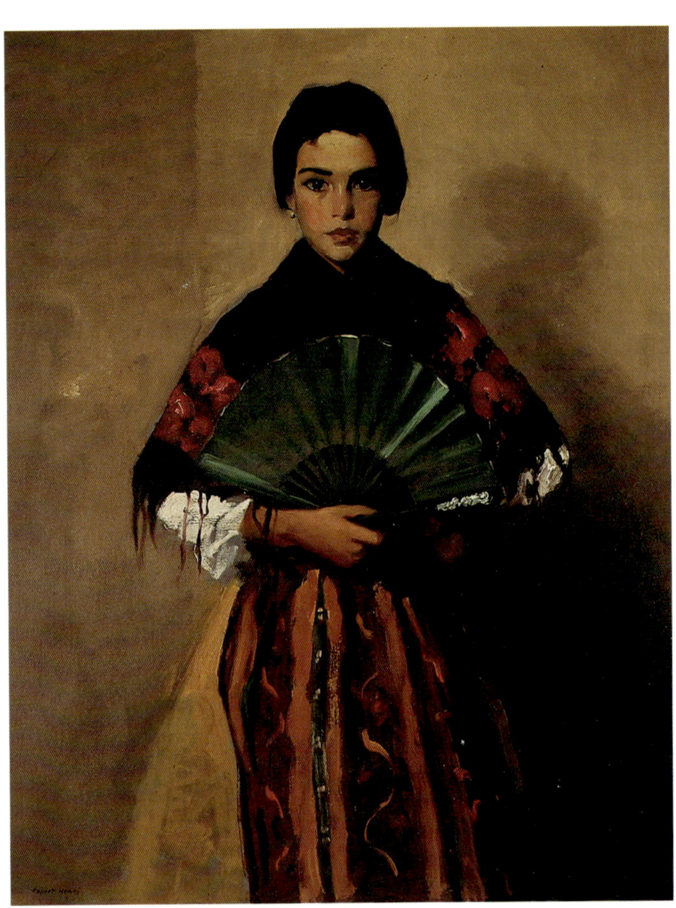

31.
THE GREEN FAN (GIRL OF TOLEDO, SPAIN), 1912
Oil on canvas, 41 x 33 in.
Signed lower left: Robert Henri
Gibbes Museum of Art/Carolina Art Association,
Charleston, South Carolina

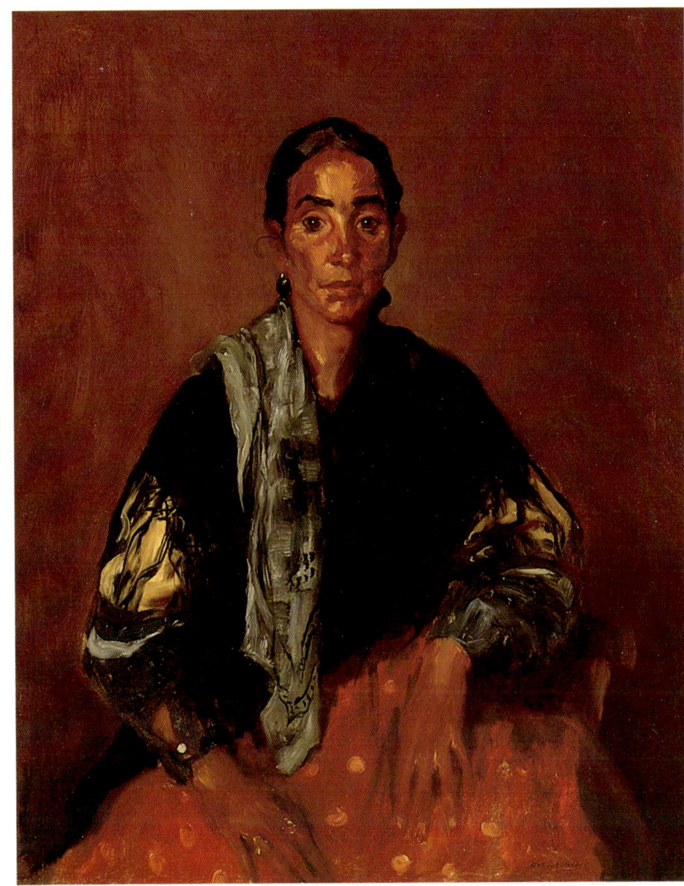

32.
MADRE GITANA (GITANA VIEJA), 1912
Oil on canvas, 41 x 33 in.
Signed lower right: Robert Henri
Westmoreland Museum of Art,
Greensburg, Pennsylvania,
Gift of Mrs. E.B. Osborn

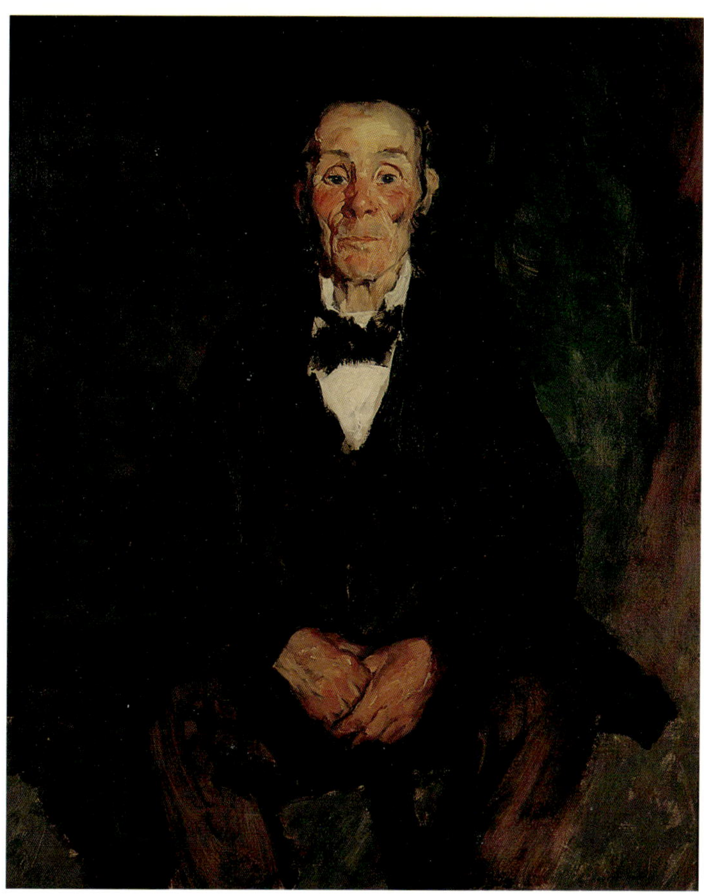

33.
THE GUIDE TO CROAGHAN (BRIEN O'MALLEY), 1913

Oil on canvas, 41 x 33 in.
Signed lower right: Robert Henri
Cummer Gallery of Art, Jacksonville, Florida,
Purchased with Membership Contributions

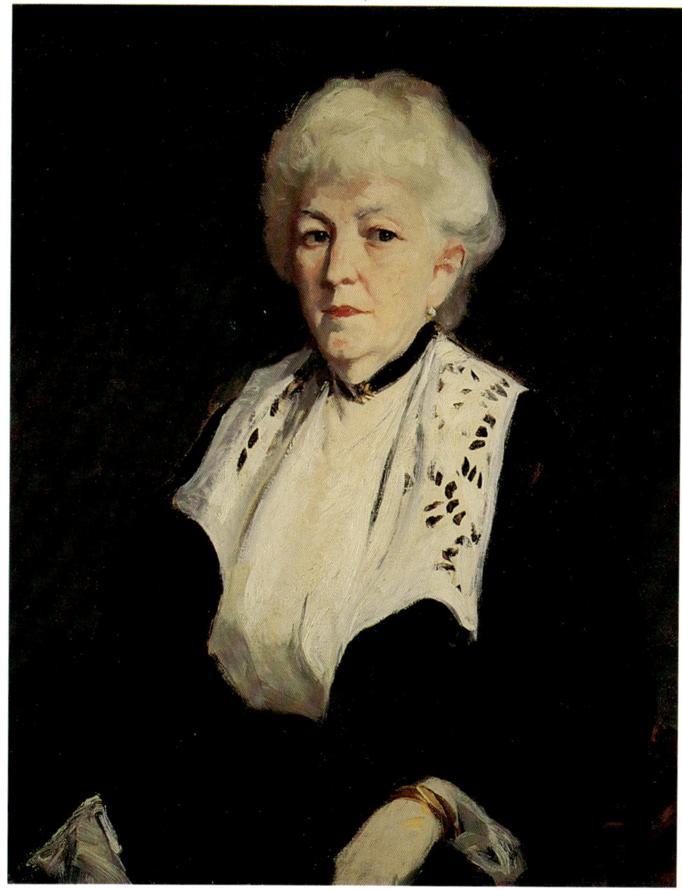

34.
PORTRAIT OF MRS. RICHARD H. LEE, 1914

Oil on canvas, 32 x 26 in.
Signed and dated on verso: Robert Henri/May 14, 1914
Sheldon Memorial Art Gallery, University of
Nebraska-Lincoln, Gift of the Cozad State Bank
and Mrs. Olga N. Sheldon

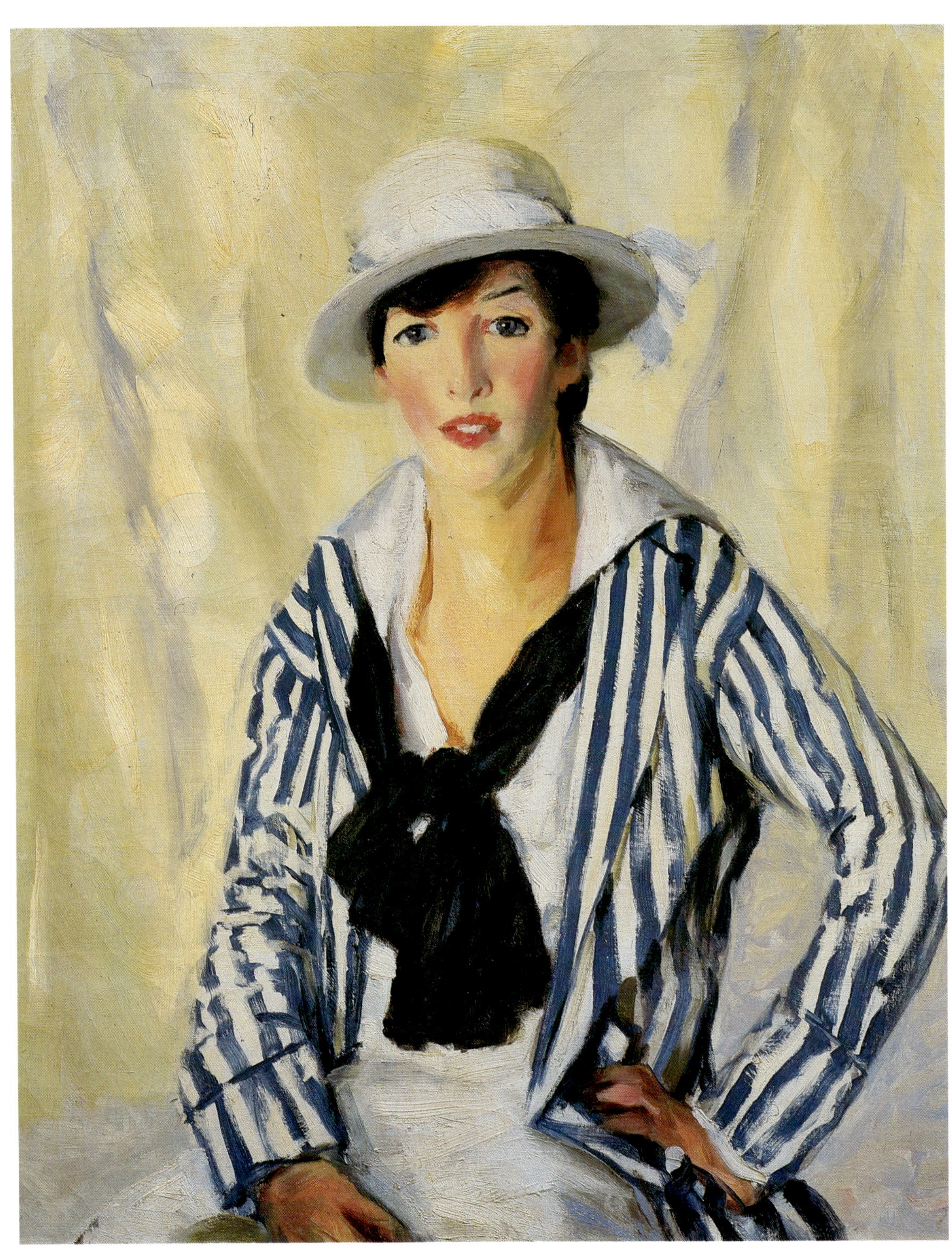

35.
VIV IN BLUE STRIPE, 1914

Oil on canvas, 32 x 26 in.
Collection of Janet Le Clair, Estate of Robert Henri

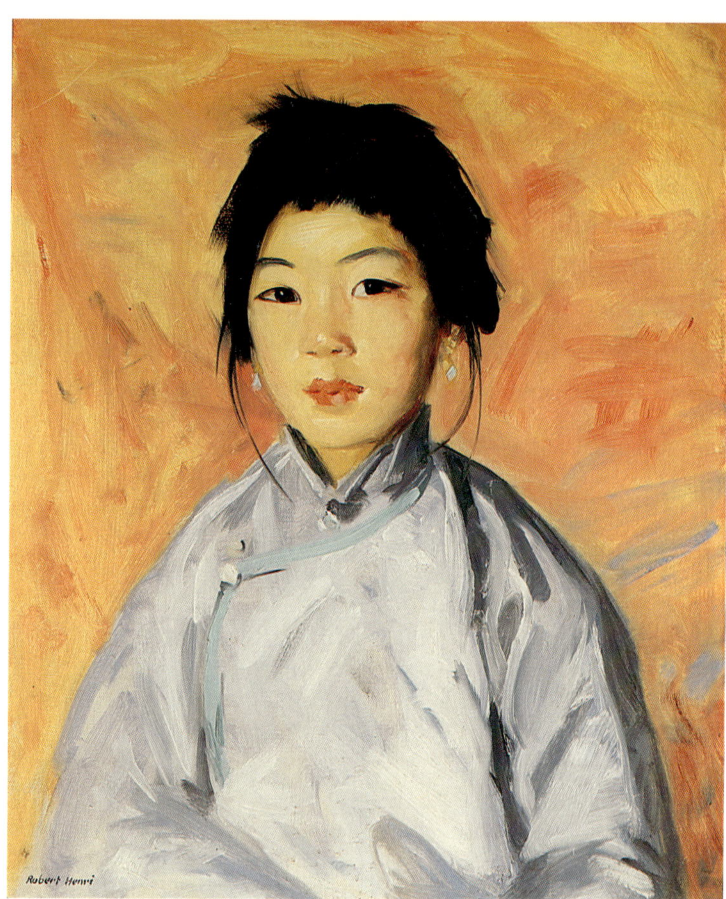

36.
TAM GAN, 1914
Oil on canvas, 24 x 20 in.
Signed lower left: Robert Henri
Albright-Knox Art Gallery, Buffalo, New York,
Sarah A. Gates Fund

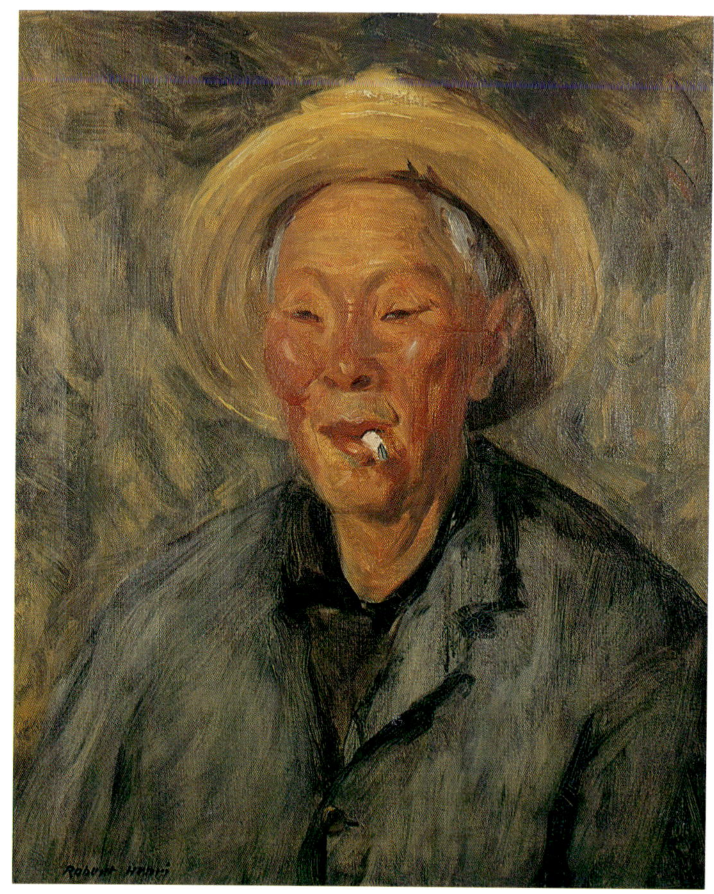

37.
JIM LEE (THE VEGETABLE MAN), 1914
Oil on canvas, 24 x 20 in.
Signed lower left: Robert Henri
Collection of Betty Cavanna Harrison

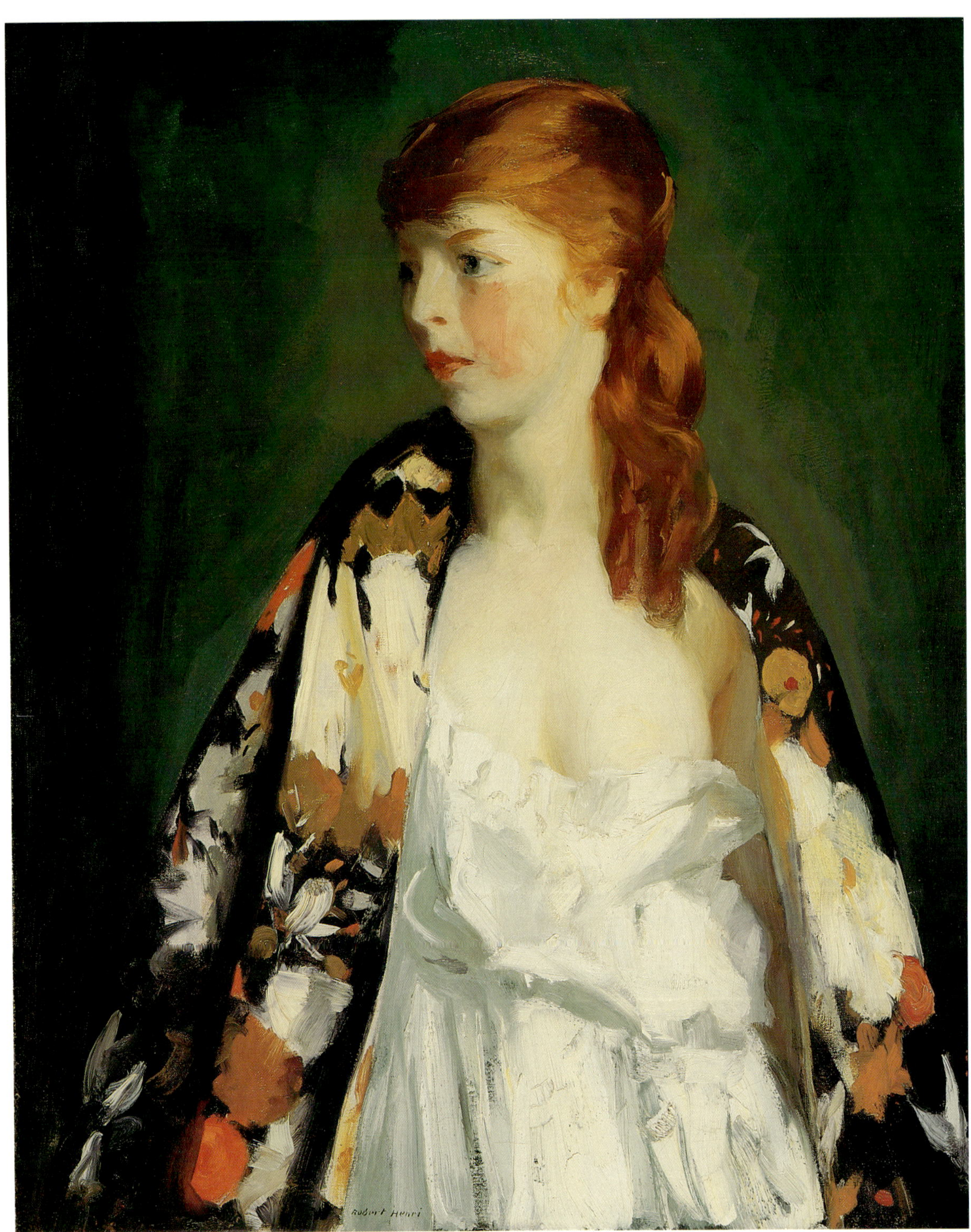

38.
EDNA, 1915

Oil on canvas, 32 x 26 in.
Signed lower center: Robert Henri
Los Angeles County Museum of Art,
Dr. Dorothea Moore Bequest, 43.15.14

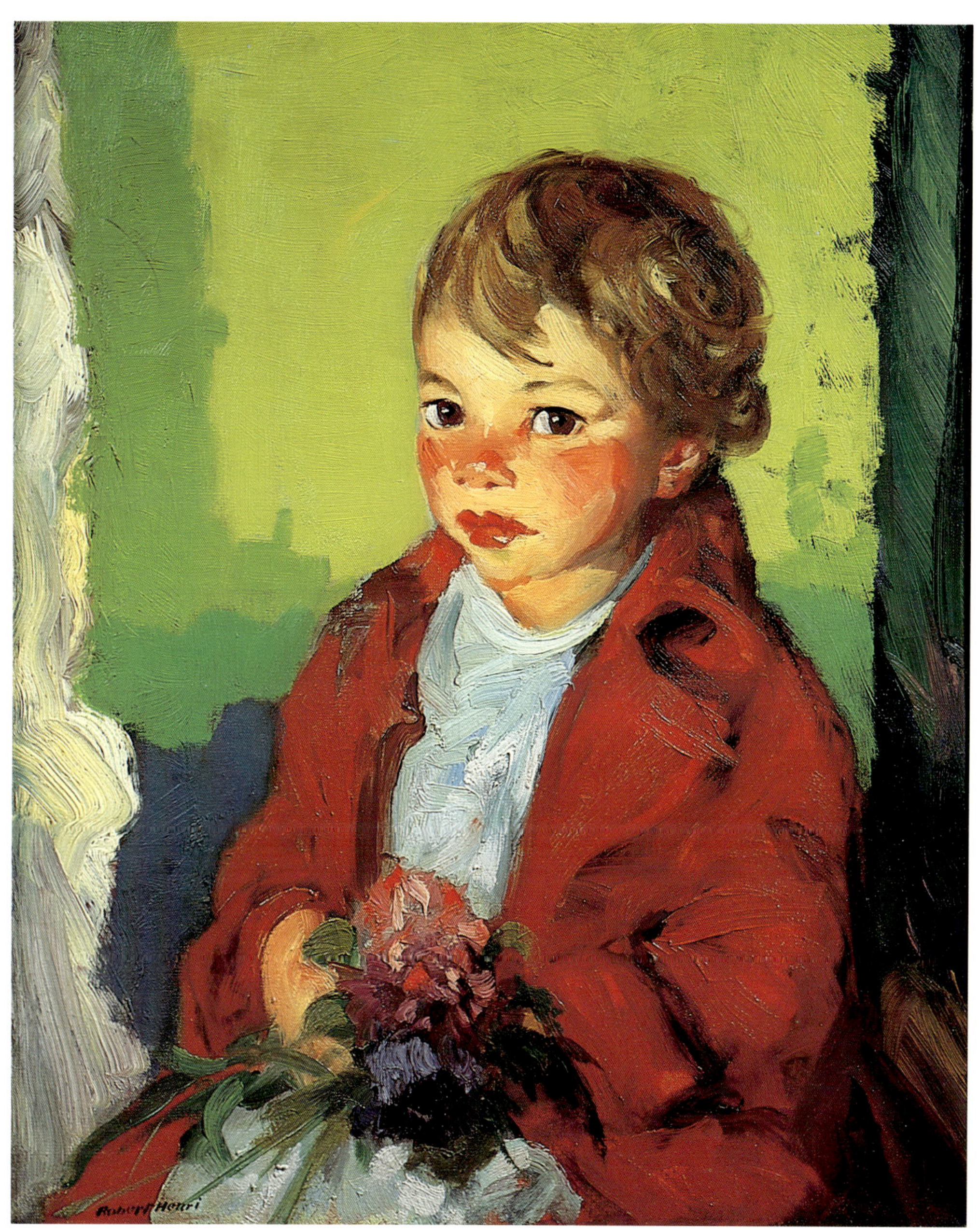

39.
VILLAGE GIRL (LILY COW), 1915

Oil on canvas, 24 x 20 in.
Signed lower left: Robert Henri
Museum of Fine Arts, St. Petersburg, Florida,
Gift of the Stuart Society in Honor of the 25th Anniversary

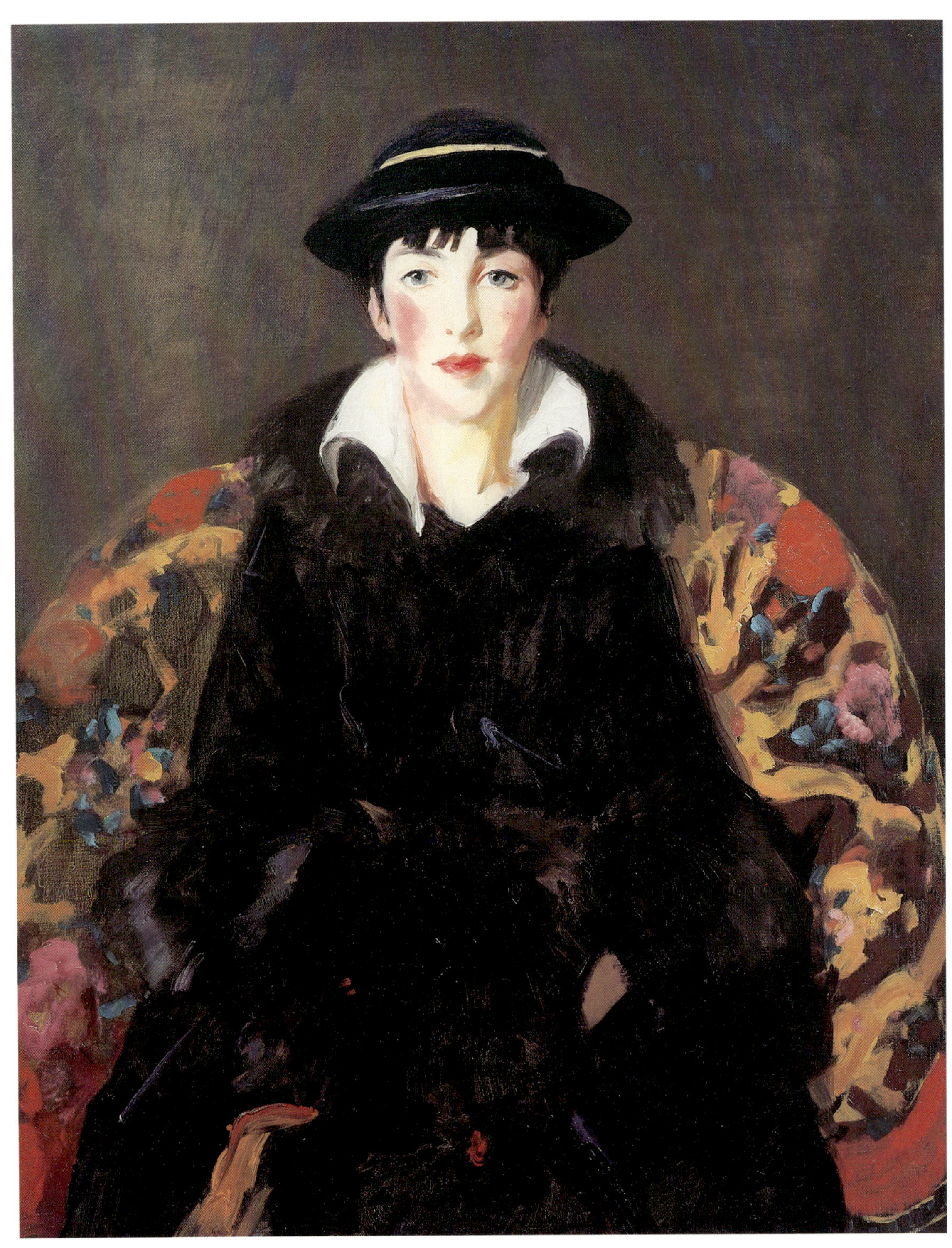

40.
VIV (NEW YORK), 1915

Oil on canvas, 41 x 33 in.
Signed on verso: Viv NY 1915/by Robert Henri
Collection of Janet Le Clair, Estate of Robert Henri

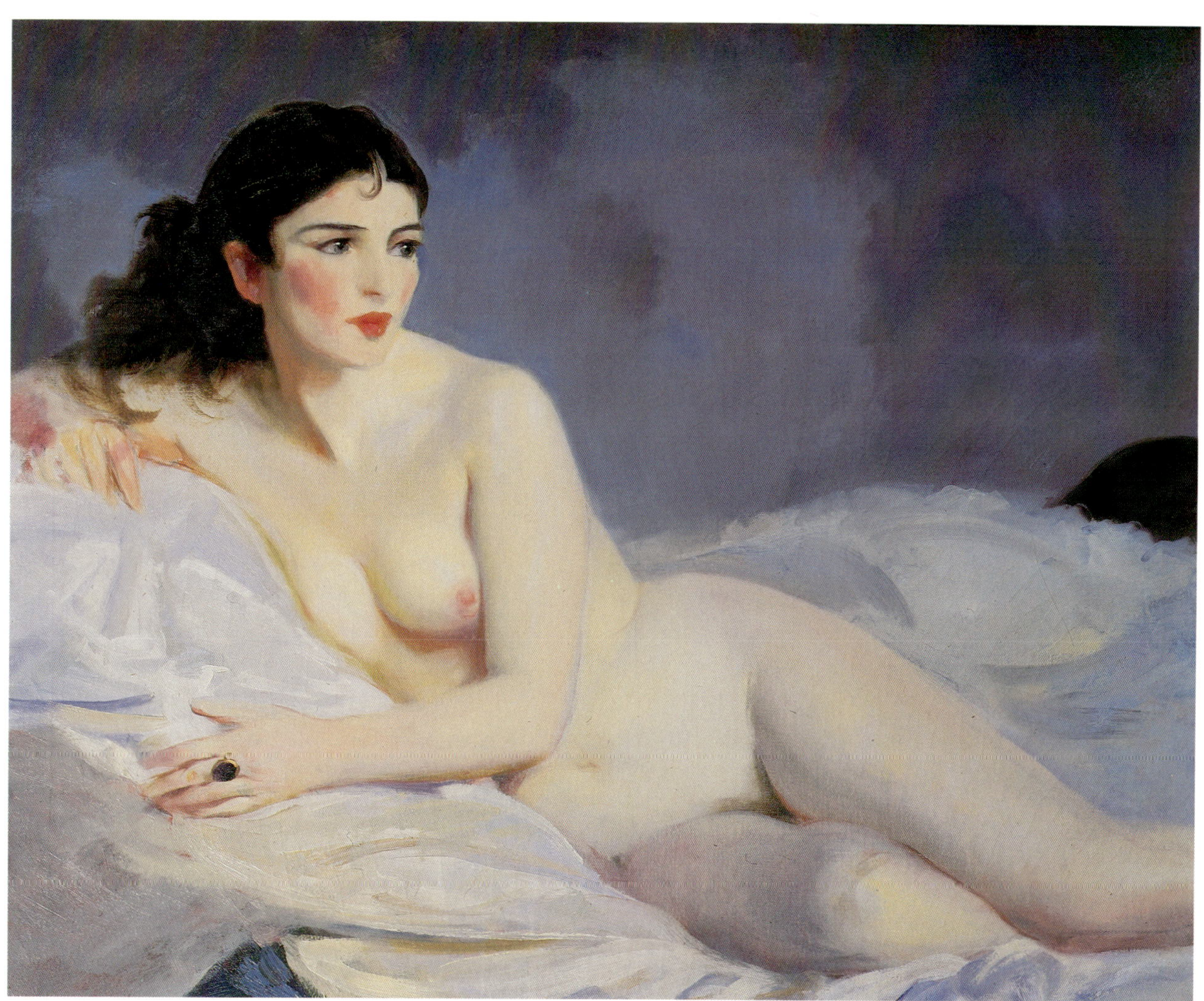

41.
BETALO NUDE, 1916

Oil on canvas, 33 x 41 in.
Signed on verso: Robert Henri
Collection of Janet Le Clair, Estate of Robert Henri

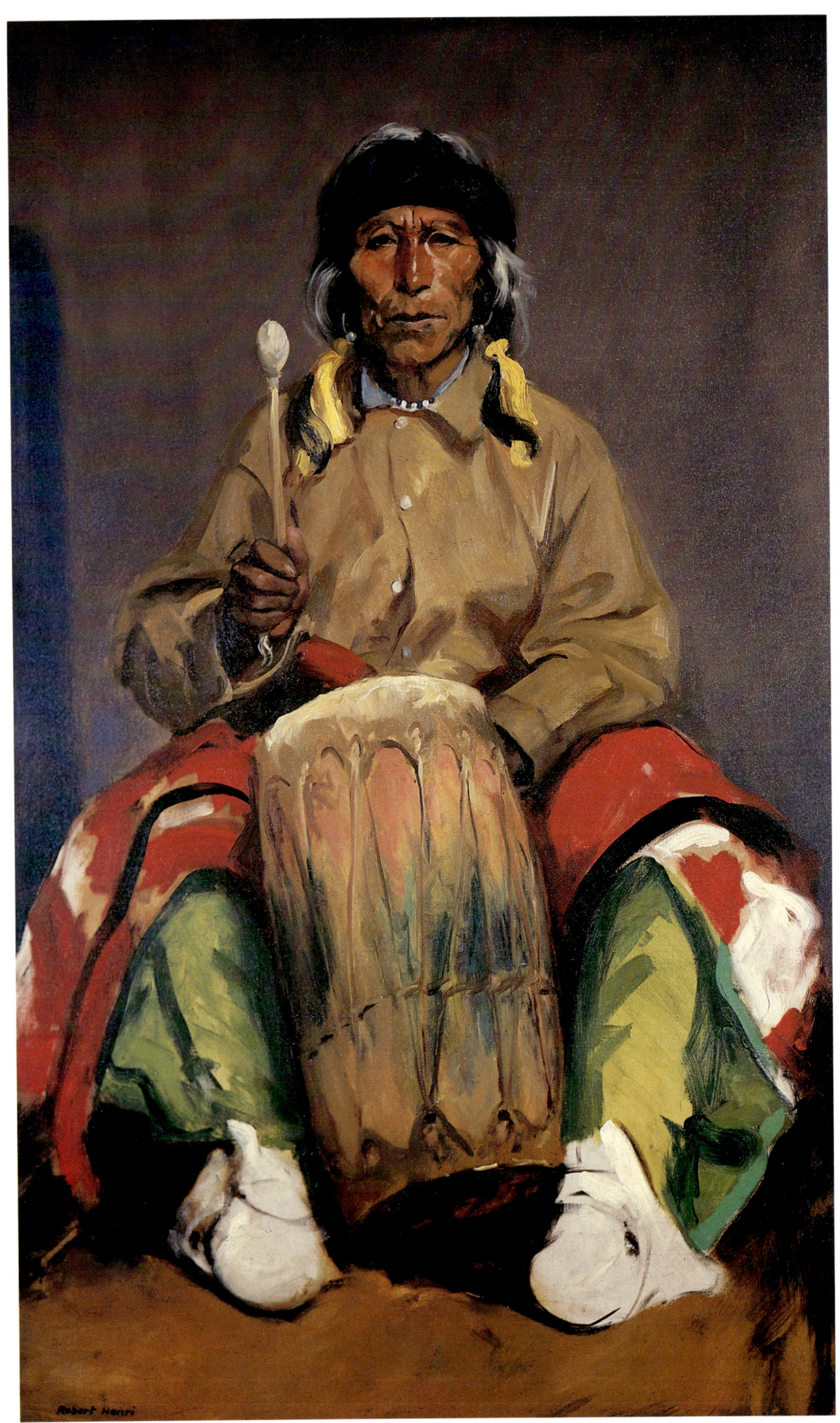

42.
PORTRAIT OF DIEGUITO ROYBAL—PO-TSE-NU-TSA, 1916

Oil on canvas, 65 3/8 x 40 1/16 in.
Signed lower left: Robert Henri
Museum of Fine Arts, Museum of New Mexico, Gift of the Artist, 1917
[exhibited at the Orlando Museum of Art only]

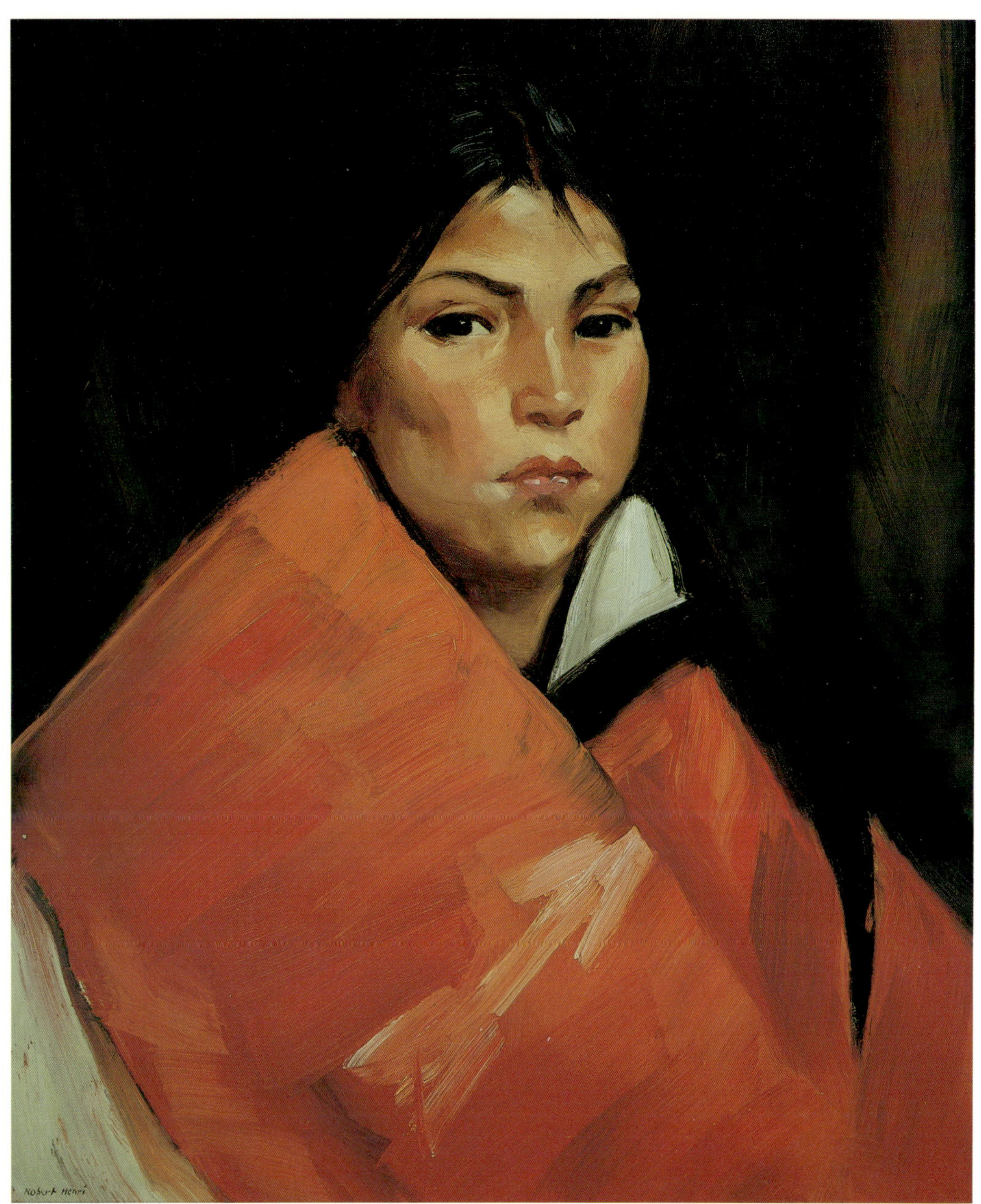

43.
INDIAN GIRL, 1916

Oil on canvas, 24 x 20 in.
Signed lower left: Robert Henri
Collection of Mr. and Mrs. Terry Stent

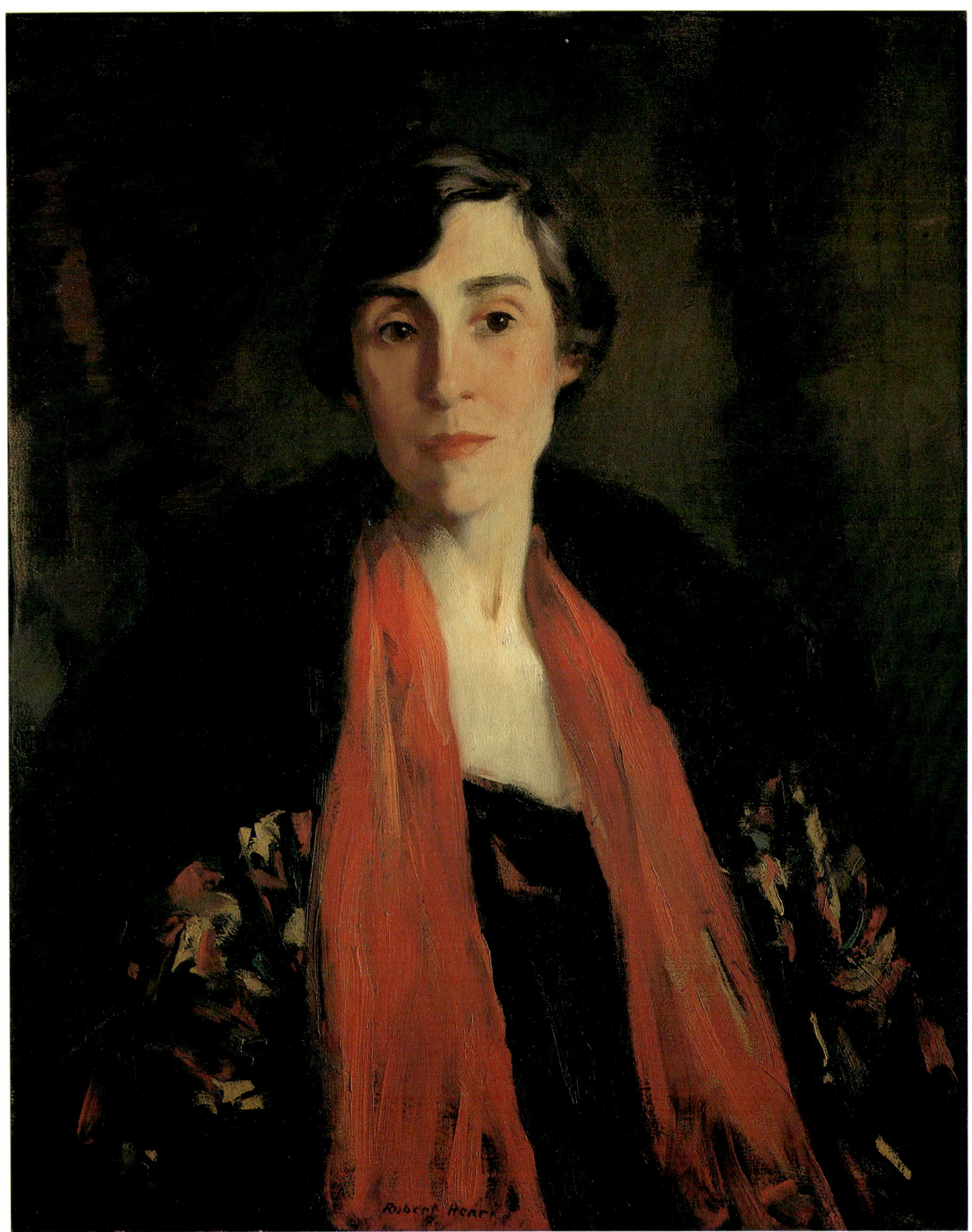

44.
PORTRAIT OF MARY FANTON ROBERTS, 1917

Oil on canvas, 32 x 26 in.
Signed lower center: Robert Henri
The Metropolitan Museum of Art, Bequest of Mary Fanton Roberts

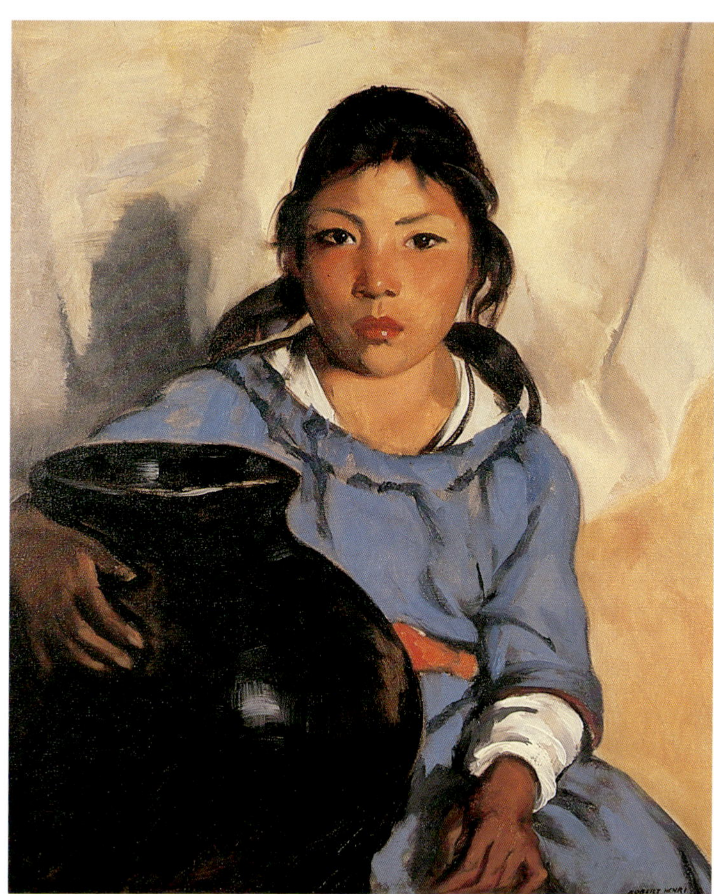

45.
GREGORITA WITH THE SANTA CLARA BOWL, 1917
Oil on canvas, 32 x 26 in.
Signed lower right: Robert Henri
Edwin A. Ulrich Museum of Art, Wichita State University, Endowment Association Art Collection

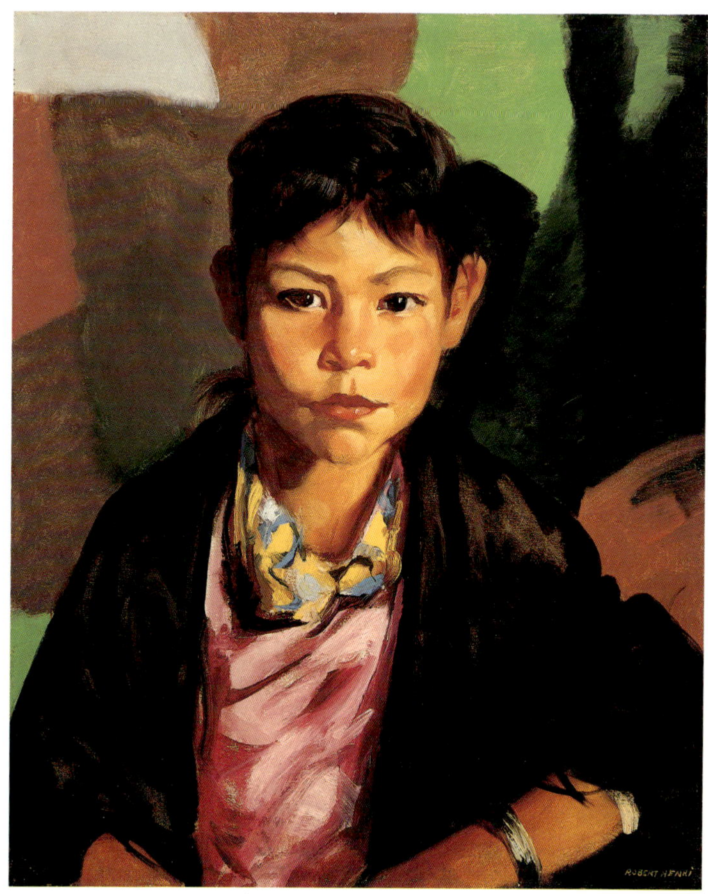

46.
PEPITA, 1917
Oil on canvas, 24 x 20 in.
Signed lower right: Robert Henri
Los Angeles County Museum of Art,
Mr. and Mrs. William Preston Harrison Collection,
20.3.2

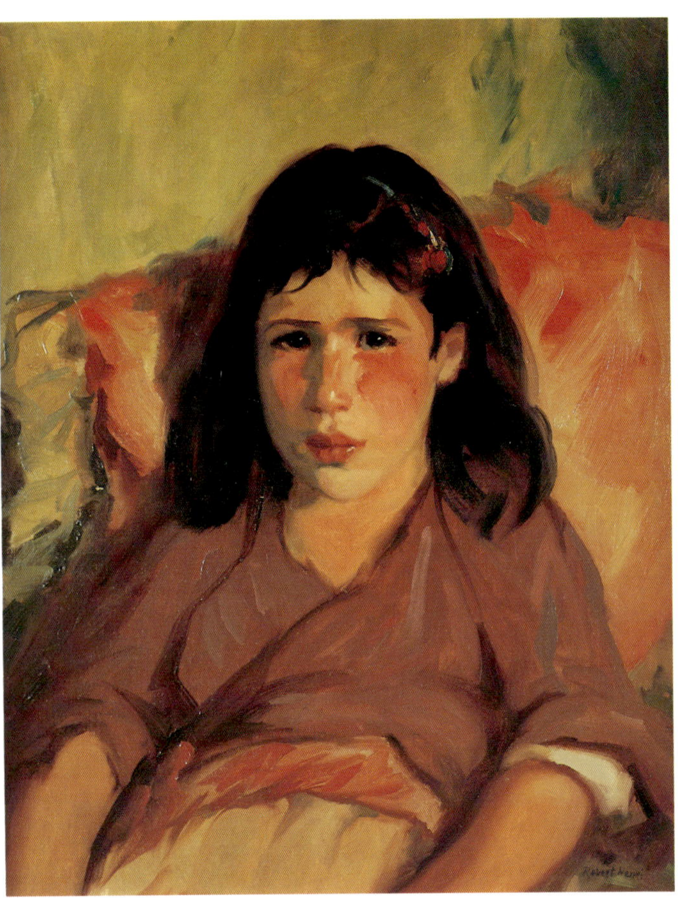

47.
TILLY, 1917
Oil on canvas, 24 x 20 in.
Signed lower right: Robert Henri
Lowe Art Museum, University of Miami, Florida,
Museum purchase through Beaux Arts

49. (Opposite)
RUTH ST. DENIS IN THE PEACOCK DANCE, 1919
Oil on canvas, 85 x 49 in.
Signed lower right: Robert Henri
Pennsylvania Academy of the Fine Arts, Philadelphia,
Gift of the Sameric Corporation in memory of
Eric Shapiro

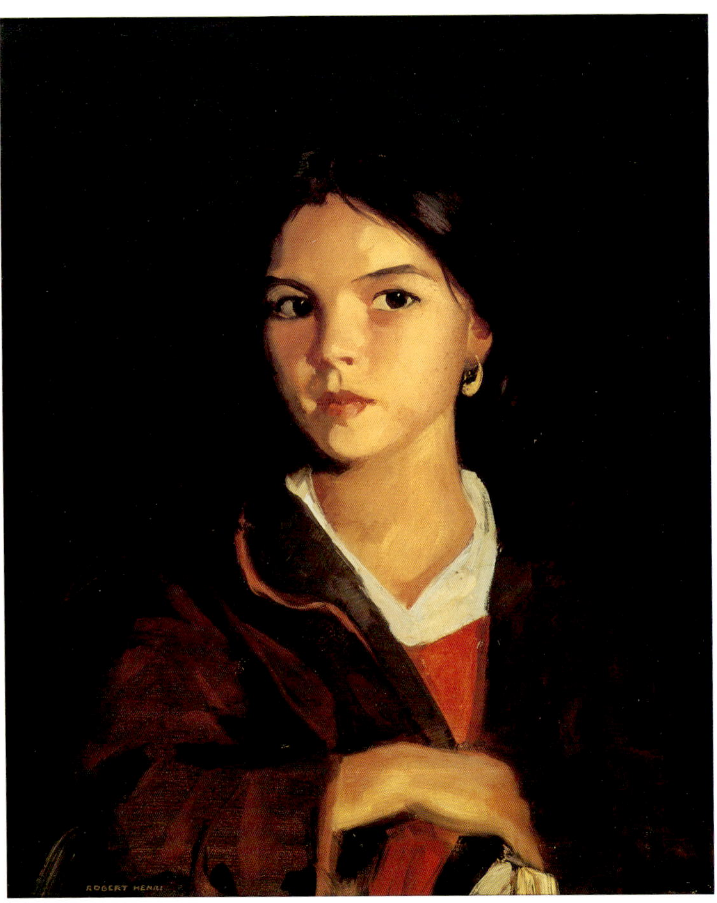

48.
BERNADITA, 1922
Oil on canvas, 24⅛ x 20¼ in.
Signed lower left: Robert Henri
San Diego Museum of Art, California,
Gift of the San Diego Wednesday Club

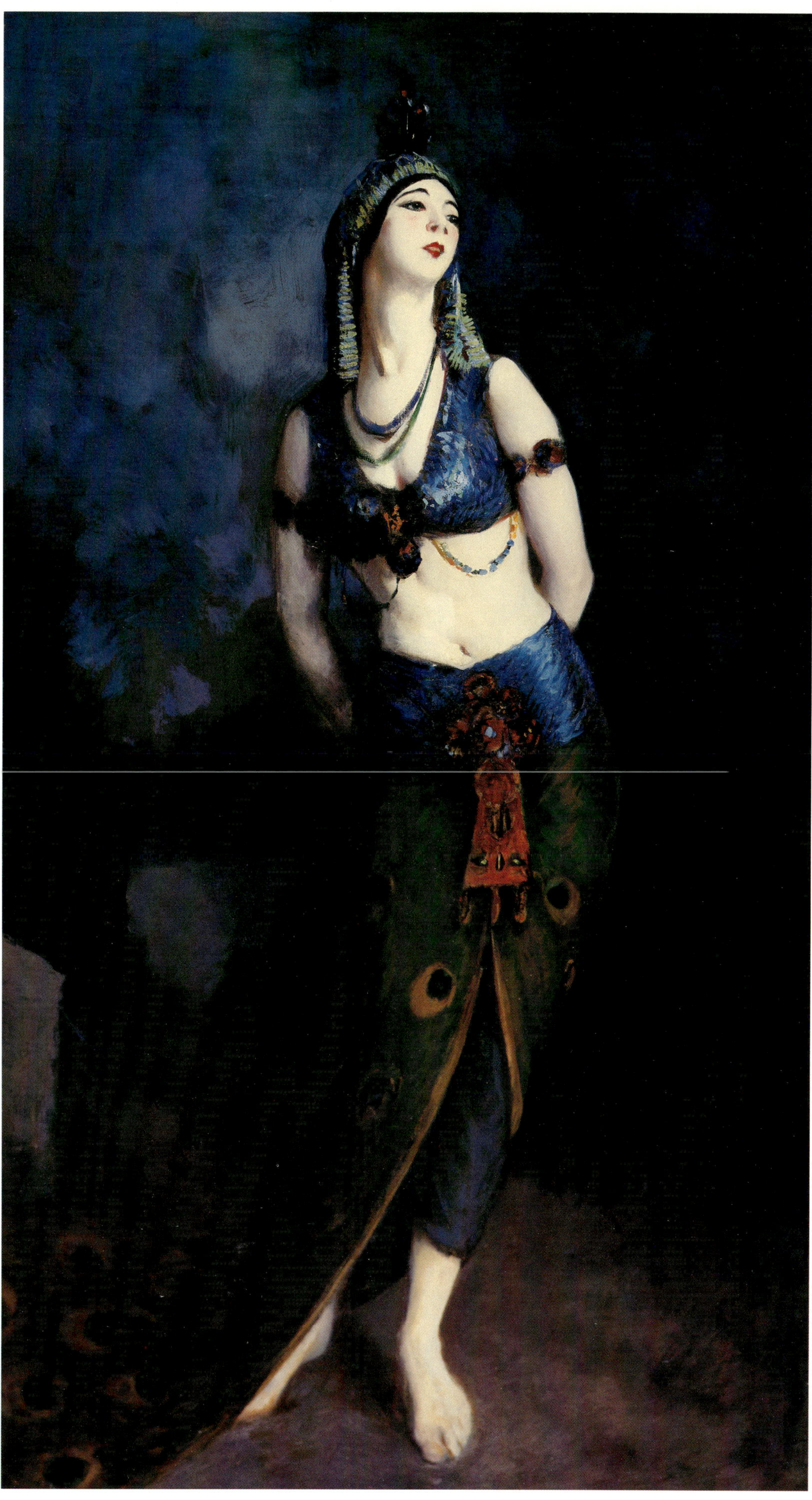

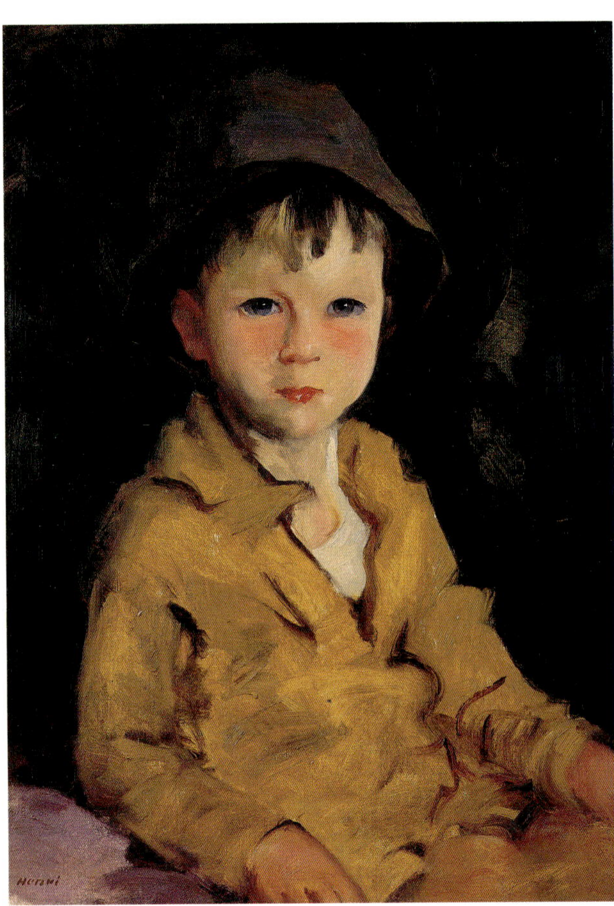

50.
JIMMIE GERRY, 1921
Oil on canvas, 22 x 17 ⅛ in.
Signed lower left: Robert Henri
Scripps College, Claremont, California,
Gift of General and Mrs. Edward Clinton Young, 1946

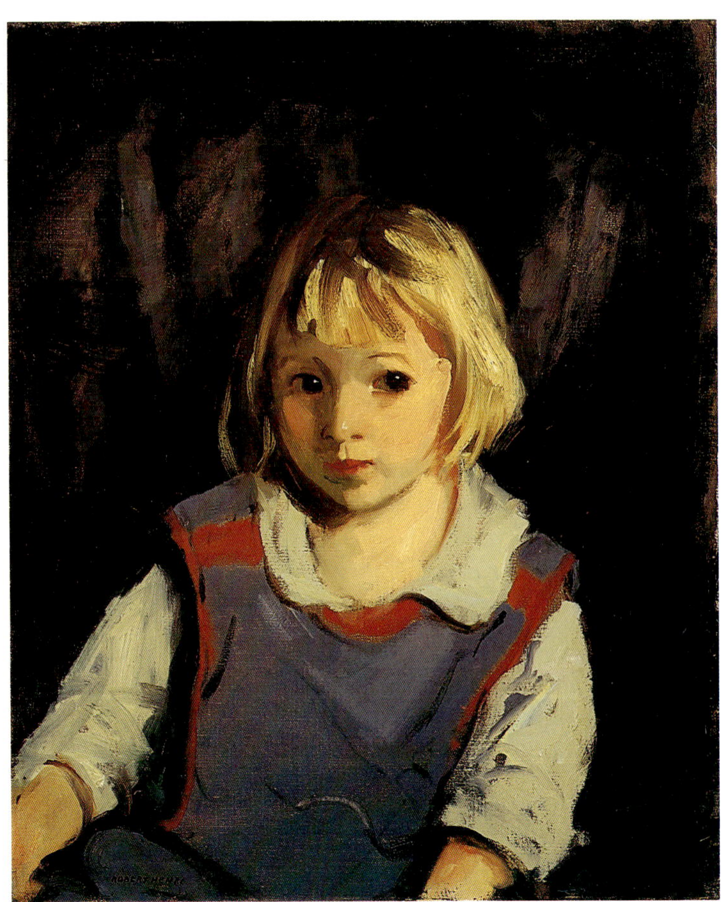

51.
CARL SLEICHER, 1921
Oil on canvas, 24 x 20 in.
Signed lower left: Robert Henri
Private collection
[exhibited at the Orlando Museum of Art only]

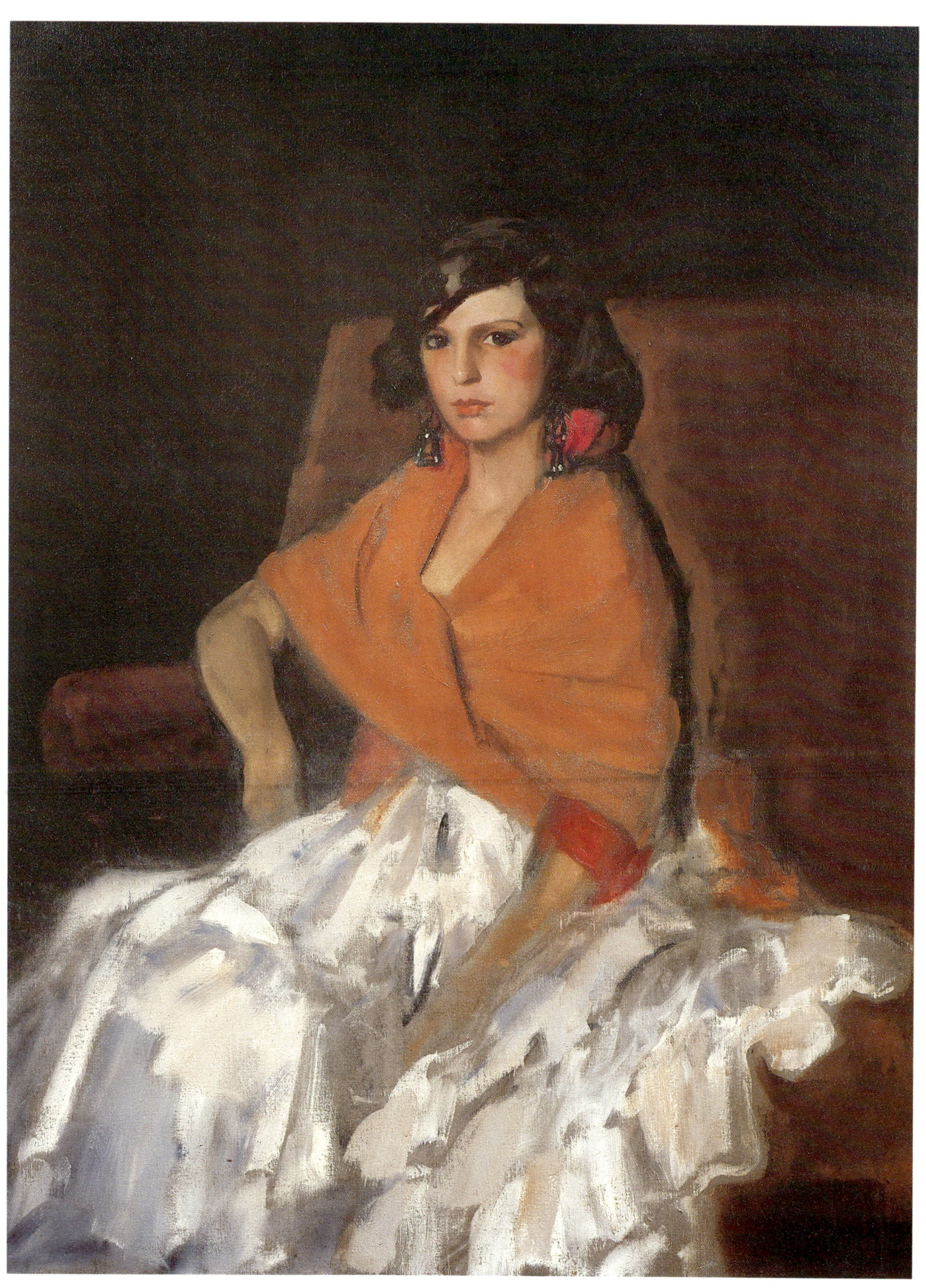

52.

DORITA, 1924

Oil on canvas, 52 x 40 in.
Collection of Janet Le Clair, Estate of Robert Henri

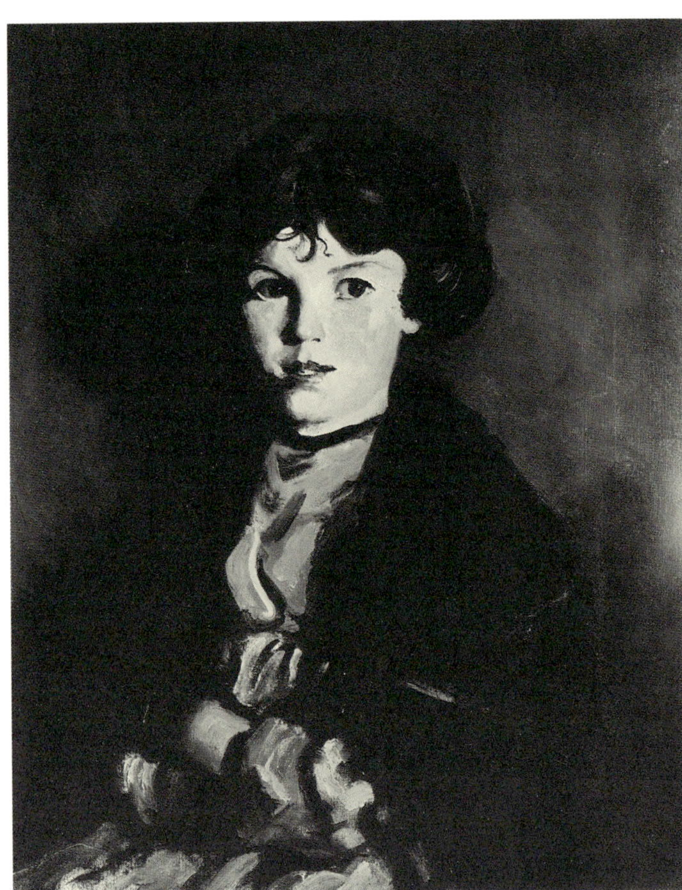

53.
MOIRA (MARY O'MALLEY), 1924

Oil on canvas, 24 x 20 in.
Signed lower left: Robert Henri
Canajoharie Library and Art Gallery,
Canajoharie, New York

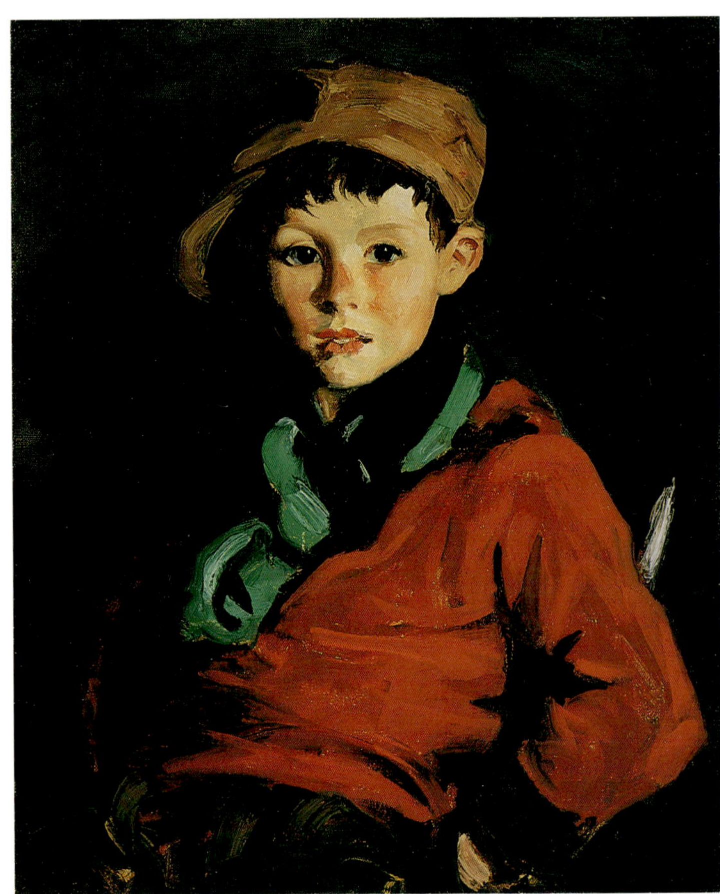

54.
TOM CAFFERTY, 1924

Oil on canvas, 22 1/4 x 20 1/8 in.
Signed lower right: Robert Henri
Memorial Art Gallery of the
University of Rochester, New York,
Gift of Mrs. Granger A. Hollister

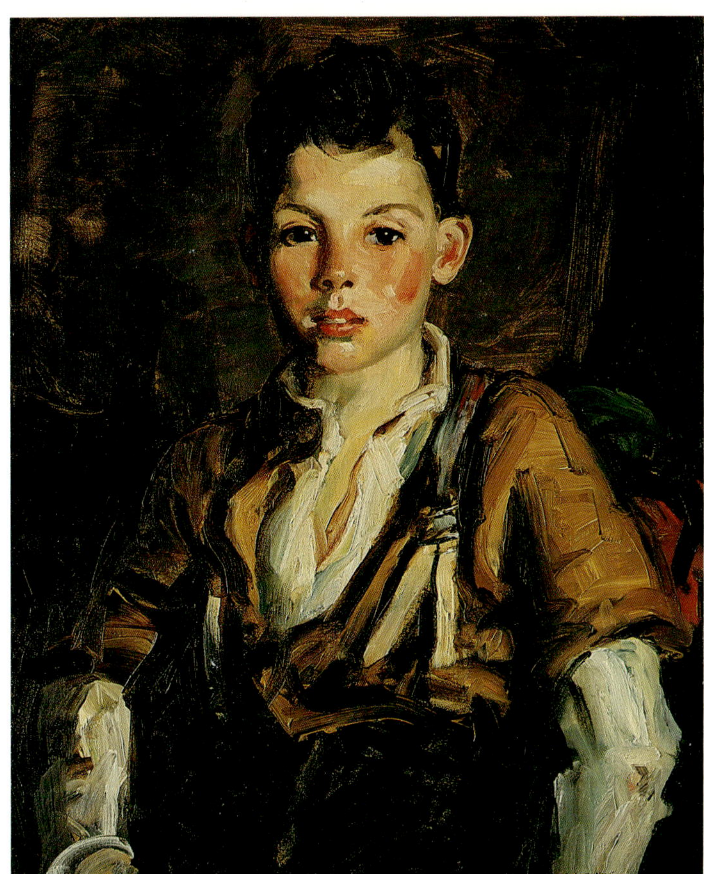

55.
THE FISHERMAN'S SON: THOMAS CAFFERTY, 1925

Oil on canvas, 24⅛ x 20 in.
Signed lower right: Robert Henri
Hirshhorn Museum and Sculpture Garden,
Smithsonian Institution, Washington, D.C.,
Gift of Joseph H. Hirshhorn

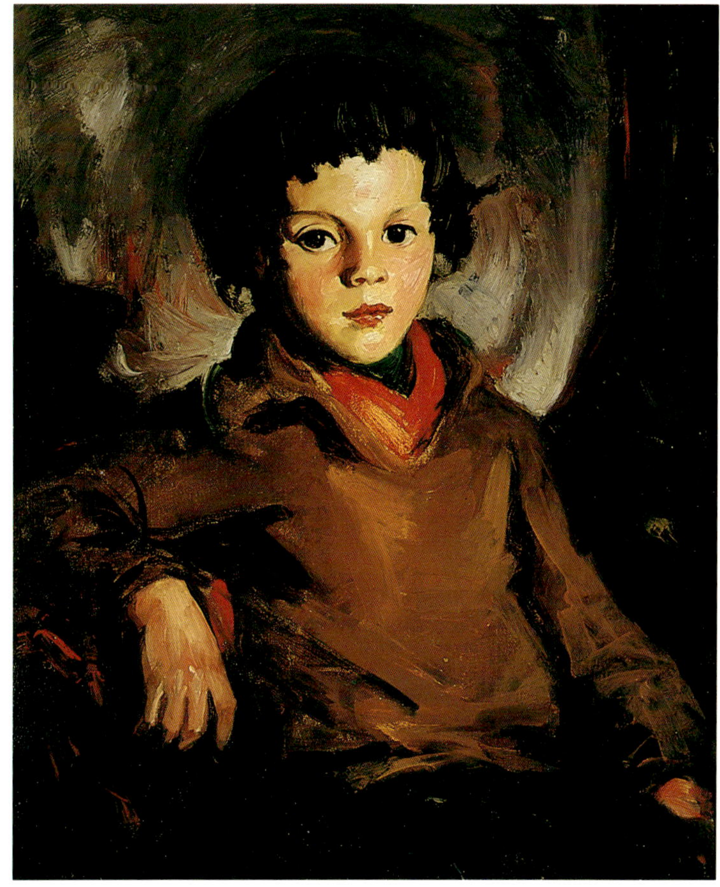

56.
YOUNG CHEVASS (MARY ANN CAFFERTY), 1925

Oil on canvas, 24 x 20 in.
Signed lower left: Robert Henri
Montgomery Museum of Fine Arts, Alabama,
Montgomery Museum of Fine Arts Association
Purchase

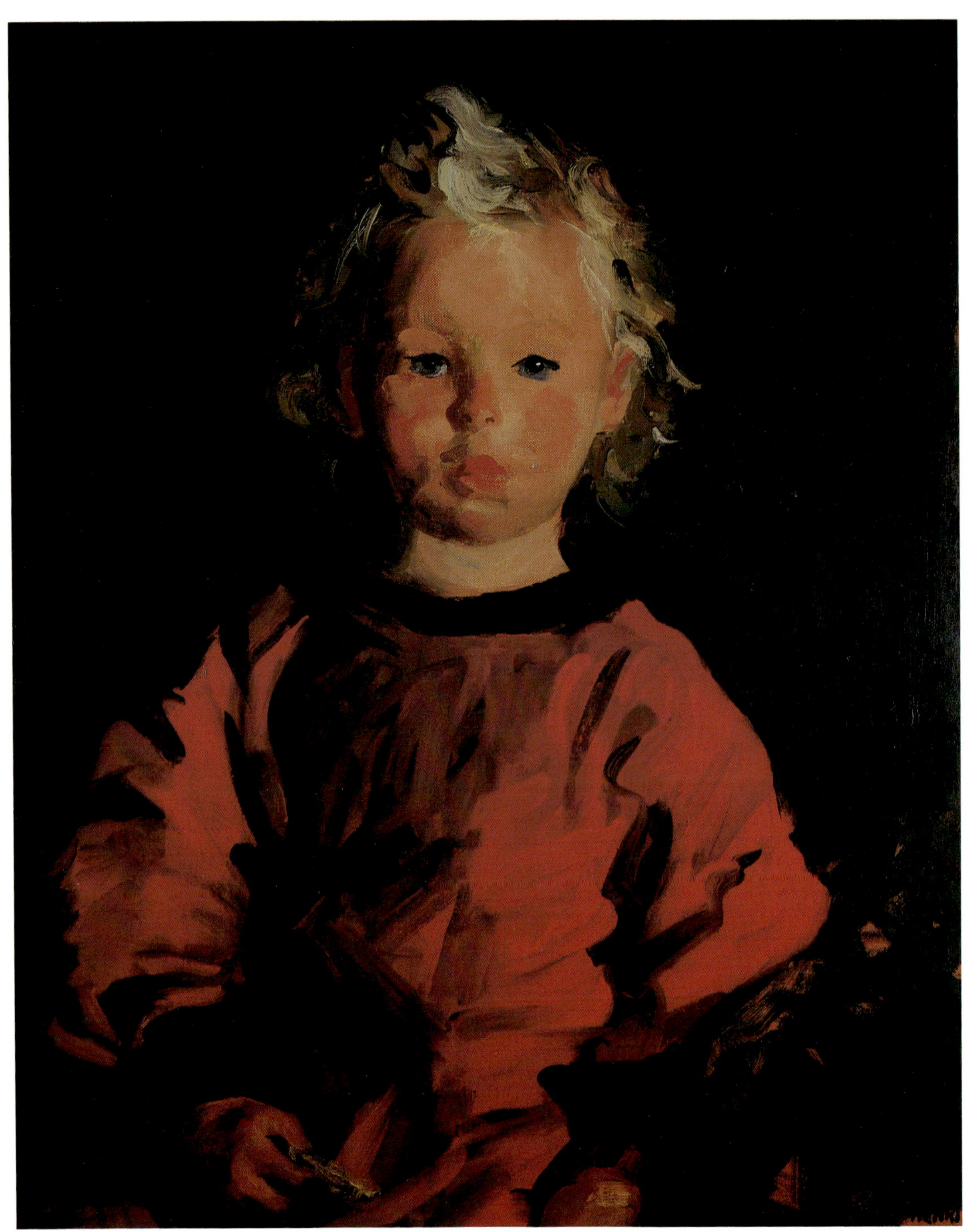

57.
THE WEE WOMAN, 1927

Oil on canvas, 24 x 20 in.
Signed lower right: Robert Henri
Collection of Mr. and Mrs. Cyrus W. Grandy V

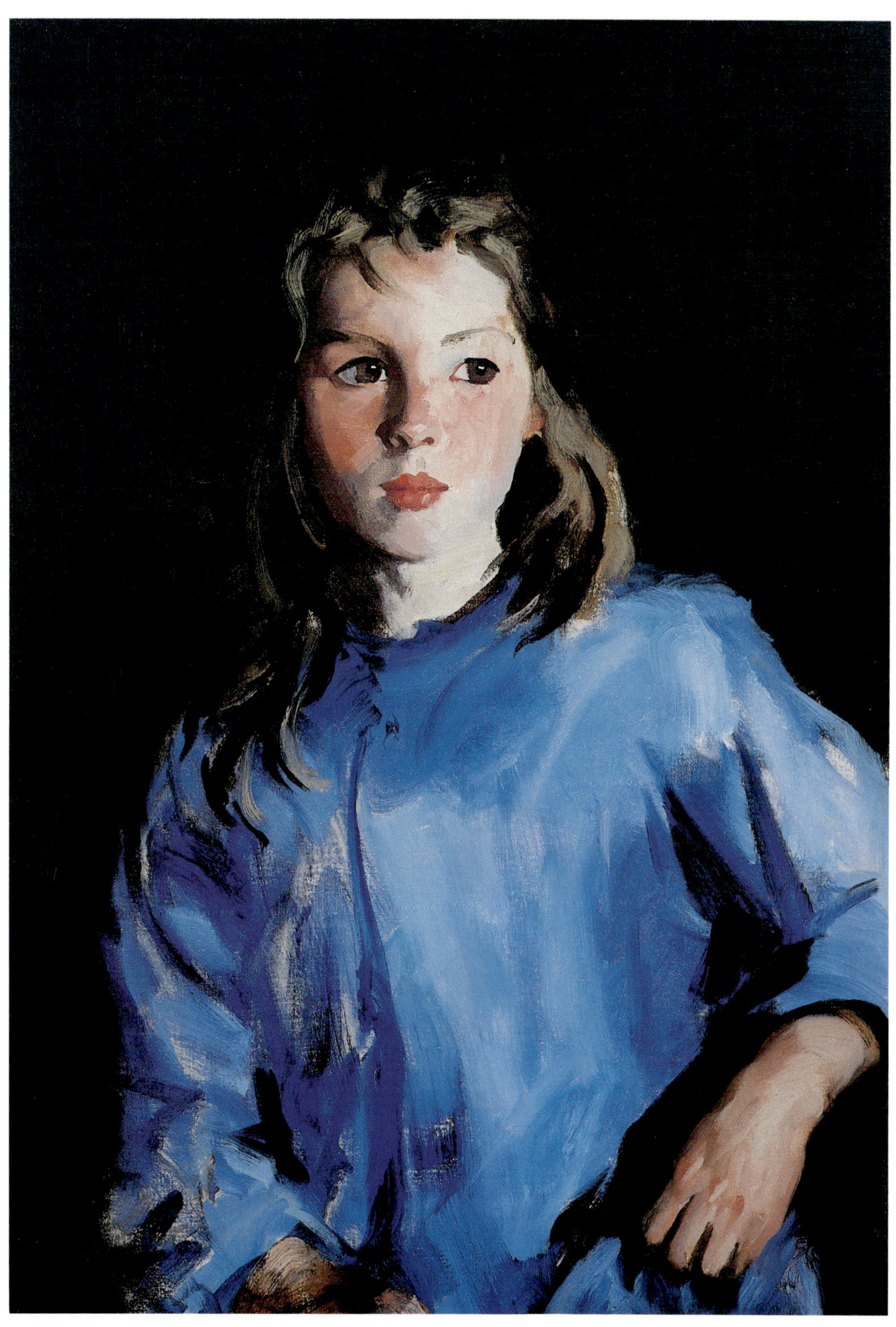

58.
BLOND BRIDGET LAVELLE, 1928
Oil on canvas, 28 x 20 in.
Collection of Mr. and Mrs. W.J. Bowen

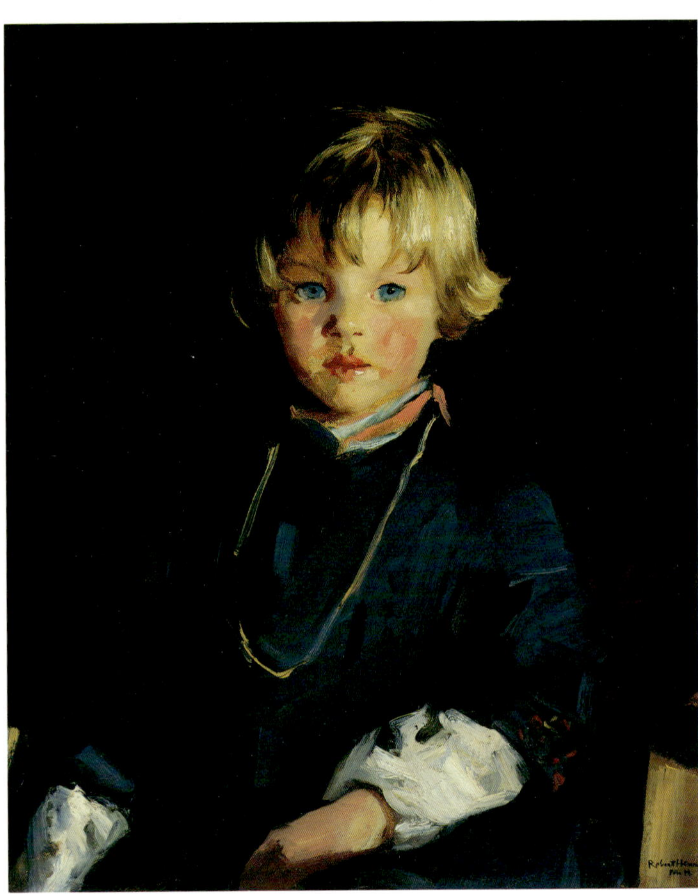

59.
WEE ANNIE LAVELLE (PET), 1927
Oil on canvas, 24 x 21 in.
Signed lower right: Robert Henri
Hunter Museum of Art, Chattanooga, Tennessee,
Gift of the Benwood Foundation

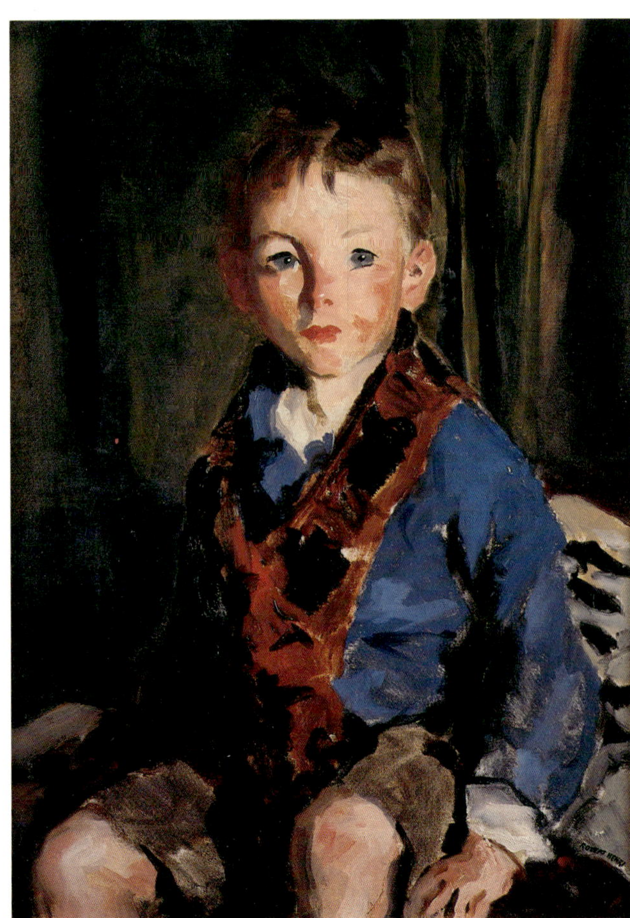

60.
FERGUS, 1928
Oil on canvas, 28 x 20 in.
Signed lower right: Robert Henri
The Columbus Museum, Georgia

Chronology

1865 Born on June 24 in Cincinnati, Ohio, as Robert Henry Cozad.

1879 Family moves to Cozad, Nebraska.

1881 Family moves to Denver, Colorado, where Henri attends public school.

1882 Father is indicted for the murder of an employee and a warrant for his arrest is issued.

1883 Family assumes new identities, Robert Henry Cozad becomes Robert Earl Henri. Parents move to Atlantic City, New Jersey, and Henri attends boarding school in New York City.

1886 Henri attends the Pennsylvania Academy of the Fine Arts, Philadelphia, studies art under Thomas Anshutz, Thomas Hovenden, and James B. Kelly, through 1887.

1888 Sails for Paris with friends in the summer. Enrolls at the Académie Julian, working under Tony Robert-Fleury and William-Adolphe Bouguereau through 1891.

1889 Fails entrance to the École des Beaux-Arts. Visits Concarneau, Pont-Aven, and Brolles.

1890 To Barbizon, St. Nazaire, Toulon, Marseilles, Monte Carlo, Rome, and Florence.

1891 Admitted to the École des Beaux-Arts. Returns to Philadelphia in September.

1892 Enrolls again at the Pennsylvania Academy of the Fine Arts, studying with Anshutz, Kelly, and Robert Vonnoh. Begins teaching at the School of Design for Women, Philadelphia, through 1895. In December meets John Sloan at a party.

1893 Founds Charcoal Club; teaches in Avalon, New Jersey, in summer.

1894 Begins private teaching; summer in Concarneau, France. Shares a studio with William Glackens in Phildelphia.

1895 Summer abroad with Glackens, Charles Grafly, and Elmer Schofield; visits Paris, Holland, and Belgium. Visits museums, conducts art class in Paris.

1896 To London to view Velázquez exhibition. Summer trip through Germany and Italy with his brother. Visits Manet retrospective at Durand-Ruel Galleries, Paris.

1897 Returns to Philadelphia in fall. In October, first one-man show at the Pennsylvania Academy of the Fine Arts; another solo show arranged by William Merritt Chase at the Chase School of Art, New York; exhibits at the Macbeth Galleries, New York

1898 Exhibits at National Academy of Design. Marries Linda Craige in June. Departs for Paris for honeymoon and extended stay abroad.

1900 Trip to Madrid; returns to New York from Paris. Teaches at Veltin School, through 1902.

1901 Rents studio in New York at the Sherwood Building, 57th Street and Sixth Avenue. Exhibits at the Pan-American Exposition in Buffalo; receives the Silver Medal, his first prize.

1902 First one-man show at the Macbeth Galleries, New York, in March. Fall, begins teaching at the New York School of Art (formerly the Chase School) and continues through 1908. One-man show at the Pennsylvania Academy of the Fine Arts in November; one-man show at Pratt Institute, Brooklyn, in December.

1903 Elected to the Society of American Artists. Summer in Maine with Edward Redfield at Boothbay Harbor and Monhegan Island.

1904 Carnegie Institute, Pittsburgh, purchases Henri's *Girl in White Waist* (subsequently destroyed in an accident), the first acquisition of his work by an American museum. Organizes show at the National Arts Club, New York, of works by Sloan, Glackens, Luks, Davies, Prendergast, and himself. Wins the Silver Medal at the Universal Exposition in St. Louis.

1905 Elected an Associate of the National Academy of Design. Wins Harris Prize at The Art Institute of Chicago. Linda Henri becomes ill and dies, December.

1906 Elected an Academician at the National Academy of Design; to Madrid in the summer with a class from the New York School of Art. In October, moves to the Beaux-Arts Building at 40th Street and Sixth Avenue. Father dies.

1907 Withdraws two of his entries from the National Academy of Design's Spring Annual following rejection of his colleagues' work; begins to formulate an alternative exhibition forum. Summer in Holland with New York School of Art class. Visits Haarlem, Volendam, and Amsterdam.

1908 Exhibition of The Eight at the Macbeth Galleries, New York, February 3–15. Marries illustrator Marjorie Organ in May. Leaves for Madrid in June with New York School of Art class; resigns in December from the New York School of Art.

1909 Opens Henri School of Art, where he continues teaching until 1912. March 3, Hardesty Maratta demonstrates his color theories and palette system for Henri; June, Henri begins to use Maratta paints and palette system. Wins Gold Medal from Philadelphia Art Club. Moves to Gramercy Park South.

1910 Rejection of works from the National Academy of Design Annual Exhibition; organizes Exhibition of Independent Artists. Receives Silver Medal at the International Fine Arts Exposition, Buenos Aires. Summer in Holland and Spain. Privately signs over ownership of the Henri School, though continues to teach classes.

1911 Organizes first jury-free exhibition at the MacDowell Club; the series of exhibitions runs until 1919. Summer in Monhegan Island, Maine, with George Bellows and Randall Davey. Begins teaching at The Modern School of the Ferrer Society through 1916.

1912 Summer in Spain with art class. September to Paris, then returns to New York. Severs connection to the Henri School.

1913 February, represented in the Armory Show with five works. June to September in Achill Island, Ireland, with Marjorie.

1914 Beck Gold Medal awarded by the Pennsylvania Academy of the Fine Arts for *Herself*. June to October, visits La Jolla, and San Diego, California.

1915 Awarded Silver Medal at the Panama-Pacific Exposition in San Francisco. Summer in Ogunquit, Maine, with George and Emma Bellows. Begins association with the Art Students League, which continues through 1927.

1916 Helps plan and participates in The Forum Exhibition. Summer to Santa Fe, New Mexico.

1917 Summer, returns to Santa Fe, New Mexico; in winter, begins studying Jay Hambidge's theory of dynamic symmetry.

1918 Summer, to Monhegan Island, Maine.

1919 Founding member, New Society of Artists, New York.

1920 Awarded prize for portraiture from the Wilmington Society of Fine Arts.

1921 Summer, Woodstock, New York, with George and Emma Bellows, Eugene and Elsie Speicher, Leon Kroll, and Marjorie.

1922 Summer, to Los Angeles, California, then to Santa Fe, New Mexico.

1923 February, death of mother. Summer, to Paris, then Madrid, through April of the following year; fall, publication of *The Art Spirit*.

1924 Spring through fall in Achill Island, Ireland.

1925 February, to Los Angeles, California; summer to Achill Island, Ireland.

1926 May to June, in Spain; July to November, in Achill Island, Ireland.

1927 May to October, in Achill Island, Ireland.

1928 May to September, Achill Island, Ireland; returns to New York, where he is admitted to hospital.

1929 Receives Temple Gold Medal from the Pennsylvania Academy of the Fine Arts for *The Wee Woman*. Dies of cancer, July 12 at St. Luke's Hospital.

1931 Memorial exhibition for Henri organized by John Sloan at The Metropolitan Museum of Art, New York.

UNPUBLISHED SOURCES

Handy, Elizabeth Armstrong. "H.G. Maratta's Color Theory and Its Influence on the Painters—Robert Henri, John Sloan and George Bellows." M.A. Thesis. Newark, Delaware: University of Delaware, 1969.

Henri, Robert. Papers, 1885–1929. Beinecke Rare Book and Manuscript Library, Yale University; and collection of Janet Le Clair.

Henri, Robert. Correspondence with John Sloan, 1893–1927. John Sloan Archives, Helen Farr Sloan Library, Delaware Art Museum, Wilmington.

Henri, Robert. Diaries, 1881–1928. Collection of Janet Le Clair.

Henri, Robert. Palette Diary/Notebook. Collection of Janet Le Clair.

Henri, Robert. Record Books, 1885–1928. Collection of Janet Le Clair.

Henri, Robert. Clipping Scrapbooks. Collection of Janet Le Clair.

Organ, Violet, "Robert Henri." 4 vols. Edited from letters, diaries, family records, etc. Collection of Janet Le Clair.

BOOKS, MONOGRAPHS, AND EXHIBITION CATALOGUES

Berman, Avis. *Rebels on Eighth Street: Juliana Force and the Whitney Museum of American Art.* New York: Atheneum Publishers, 1990.

Braider, Donald. *George Bellows and the Ashcan School of Painting.* Garden City, New York: Doubleday & Company, 1971.

Brooks, Van Wyck. *John Sloan: A Painter's Life.* New York: E. P. Dutton and Company, 1955.

Brown, Milton W. *American Painting from the Armory Show to the Depression* (1955). Reprint. Princeton, New Jersey: Princeton University Press, 1970.

——. *The Story of the Armory Show* (1963). Reprint. New York: Abbeville Press, 1988.

Cortissoz, Royal. *American Artists.* New York: Charles Scribner's Sons, 1923.

Du Bois, Guy Pène. *Artists Say the Silliest Things.* New York: American Artists Group, Duell, Sloan and Pearce, 1940.

Ely, Catherine Beach. *The Modern Tendency in American Painting.* New York: Frederick F. Sherman, 1925.

Elzea, Rowland. *John Sloan's Oil Paintings: A Catalogue Raisonné.* 2 vols. Newark, Delaware: University of Delaware Press, 1991.

Glackens, Ira. *William Glackens and the Ashcan Group.* New York: Crown Publishers, 1957.

Goodrich, Lloyd. *John Sloan, 1871–1951.* New York: Whitney Museum of American Art, 1952.

Hambidge, Jay. *Dynamic Symmetry in Composition As Used by the Artists* (1923). Reprint. New Haven: Yale University Press, 1948.

——. *The Elements of Dynamic Symmetry* (1926). Reprint. New Haven: Yale University Press, 1948.

Hartmann, Sadakichi. *A History of American Art* (1901). 2 vols. Reprint. New York: Tudor Publishing Company, 1934.

Homer, William Innes. *Robert Henri and His Circle* (1969). Reprint. New York: Hacker Art Books, 1988.

Isham, Samuel. *The History of American Painting* (1905). Reprint. New York: The Macmillan Company, 1944.

Maratta, H.G. *The Web of Equilateral Triangles.* New York: 1915.

Morgan, Charles H. *George Bellows: Painter of America* (1965). Reprint. Millwood, New York: Kraus Reprint Company, 1979.

Perlman, Bennard B. *Painters of the Ashcan School: The Immortal Eight* (1979). Reprint. New York: Dover Publications, 1988.

——. *Robert Henri: His Life and Art.* New York: Dover Publications, 1991.

Pousette-Dart, Nathaniel. *Robert Henri.* New York: Frederick A. Stokes Company, 1922.

Quick, Michael. *The Paintings of George Bellows* (exhibition catalogue). Fort Worth: Amon Carter Museum; Los Angeles: Los Angeles County Museum of Art, 1992.

Read, Helen Appleton. *Robert Henri.* New York: American Artists Series, Whitney Museum of American Art, 1931.

Ross, Denman. *On Drawing and Painting.* Boston and New York: Houghton Mifflin Company, 1912.

——. *The Painter's Palette.* Boston and New York: Houghton Mifflin Company, 1919.

——. *A Theory of Pure Design: Harmony, Balance, Rhythm.* New York: Peter Smith, 1907.

Sloan, John. *The Gist of Art* (1939). Reprint. New York: Dover Publications, 1977.

——. *John Sloan's New York Scene.* Edited by Bruce St. John. New York: Harper & Row, 1965.

Young, Mahonri Sharp. *The Eight: The Realist Revolt in American Painting.* New York: Watson-Guptill Publications, 1973.

Yarrow, William, and Louis Bouché. *Robert Henri: His Life and Works.* New York: Boni & Liveright, 1921.

EXHIBITION CATALOGUES OF MAJOR ONE-MAN SHOWS

Lincoln, Nebraska, Sheldon Memorial Art Gallery, University of Nebraska. *Robert Henri 1865–1929,* 1971. Catalogue by William Innes Homer.

——. *Robert Henri 1865–1929–1965,* 1965.

New York, Berry-Hill Galleries. *Robert Henri,* 1986. Catalogue by Bruce W. Chambers.

New York, Chapellier Galleries. *Robert Henri,* 1964.

——. *Robert Henri 1865–1929,* 1976. Catalogue by Donelson F. Hoopes.

New York, Hirschl & Adler Galleries. *Robert Henri 1865–1929—Fifty Paintings,* 1958. Catalogue by Leslie Katz.

——. *Full-Length Portraits and Paintings of Children by Robert Henri 1865–1929,* 1960.

New York, Maynard Walker Gallery. *An Exhibition of Early Works by Robert Henri,* 1962.

New York, The Metropolitan Museum of Art. *Robert Henri Memorial Exhibition,* 1931.

New York, New York Cultural Center. *Robert Henri: Painter-Teacher-Prophet,* 1969.

Wilmington, Delaware Art Museum. *Robert Henri: Painter,* 1984. Catalogue by Bennard B. Perlman.

CATALOGUES OF MAJOR GROUP EXHIBITIONS

Jacksonville, Florida, The Cummer Gallery of Art. *Henri—Bellows,* 1981.

Milwaukee Art Museum. *Painters of a New Century: The Eight & American Art,* 1991. Catalogue by Elizabeth Milroy.

New York, American Academy of Arts and Letters. *Robert Henri and His Circle,* 1965.

New York, The Century Association. *Robert Henri and Five of His Pupils: George Bellows, Eugene Speicher, Guy Pène du Bois, Rockwell Kent, Edward Hopper,* 1946.

New York, Macbeth Galleries. *The Eight,* 1908.

New York, Whitney Museum of American Art. *New York Realists—1900–1914,* 1937.

——. *The 75th Anniversary of The Eight,* 1983. Catalogue by Bennard B. Perlman.

Philadelphia, Moore College of Art Gallery. *John Sloan/Robert Henri: Their Philadelphia Years 1886–1904,* 1976.

Vero Beach, Florida, Center for the Arts. *William Merritt Chase and Robert Henri: American Master Painters,* 1986.

BY ROBERT HENRI

"An Appreciation by Robert Henri," *The New York Times Magazine,* November 11, 1917.

"The Artist's Partnership with His Public," *Literary Digest,* 80 (January 5, 1924), pp. 27–28.

"An Artist's Social Maxim," *Survey,* 50 (1923), pp. 279–82.

The Art Spirit. Compiled by Margery Ryerson. Philadelphia: J.B. Lippincott, 1923.

"As to Books and Writers," *Conservator,* 26 (May 1915), pp. 40–41.

"The 'Big Exhibition,' the Artist and the Public," *Touchstone,* 1 (June 1917), pp. 174–77, 216.

Foreword to New York, Anderson Galleries. *The Forum Exhibition of Modern American Painters,* 1916, pp. 30–32.

"To Free Art from Prizes and Juries," *Literary Digest,* 42 (January 21, 1911), p. 114.

"My People." *The Craftsman,* 27 (February 1915), pp. 459–69.

"The New York Exhibition of Independent Artists." *The Craftsman,* 18 (May 1910), pp. 160–72.

"A Practical Talk to Those Who Study Art," *Philadelphia Sunday Press,* May 12, 1901.

"Progress in Our National Art Must Spring from the Development of Individuality of Ideas and Freedom of Expression: A Suggestion for a New Art School," *The Craftsman,* 15 (January 1909), pp. 387–400.

"What About Art in America?," *Arts & Decoration,* 24 (November 1925), pp. 35–37, 75.

ARTICLES

"Around the Galleries." *The Sunday Sun,* April 6, 1902.

Barrell, Charles Wisner. "Robert Henri: Revolutionary." *Independent,* 64 (June 25, 1908), pp. 1427–32.

Bellows, George. "'The Art Spirit' by Robert Henri." *Arts & Decoration,* 20 (December 1923), pp. 26, 87.

Breuning, Margaret. "Memorial Exhibit of Robert Henri's Work." *The New York Post,* March 14, 1931.

——. "Realism at the Whitney." *Magazine of Art,* 30 (March 1937), pp. 174–75.

Brooks, Van Wyck. "The Eight's Battle for U.S. Art." *Art News,* 53 (November 1954), pp. 41–43, 69.

Burrows, Carlyle. "Robert Henri and His Service to Painting." *New York Herald Tribune,* July 21, 1929.

"California Types Painted by Mr. Robert Henri." *Town and Country,* November 28, 1914, pp. 27, 38.

"The Career and Work of Robert Henri." *Vanity Fair,* 6 (August 1916), p. 38.

Cary, Elisabeth Luther. "Robert Henri." *Bulletin of The Metropolitan Museum of Art,* 26 (March 1931), pp. 58–62.

C.A.Z. [Carl A. Zigrosser]. "Henri and Manship." *Little Review,* 2 (October 1915), pp. 38–39.

"Chase, Nettled, Leaves Art School He Founded." *The World* (New York), November 21, 1907.

Cheyney, E. Ralph. "The Philosophy of a Portrait Painter: An Interview with Robert Henri." *Touchstone,* 5 (June 1919), pp. 212–19.

Cline, Leonard Lanson. "Paintings by Henri at the Art Museum, Color and Candor Shocking, But Underneath Evidence of Notable Rebel," *Detroit News,* July 11, 1919.

Cortissoz, Royal. "Robert Henri." *The Herald Tribune,* January 15, 1939.

Cournos, John. "Three Painters of the New York School." *International Studio,* 56 (October 1915), pp. 239–41.

——. "What Is Art? Answered by Henri, Art 'Insurgent.'" *Philadelphia Record,* December 25, 1910.

Craven, Thomas Jewell. "Realism and Robert Henri." *Dial,* 72 (January 1922), pp. 84–88.

De Kay, Charles. "Six Impressionists: Startling Works by Red-Hot American Painters." *The New York Times,* January 20, 1904.

——. "Wolves That Stalk the Academic Sheep Fold: Academy Threatened by a Realistic Eight." *The New York Times,* May 19, 1907.

Dinnerstein, Harvey, and Burt Silverman. "New Look at Protest: The Eight Since 1908." *Art News,* 56 (February 1958), pp. 36–39.

Du Bois, Guy Pène. "Exhibitions—Robert Henri." *Arts,* 17 (April 1931), pp. 495–99.

——. "Robert Henri." In *The One Hundred Fiftieth Anniversary Exhibition.* Philadelphia: Pennsylvania Academy of the Fine Arts, 1955, pp. 68–74.

——. "The Henri, Bellows, Speicher Union." *Harper's Bazaar,* 75 (March 1, 1941), pp. 64–65, 120.

——. "Robert Henri: The Man." *Arts & Decoration,* 14 (November 1920), pp. 36, 76.

——. "Robert Henri—Realist and Idealist." *Arts & Decoration,* 2 (April 1912), pp. 213–15, 230.

Edgerton, Giles [Mary Fanton Roberts]. "Is America Selling Her Birthright in Art for a Mess of Pottage?" *The Craftsman,* 11 (March 1907), pp. 656–70.

——. "The Younger American Painters: Are They Creating a National Art?" *The Craftsman,* 13 (February 1908), pp. 512–32.

"Eight Independent Painters." *The Sun* (New York), May 15, 1908.

"'The Eight' Stir Up Many Emotions." *Newark News,* May 1909.

Ely, Catherine Beach. "The Modern Tendency in Henri, Sloan, and Bellows." *Art in America,* 10 (April 1922), pp. 132–43.

Emmart, A.D. "One of the Most Important and Useful Shows of Season." *Baltimore Morning Sun,* May 3, 1931.

"Exhibitions at the Art Institute—Sculpture by Paul Manship—Paintings by Robert Henri." *Fine Arts Journal,* 33 (October 1915), pp. 426–37.

"Extracts from the Teachings of Robert Henri." *Art Instruction,* 3 (April 1939), pp. 5–10.

"Famous American Artist Passes Away at Age of Sixty-Four." *The New York Times,* July 13, 1929.

[Fitzgerald, Charles]. "The Society of American Artists." *New York Evening Sun,* April 3, 1903.

Fitzgerald, Riter. "Robert Henri's Works: The Eccentric Artist Improving." *Philadelphia Item,* December 1, 1902.

Flint, Ralph. "Robert Henri Memorial Show at Metropolitan." *Art News,* 29 (March 14, 1931) pp. 3, 6.

F. W. [Forbes Watson]. "Robert Henri." *The Arts,* 16 (March 1930), pp. 501–03.

"Glamour About Name of Sargent, Painter: His Work Draws All Eyes at the American Artists' Show, Yet Not as Good as Henri's." *New York Press,* March 27, 1904.

Goodman, Helen. "Robert Henri." *American Magazine of Art,* 23 (June 1931), pp. 437–46.

——. "Robert Henri, Teacher." *Arts,* 53 (September 1978), pp. 158–60.

Hanson, H. Thurland. "Robert Henri—Some of His Ideas." *Art Center Bulletin* (New York), 4 (January 1926), pp. 144–47.

[Hartmann, Sadakichi]. "On Robert Henri." *Art News,* 1 (April 1897), p. 4.

——. "Studio Talk." *International Studio,* 30 (December 1906), pp. 182–83.

Heitkamp, Ernest. "Paintings by Robert Henri." *Detroit Institute of Arts Bulletin,* 1 (1920), pp. 70–71.

Henderson, Rose. "Robert Henri." *American Magazine of Art,* 21 (January 1930), pp. 3–12.

"The Henri Hurrah." *American Art News,* 5 (March 23, 1907), p. 4.

"Henri Is Dead." *Art Digest,* 3 (July 1929), p. 11.

"Henri Memorial Show for Detroit." *Art News,* 28 (February 8, 1930), p. 6.

"Henri, 'Typically American,' a 'Born Insurgent.'" *Literary Digest,* 102 (August 3, 1929), pp. 19–20.

[Hoeber, Arthur]. "Art and Artists: A Most Lugubrious Show at the National Club." *The Commercial Advertiser* (New York), January 21, 1904.

Howard, W. Stanton. "A Portrait by Robert Henri." *Harper's Monthly Magazine,* 117 (August 1908), pp. 430–31.

——. "Robert Henri." *Harper's Monthly Magazine,* 125 (October 1912), pp. 706–07.

H. St.-G. [Homer Saint-Gaudens]. "Robert Henri." *Critic,* 49 (August 1906), p. 131.

Hunter, Sam. "'The Eight'—Insurgent Realists." *Art in America,* 44 (Fall, 1956), pp. 20–22, 56–58.

Jewell, Edward Alden. "Drama of Current Week of Art in New York: A Memorial and a Reunion." *The New York Times,* March 15, 1931.

——. "Exhibition Is Made of Irish Paintings." *The New York Times,* October 25, 1934.

Kwiat, Joseph J. "Robert Henri and the Emerson-Whitman Tradition." *Publications of the Modern Language Association,* 81 (September 1956), pp. 617–36.

Maratta, H.G. "Colors and Paints." *Touchstone,* 7 (June 1920), pp. 249–50.

——. "The Maratta System of Color." *Scientific American Supplement,* 68 (November 13, 1919), p. 311.

——. "A Rediscovery of the Principles of Form Measurement," *Arts & Decoration,* 4 (April 1914), pp. 230–32.

Marlais, Michael Andrew. "Robert Henri: La Reina Mora." *American Art Review,* 5 (Fall 1993), pp. 84–85, 159.

Mather, Frank Jewett, Jr. "Some American Realists." *Arts & Decoration,* 7 (November 1916), pp. 13–17.

McBride, Henry. "Robert Henri's California Paintings." *The Sun* (New York), November 22, 1914.

M'Cormick, William B. "Mastery of Medium Shown in Henri's Exhibit of Far Western Types at Macbeth's." *The New York Press,* November 22, 1922.

"Metropolitan Shows Art of Henri, Leader of Independents." *Art Digest,* 5 (March 15, 1931), p. 8, 22.

"Mr. Henri Off 'Academy' Jury." *New York Herald,* April 12, 1907.

"National Academy Stirred by Mr. Henri's Withdrawal of Pictures." *The Sun* (New York), March 14, 1907.

"Notable Specimens of Robert Henri's Brush on Exhibition." *The American* (Philadelphia), November 16, 1902.

Pattison, James William. "Robert Henri—Painter." *House Beautiful,* 20 (August 1906), pp. 18–19.

Perlman, Bennard B. "Practicing Preacher." *Art & Antiques,* 7 (November 1990), pp. 84–89, 108.

——. "Prophet of the New." *Art News,* 83 (Summer 1984), pp. 94–99.

——. "Robert Henri." *Arts Digest,* 28 (August 1, 1954), pp. 14–15.

——. "Robert Henri, Emancipator." *Art Voices,* 5 (Winter, 1966), pp. 42–47.

——. "The Years Before [the Armory Show]." *Art in America,* 51 (February 1963), pp. 38–43.

"Portrait Painters of Today: Robert Henri." *Vogue,* 29 (January 3, 1907), p. 3.

"Portraits of Children in Old and Modern Art." *Arts & Decoration,* 12 (November 1919), pp. 86–87.

Read, Helen Appleton. "'I Paint My People' Is Henri's Art Key." *The Brooklyn Eagle,* February 12, 1916.

——. "Robert Henri." *Vogue,* 74 (November 9, 1929), pp. 98–99.

"Robert Henri." *American Magazine of Art,* 20 (September 1929), p. 541.

"Robert Henri." *Art News,* 27 (August 17, 1929), p. 13.

"Robert Henri." *Broadway Magazine,* 19 (February 1908), pp. 589–90.

"Robert Henri." *Dictionary of American Biography,* 8 (New York, 1932), pp. 544–55.

"Robert Henri." *Kennedy Quarterly,* 4 (December 1963), p. 73.

"Robert Henri." *The National Cyclopedia of American Biography,* 15 (1916), pp. 146–57.

"Robert Henri: An Apostle of Artistic Individuality." *Current Literature,* 52 (April 1912), pp. 464–68.

"Robert Henri Calls Art the Manifestation of Race." *Milwaukee Art Institute Art Quarterly,* 5 (October 1916), pp. 7–8.

"Robert Henri Dies; Ill Eight Months." *The New York Times,* July 13, 1929.

"Robert Henri Has Left Indelible Imprint Behind." *Toledo Ohio Times,* July 21, 1929.

"Robert Henri: One of the Big Figures in American Painting." *Current Opinion,* 71 (December 1921), pp. 793–96.

"Robert Henri—Painter." *Index of Twentieth Century Artists,* 2 (June 1935), pp. 49–60, plus supplement.

"Robert Henri's New School." *American Art News,* 7 (January 16, 1909), p. 2.

Roberts, Mary Fanton. "Art Reviews: A Point of View." *Arts & Decoration,* 28 (March 1928), p. 69.

——. "A Distinguished Group." *Touchstone,* 6 (January 1920), pp. 200–08.

——. "Speaking of Art: The Henri Memorial Exhibition." *Arts & Decoration,* 34 (March 1931), pp. 44–45.

——. "Visiting the Art Galleries." *Arts & Decoration,* 32 (November 1929), pp. 70–71.

Shepherd, Richard. "Henri and His Boys." *Art News,* 45 (May 1946), pp. 42–43.

Swift, Samuel. "Revolutionary Figures in American Art." *Harper's Weekly,* 51 (April 13, 1907), pp. 534–36.

"The 'Thirty' and Mr. Henri: Why the Painter Withdrew His Academy Canvases." *The Evening Post* (New York), March 13, 1907.

Tonks, Oliver. "Robert Henri—An Appreciation." *American Magazine of Art,* 7 (October 1916), pp. 473–79.

"Two Admired of Mr. Robert Henri." *New York Herald,* March 31, 1907.

"A Varnishing Day Crush." *The Evening Post* (New York), March 16, 1907.

Vaughan, Malcolm. "Eight Who Made History in Art." *The New York Times Magazine,* November 28, 1943.

Walter, Paul A. F. "The Santa Fe-Taos Art Movement." *Art and Archaeology,* 4 (December 1916), pp. 330–38.

Watson, Forbes. "Robert Henri." *The Arts,* 16 (September 1929), pp. 2–8.

"Who's Who in American Art." *Arts & Decoration,* 6 (November 1915), p. 33.

"Wm. M. Chase Forced Out of N.Y. Art School: Triumph for the 'New Movement' Led by Robert Henri." *New York American,* November 20, 1907.

"Works from Brush of Artist Henri Reveal Unusual Skill." *Grand Rapids Press,* February 5, 1916.

"A Worthy Henri." *Art Digest,* 4 (November 1, 1929), p. 17.